GOVERNANCE
AND THE
PUBLIC GOOD

SUNY SERIES, FRONTIERS IN EDUCATION
Phillip G. Altbach, editor

Governance
and the
Public Good

Edited by
William G. Tierney

STATE UNIVERSITY OF NEW YORK PRESS

Published by
State University of New York Press, Albany

For information, address State University of New York Press,
194 Washington Avenue, Suite 305, Albany, NY 12210-2384

Production by Michael Haggett
Marketing by Susan M. Petrie

Library of Congress Cataloging in Publication Data

Tierney, William G.
  Governance and the public good / William G. Tierney.
      p. cm. — (SUNY series, frontiers in education)
  Includes bibliographical references and index.
  ISBN-13: 978-0-7914-6875-3 (hardcover : alk. paper)
  ISBN-10: 0-7914-6875-5 (hardcover : alk. paper)
  ISBN-13: 978-0-7914-6876-0 (pbk. : alk. paper)
  ISBN-10: 0-7914-6876-3 (pbk. : alk. paper) 1. Education,
Higher—United States—Administration. 2. Education, Higher—Political
aspects—United States. 3. Education, Higher—Social aspects—United
States. I. Title. II. Series.

  LB2341.T586 2006
  378'.050973—dc22
                                            2005031412

10 9 8 7 6 5 4 3 2 1

Contents

Introduction

The Examined University

Process and Change in Higher Education

William G. Tierney

If I tell you that the unexamined life is not worth living for a human being,
you will be even less likely to believe what I am saying. But that's the way it
is, gentlemen, as I claim, though it's not easy to convince you of it.

Socrates, in Plato, *Apology 38A*

CHICKENS AND EGGS

Any observer of higher education over the last decade will undoubtedly point
out three trends that appear to be taking shape, and two tensions that have
subsequently arisen. The trends pertain to privatization, politicization, and
restructuring. The tensions refer to increased demands for accountability and
questions regarding autonomy. Whether the tensions have created the trends
or the trends have caused the tensions is a bit like asking which came first: the
chicken or the egg. Although an argument over whether there is a linear relationship between the tensions and trends might be of interest to academics
interested in organizational and system theory, such a discussion is of limited
utility. Organizational life is rarely unicausal, such that a move toward privatization takes place only because of one stimulus, or a concern about accountability arises solely because of another.

Accordingly, rather than engage in a jejune debate about causality, I have
assembled here a thoughtful group of scholars that grapples with these trends
and tensions in order to provoke a discussion about the academy. All five topics
warrant investigation and analysis because understanding them will help
determine the role of the twenty-first century research university. By suggesting that topics such as accountability and autonomy are worthy of discussion
and analysis, I walk a fine line between those who are more interested in

1

abstract theoretical discussions about organizational life and those who desire immediate solutions to what academe should be doing during a time of great flux.

On the one side are those who have little interest in the specific actions of the university and are more interested in the university as an idea and organizational change as a theory. On the other side are those who seek immediate answers to the complex problems that institutions face and who are impatient with reflexive deliberation. In this book, however, we seek to examine higher education in a manner akin to what Socrates has argued about life. Indeed, although we surely do not wish to personify an idea—the university—we readily acknowledge that higher education holds a special place in the life and well-being of the United States. Academic institutions are not simply another organization that is undergoing the trials and tribulations of change due to globalization. Yes, colleges and universities must contend with economic, social, and cultural forces that are impacting virtually all organizations and systems, but postsecondary institutions are related to America's concept of the "public good" in ways that corporations and businesses are not.

As Brian Pusser points out in chapter 1, the public good is not merely an economic idea of goods and services—who can deliver and provide a particular good to whom—it is also an ideology and a belief about how things get done and whether the "public" provides those services in ways different from those in the private sector. In higher education, then, to discuss the public good inevitably leads to discussions about governance. Conversely, to entertain proposals about reforming one or another governance structure in higher education (as seems to occur on an almost daily basis) and not to take into consideration what is meant by the public good seems to overlook the *raison d'etre* of academic life. Education writ large and public higher education in particular, as Pusser reminds us, derive from a fealty to the public good—not simply to educate the citizenry for jobs, skills, and citizenship but also to be a public place where thoughtful debate and examination about the polis might occur.

Unfortunately, the phrase "public good" has gained a currency and cachet equivalent to other deceptively simple concepts that make it into the public domain stripped of all meaning other than what can be found in a sound bite. The public good also has the positive ring of authenticity. To betray the public good is bad; to speak on behalf of the public good is, well, good. The public good has become like motherhood and apple pie. Everyone supports the public good, even while not understanding the history of the term or its current trajectory very well.

In what follows, we seek to tie the notion of the public good in higher education to that of governance. We ask, if one accepts the notion of higher education as a public good, what does it suggest for how one thinks about the governance of America's colleges and universities? The assumption is that asking the question is what matters right now, more so than developing an answer, for no single answer that pertains to all institutions and all individuals may exist. We need to interrogate the interrelationships between governance and the public good with the intent that such an examination will lead to a more informed polity. A more informed polity is likely to develop a plurality of responses for governance in higher education that is responsive to the multiple needs of the citizenry.

The chapters that follow generally develop complementary arguments about governance and the public good, but I by no means tried to put together a lock-step argument that proceeds in deterministic fashion. Instead, I invited authors with a particular expertise to focus on questions of vital concern: What is the role of a twenty-first century college or university? What does the changing definition and interpretation of the public good suggest for that role? How is governance impacted by these questions, and how does it impact them?

In order to provide focus for the text, I have not entertained a discussion about community colleges or for-profit providers, but I certainly acknowledge that both institutional types deserve thorough analysis in a manner akin to what we are attempting here. Instead, we have focused on four-year institutions in general, in particular, public institutions. Public colleges and universities still serve a majority of the students who attend four-year institutions, so they deserve particular attention—especially with regard to governance and the public good. The chapters derive from a mixture of data-driven sources as well as hands-on experience of authors who are living these questions in the "real world." Before turning to Pusser's discussion of the public good, I offer here a road map that discusses the trends and tensions that currently exist and what the authors have to say about them.

TRENDS

Privatization

Privatization has impacted postsecondary institutions in many ways but most significantly with regard to basic funding, faculty work, and student tuition. A century ago, public universities relied largely on the munificence of the state to fund their operations; even during the Great Depression, public institutions still received virtually all of their support from state governments. Private institutions relied largely on tuition, and over the last century, tuition has been increasingly supported through grants and loans provided by the state and federal governments. In the twenty-first century, however, public and private institutions have been required to significantly diversify their funding bases. Although many private institutions still receive an overwhelming amount of their income through tuition, and public institutions through state support, the trend is toward privatization and funding diversification.

Similarly, prior to World War II, faculty were largely full-time tenure track professors who primarily saw their role as teaching undergraduate students combined with a modicum of research and service to the institution. A handful of individuals, mostly in the natural sciences at research universities, sought funding from foundations and the government. Today, more part-time faculty are hired than full-time professors. The trend is away from full-time faculty. Those who are full-time tenure track faculty are increasingly expected to generate revenue. Whereas tenure once implied 100 percent of a professor's salary, the possibility increasingly exists that tenure actually means a certain percentage of an individual's salary, the rest to be generated by the individual or the home department. The strength of this suggestion resides on the possibility of an individual (or a department) generating more income than would have been set if a cap existed, so that one's salary can dramatically increase. The downside, of course, is that job security for a job that does not pay one's full salary provides a new meaning to "job security."

Research where patents are developed and distance learning is employed also has generated discussions over the nature of intellectual property. The Bayh-Dole Act, coupled with the invention of the Internet and the potential of serving thousands of students without ever seeing them, has raised questions about who owns what. Only a generation ago, if someone had asked professors who owned their scribbled lesson plans, the question would have been seen as absurd. Who could be troubled to read an English professor's yellowed pages about Chaucer? However, in an age when a lesson plan suggests a carefully crafted series of lectures provided via Web pages that do not necessitate the actual professor to be in attendance, one can understand the argument. A professor, and perhaps the majority of those who thought about it as well, always assumed that the ideas developed for a class were her or his property. In a world where privatization has taken hold, however, such an assumption is no longer secure. If a private institution is akin to a company, and a public institution is owned by the state, then an argument may be made that the business owns what the worker develops, not the individual.

Tuition also has risen dramatically; the reason being is twofold. On the one hand, one need not be an economist to recognize that when fiscal support in one area drops—state support—then the organization needs to generate revenue in another area, such as tuition. On the other hand, the sense that the collective as defined by state support should provide all of the necessary funds for individuals to attend college has come into disfavor. Once again, the idea of the public good has come into question. The result is that individuals increasingly have to shoulder the burden for paying for a college education. The implicit assumption is that a postsecondary degree is a private good rather than a public good. Thus the state or federal government may try to provide loans for citizens so that they are able to attend college, but the individual should assume the cost of an education rather than the state.

Karen Whitney, in "Lost in Transition," traces the shift in state funding of higher education and points out the relationship between who governs or controls public institutions and who provides the funding. She suggests that privatization is likely to continue and to bring with it less control by the state. She provides a historical overview to privatization and points out that governing bodies have long made attempts at privatization by raising fees for one or another activity, though the recent move toward privatization seems more dramatic and is coupled with a fundamental shift in philosophy. That shift is from the assumption that education is a public good toward the belief that it is a private benefit. Whitney also suggests, however, that the current movement toward privatization is not only a philosophic shift but also a political one. The state has been prone to de-fund higher education, she argues, because of academe's ability to generate funds from a wide range of sources.

In "Rethinking State Governance of Higher Education," Jane Wellman does not so much disagree with Whitney as add to the argument. Wellman maintains that state governance is historically disorganized and inefficient; the recent political and economic contexts in which states exist have made a messy relationship only more disorganized and inefficient, if not dysfunctional. She also argues that the state is frequently at odds with the manner in which colleges and universities define their priorities and conduct their work. The state is concerned with access to undergraduate education and economic competitiveness, she notes, whereas postsecondary institutions frequently seem more concerned about graduate education, research, and autonomy. Wellman suggests that state governing bodies that deliberate over policy appear to be on a collision course with institutions that will be framed through a contentious political environment. The result, she contends, is a move toward privatization. In this sense, then, Wellman is suggesting that the definition of the "public good" has shifted, and that mission redefinition by institutions has resulted in privatization. The vehicle for that redefinition has been the decision-making structures employed by the state and the institutions themselves.

Politicization

Colleges and universities have long been contentious and conflict ridden. Indeed, the rise of tenure in part came about because boards of trustees and state governments sought to fire professors for making statements that went against the grain. One cannot think of the protests that engulfed the country over Vietnam in the 1960s without considering that the site of many of those protests was a college campus. Berkeley and the Free Speech Movement, the rise of Students for a Democratic Society (SDS) at Columbia University, and the Student Nonviolent Coordinating Committee (SNCC), originating at Shaw University in North Carolina, all used colleges and universities as main theaters for action.

Campuses also have been inherently political in the manner in which they have governed themselves. The rise of faculty senates and the increase in collective bargaining are examples of formalized arenas for politics. But any faculty member will also surely attest to the numerous informal arenas for politics, whether a departmental meeting where who teaches what when gets debated or in never-ending discussions about office space, parking, and an array of benefits and/or rights that faculty, staff, and students believe they deserve.

However, the current politicization of the campus differs somewhat from the past. Boards of trustees and regents have inserted themselves into the life of the institution in a manner to an extent that has not previously been seen. Wellman points out that several external groups, such as the Association of College Trustees and Alumni (ACTA), the National Association of Scholars (NAS), and the National Committee for Responsive Philanthropy (NCRP), have been created with the mission to encourage governing boards to engage in activist oversight of academic quality. An "academic bill of rights" has been championed by the conservative David Horowitz, which has brought into question hiring policies and tenure. The bill has been seriously considered at the federal and state levels. Whether one applauds or abhors such events is not my point here; rather, I simply wish to note that along with a trend toward privatization is one toward politicization as well.

Ken Mortimer and Colleen O'Brien Sathre offer a case study of a public university that closed a professional school—an inherently political act. The authors suggest that an inevitable tension exists in academic governance between staying focused on core missions while at the same time recognizing the political environment in which they operate. The interactions of the board, administration, faculty, and public have to be seen through a political lens where conflict is inevitable and focus is essential. David Longanecker, in his chapter, agrees with Mortimer and Sathre, but he argues that all too often governing boards do not stay focused and frequently become political. Longanecker points out, using current data from states and public institutions, how easy it is for the mission of an institution to fall by the wayside as a governing board pursues an unrealistic goal that ultimately does not serve the state very well. Board members act as entrepreneurs, points out Longanecker, and they may be well versed as businesspeople in their own particular businesses, but they are commonly neophytes in the academic arena. The result is an unfocused system that is neither efficient nor effective but decidedly political.

One ought not to bemoan that politics exists but instead accept it as a social fact. Indeed, insofar as higher education has been thought of as a public good, why would one expect that it is not to be ardently debated? A public good means that the "public" has some involvement in the definition and delivery of the good. The public has much less say regarding private goods in a country dedicated to individual liberties and rights. "A man's home is his castle" goes the cliché, and within that castle is the assumption that the individual has broad leeway to live in it in a manner that the individual decides, without external interference. If higher education is a public good, however, then those who govern the campus do not get to do just as they please. Rather, multiple constituencies will be involved in determining what to do. Thus debates about mission and attempts by governing boards to expand an institution's role inevitably involve arguments over higher education as a public good.

Restructuring

The rise of administration and bureaucracy is a hallmark of American higher education in the twentieth century. Whereas a century ago a thin administrative veneer populated most institutions, today an elaborate structure exists that encompasses tasks and activities that could not be conceived at the turn of the last century. Directors of libraries have become vice presidents of information services. Deans of graduate schools frequently have the research aspect of their work separated off into another office. Offices of human subjects, intellectual property, and business development have become as large, if not larger, than a classics and philosophy department. Restructuring, of course, is inherently political; an individual assumes an office and sets out to increase the power and authority of the office through an increase in size and accumulation of resources.

Restructuring, however, has taken on a different shape in the new economy. To be sure, as Mortimer and Sathre suggest, politics is ever present, and much restructuring resembles the rough and tumble of any organizational change. And yet when coupled with privatization, an odd centralization/decentralization of authority appears to be taking place. One would assume that a public good demands greater external supervision and that a private one has less external involvement. And yet the federal government seeks greater oversight of graduation rates and time to degree when it simultaneously loosens federal regulations pertaining to for-profit institutions. Regional accreditation agencies seek increased authority at the same time institutions are expanding their reach beyond regional boundaries and questioning the need for accreditation. States decrease their support for public colleges and universities but expand their demands for accountability. Boards

insert themselves in campus activities in ways unheard of in the past but
resist measures to conform to their own oversight and accountability. Budgeting measures such as revenue centered management (RCM) are lauded as
good tools because they make institutions more entrepreneurial and decentralized, but the institutions are then criticized because they do not respond
to state and public needs that call for centralization.

Restructuring always implies new governance arrangements, of course,
and the most recent wave of restructuring usually has called for less faculty
input. Decision making needs to be more "nimble," we are told; faculty governance may be many things, but it is not nimble. Concomitantly, boards and
presidents presumably need greater authority with which to make decisions. In
a helpful chapter that is based on events in Australia, Craig McInnis questions
such assertions. He points out that a key assumption pertaining to restructuring is that streamlined smaller bodies, with more external expertise and less
internal faculty involvement, can best provide focused whole-of-institution
leadership. Ironically, the role of academic expertise and authority, however, is
needed now more than ever before, argues McInnis. He is not a proponent of
the status quo.

In the context of recent national reforms in Australia, McInnis argues for
an increase in ad-hoc (or "short cycle") working groups composed largely of
faculty. The challenge of implementing such a suggestion, however, is similar
regardless of where the reform is implemented. There are those external to the
organization who have no interest in gaining faculty input in governance and
decision making; there are faculty within the institution who see any attempt
to change traditional governance structures as, at a minimum, misguided and,
at worst, subterfuge. Until such an agreement is reached, suggests McInnis, the
road to joint agreements is going to be rocky indeed.

TENSIONS

Accountability and Autonomy

Jay Dee offers a unique way of thinking about accountability in his chapter on
"Institutional Autonomy and State-Level Accountability: Loosely Coupled
Governance and the Public Good." Dee calls upon a well-utilized organizational term, "loose coupling," to examine the tensions that exist around
accountability and autonomy. Accountability here refers to the responsibilities
that an organization assumes in order to respond to external entities that have
some form of control over the unit. Until recently, accountability was most
often defined as accreditation and a loose confederation of institutions fre-

quently held together by a coordinating board to avoid duplication of services. In large part, self-regulation was what the state and federal government requested and what institutions desired. Along with the trends listed earlier, external demands have grown over the last two decades such that the state and federal governments now require institutions to collect data on any number of topics; the most hot-button topic pertains to undergraduate students. Retention, graduation rates, time to degree, job placement, and a host of other topics are now demanded of institutions. The shift to performance-based funding has forced institutions scurrying in order to bolster institutional research with the hopes of providing data that justify not so much a budget increase but at least not a budget decrease.

Dee points out that loose coupling, a term generally used within an organization to determine how structures interact with one another, may be a useful way to think about how the organization and external entities such as the state should interact with one another. In a loosely coupled system, Dee observes, the tendency is to tighten the coupling; such an action is inappropriate if one wants to improve effectiveness. Rather than spend money and time to ensure that all components have little independence, the emphasis should be on giving different elements of the organization the flexibility to respond to the abstruse demands and opportunities of the environment while at the same time having some sense of organizational cohesion.

From Dee's perspective, a loosely coupled governance structure would focus, for example, more on policy inducements than on policy mandates. Performance measures would be customized rather than cookie-cutter style. The basis for such responsiveness would be the ability of the state and the organizations to create shared commitments. Such commitments, maintains Dee, are more than simply platitudes about academic quality. Commitments suggest that higher education is a public good, and that the state and the campuses have a relationship with one another. Shared commitments point the organization and the state toward purposive action that creates a unique equilibrium between accountability and autonomy.

Enter Judith Ramaley. In "Governance in a Time of Transition," she takes Dee's argument one step farther. Although she concurs with Longanecker's assessment, that too often boards lose sight of the mission of the institution and are susceptible to mission creep, she argues that no function of a board is more important that ensuring that institutions contribute to the public good. Ramaley in part agrees with Wellman's assessment that constituencies external to postsecondary institutions question academe's commitment to pursue public goals rather than personal agendas. She frames her argument by way of an analysis of "Pasteur's Quadrant," an intellectual space in which theory and practice come together to create the capacity for colleges and universities to address societal problems.

Dee (and Pusser) may well disagree with Ramaley's (and Wellman's) assessment that colleges and universities are not being responsive to the public. They conceivably might argue that trends occurring in the environment have forced institutions to respond in ways that are counter to the public good. Once again, I am unconvinced that the argument moves any farther if we simply assign blame to one or another group. A circle seems to have been set in place where decreased funding has forced organizations to act in a manner that begets calls for greater accountability that suggests that privatization is the answer, and so on.

One point the authors agree on is the need for a shared commitment. Indeed, such a need is the very essence of a public good. By definition, a public good is shared by the public. Fiscal and academic flexibility is necessary, Whitney reminds us, but flexibility does not mean that an institution can be all things to all people, or that the state ought to expect that of an institution. How best then to develop a shared commitment?

By way of a case study of a large research university, in my chapter I discuss the idea of trust in the academy as an integral component of this shared commitment. If I expressed concern about the conceptual looseness of the term "public good," then I am even more troubled by the vagueness of a notion such as trust. "I can't trust him as far as I can throw him" is a negative comment; "she personifies trustworthiness" sure sounds good. However, in the chapter I argue that during periods of change and transformation, trustworthy behavior is essential for governance. I offer a contrasting theoretical framework from organizational theory pertaining to the idea of trust, and I then expand on the notion from a cultural perspective. As with the intent of the book in general, the purpose of the chapter is not to offer a comprehensive framework for trust. Instead, I advance the notion of trust in governance for consideration as a way out of the morass that we currently seem to be in, and as a way to develop shared commitments that reframe the notion of the public good. In the conclusion, Karri Holley illustrates the importance of redefining our understanding of public higher education as well as the role of the state and the significance of the public good. By offering the reader a summary of the preceding chapters, Holley underscores the dual response needed by colleges and universities: to define and advance the institutional mission as well as to respond to social, economic, and political demands. The nature of the response means that the status quo is unrealistic and unacceptable. The question is not if higher education will change as a result of these demands, but how colleges and universities will confront the need for change.

Reconsidering Higher Education and the Public Good

The Role of Public Spheres

Brian Pusser

One of the enduring dilemmas in higher education research has emerged from efforts to conceptualize the role of higher education in serving the public good (Marginson, 2004; Pusser, 2002). The public good (alternatively, and not necessarily synonymously, "public goods") is at the center of contemporary debates over university organization and governance, resource allocation, access, autonomy, and legitimacy. In light of the current turbulence in the broader political economy of higher education (Tierney, 2004), the concept is also at the center of arguments over market-based and neoliberal approaches to reform as well as proposals and policies shaping the privatization and restructuring of the postsecondary arena.

Over the past decade, researchers working on the question of public and private goods have turned significant attention to the nature of production in higher education (Ehrenberg, 2000) and, more specifically, to the public and private benefits generated by postsecondary institutions and their graduates (Marginson, 1997; Powell and Clemens, 1998; Pusser, 2002; Turner and Pusser, 2004). Much of this literature has been generated in response to changes in the broader political economy that have challenged higher education institutions and policy makers to justify existing understandings of provision, finance, and outcomes in higher education (Geiger, 2004; Slaughter and Leslie, 1997). In the policy arena, a majority of the debate over public and private goods in contemporary higher education has revolved around the issue of whether the public benefits generated by postsecondary education justify public investment in those benefits (Breneman, 2003; Pusser, 2002). The increase in attention to this issue mirrors similar debates in other sectors of higher education, particularly those with essential political contests at their core, as with admissions policy and the growth of the research enterprise (Pusser, 2004; Slaughter and Rhoades, 2004). In a similar fashion, a considerable body of policy literature in economics has framed the debate through cost-benefit approaches to production in higher education and to classical economic definitions of public goods (Marginson, 2004; Winston, Carbone, and Lewis, 1998).

A number of concerns have been recently expressed about the rising conflict over privatization initiatives and market forces (Pusser and Doane, 2001; Kirp, 2004; Geiger, 2004), over state intrusion into university autonomy (Bok, 2003), and over institutional efforts to benefit from emerging forms of resources and legitimacy (Slaughter and Rhoades, 2004). In each of these cases, the nature of the public good in higher education is central to understanding the conflict. In light of the importance of the debate and the lack of consensus on the public good, this chapter argues for a reconceptualization of the research agenda and the dominant discourse on higher education and the public good. Based on historical analyses and case studies of political conflict in universities over the past five decades, I argue here that we have long relied on a narrow definition of the public good produced in postsecondary education, one that increasingly privileges economic development over citizenship training, establishing common values, and democratic participation (Pusser, 2002; Cuban and Shipps, 2000). Marginson (2004) contends that the debate over the public good in higher education has been most recently influenced by a reliance on models derived from economic literature, with a focus on rivalry and excludability and such benefits as higher personal incomes, increased tax revenues, and greater productivity (Becker, 1964; Marginson, 1997, 2004; IHEP, 1998).

The analysis presented in this chapter suggests that the enactment of the public good through higher education is better understood as a multifaceted process that begins with the conceptualization, in Habermas's terms, of a public sphere enacted through the higher education process (Habermas, 1962, 1996; Ambrozas, 1998). The preservation of a public sphere through higher education is an essential public good and arguably the one that makes the more traditionally defined public goods possible. Understanding the concept of public spheres through higher education also offers significant potential for better understanding the recurrent political contests and social movements that have long been centered in postsecondary institutions. Perhaps most importantly, public spheres enacted through higher education can also be seen as a primary mechanism for converting the right to an education into access and opportunity at the postsecondary level (Pusser, 2004; Sunstein, 2004).

What We Talk about When
We Talk about the Public Good

Mansbridge (1998) suggests that the debate over the concept of the public good in social and political life has been engaged at least since Plato's Republic, engendering multiple understandings about the concept of the public good that persist to this day. She notes that some scholars interpret Plato as advocating for the public good to be understood as a "body of substantive truths or principles" (Flathman, in Mansbridge, 1998, 7). That vision stands in contrast to the one put forth by Aristotle, who considered the public good as encompassing virtue, justice, and material well-being. More germane to thinking about the public good and higher education, the Greek philosophers considered the public good a contested space, one that was disputed philosophically, discursively, and politically (Mansbridge, 1998).

It was not until the Middle Ages that philosophers focused on the duality and conflict between common good and private gain. The philosophical dialogues of the thirteenth century stressed the contrast: private gains of the ruling classes, as opposed to the good of the public. Throughout the sixteenth and seventeenth centuries, such philosophers as More, Hobbes, and Locke continued to make a distinction between private good, generally attributed to monarchs, and the public good, those actions designed to benefit the broader community (Mansbridge, 1998). It is important to note that the public good at that time was not defined as some aggregate of individual goods, or of individual action. That concept would emerge in the seventeenth century, as embodied in the writing of Adam Smith and others who argued that private action could enhance the public good (Marginson, 1997).

From that clear delineation of private good and public good, political philosophers soon countenanced the possibility of an interaction between private interests and public goods. At first, this was conceived as an individual's obligation to serve the public good through contributing to public welfare as a matter of duty, a devotion that (while sometimes, but not always, linked to religious duty) also both benefited the individual as a member of the broader public and elevated the individual's personal and social standing (Mansbridge, 1998). Thomas Jefferson referred to that process of individual gain through devotion to the common good as a "coincidence of interests," though he advocated for the public good above private interest, suggesting it was "false pride which postpones the public good to any private or personal considerations" (Jefferson, 1812). In that spirit, the first graduation day at the University of Virginia was known as "public day" (Rudolph, 1965).

The understanding of the role of the university and the public good in the colonial colleges was considerably different than it is in those institutions today. In 1803, President Joseph McKeen of Bowdoin College commented, "It ought always to be remembered that literary institutions are founded and endowed for the common good and not for the private advantage of those who resort to them for education" (McKeen, in Rudolph, 1965, 58–59). McKeen also alluded to the sense of noblesse oblige that shaped the missions of colonial colleges. "If it be true no man should live for himself alone, we may safely assert that every man who has been aided by a public institution to acquire an education and to qualify himself for usefulness, is under peculiar obligations to exert his talents for the public good" (ibid.). Rudolph later illuminated the understanding of the public good in the early nineteenth century: "The college which President McKeen represented and all other colleges of early nineteenth century America were committed to social needs rather than to individual preference and self-indulgence" (ibid., 59). Bowdoin, like other early higher education institutions, was charged with developing leaders for a new republic, a practice that embodied private development for public good. At the same time, the early American colleges occupied a key symbolic space, as they would later serve as key physical spaces, in an essential arena, the public sphere.

The early nineteenth century was something of a high watermark for the noblesse oblige understanding of the public good in higher education, a period that encompassed a general decline in the spirit of obligation that shaped the early colleges. As the public constituency of higher education expanded and the nature of public action and participation in the leadership of the broader society moved beyond university-educated elites, the sense of noblesse oblige and the importance of the public service role embedded in the training of university students diminished. As a culture of individualism grew in American society, it was accompanied by a general spirit of anti-intellectualism. Rudolph summed up the change this way: "In time going to college would come very close to being an experience in indulgence rather than an experience in obligation" (ibid., 60).

Throughout the nineteenth century, the university's contribution to the public good continued to evolve. Prior to the founding of the land grant colleges, a primary public good produced by the universities was the number of professionals produced therein (Goldin and Katz, 1998; Rudolph, 1965). The vision of the university as something beyond the reach of private interests and state control was embodied in the nineteenth-century founding documents of a number of public universities, including the University of California, which was chartered in the state constitution as a "public trust" (Douglass, 2000). Land grant institutions widened the scope of collegiate offerings and gave birth to what could be characterized as a "social contract" for research (Feller,

2000). In exchange for federal resources and legitimacy, the colleges would produce research for the common good and the training of agronomists, engineers, teachers, and public servants. In a similar manner, at the turn of the twentieth century, the progressive movement revived the notion of the university's role in service to wider communities, although the progressives also initiated the long-standing critique of partnerships between universities and the business community (Slaughter, 1990).

THE RIGHT TO AN EDUCATION

Despite the attention and the evidence of a commitment to the public good in higher education at the beginning of the twentieth century, it was still the case that higher education was largely limited to a few, affluent students. Few argued that one had a "right" to a postsecondary education, even though enrollments in two-year and four-year programs throughout the first half of the century had grown significantly. As the end of World War II approached, President Roosevelt addressed that concept as he set out to enunciate a "second bill of rights," an extension of the New Deal's efforts to add liberation from economic oppression to the freedom from political repression embodied in the original Bill of Rights (Sunstein, 2004).

In Roosevelt's State of the Union address, on January 11, 1944, he enumerated eight rights essential to individual freedom. Among these was "the right to a good education" (Sunstein, 2004, 13). Sunstein suggests Roosevelt justified the elevation of a good education to a right on three essential grounds: that "education is indispensable to decent prospects in life," that "education is a basic safeguard of security," and that education is necessary for citizenship itself (186). Education has long held a place of privilege in nearly every state constitution, and Roosevelt sought to add national recognition to that of the individual states. While he did not live to see these rights formally enacted, his second bill was instrumental in shaping the passage of the GI Bill as well as the 1948 Universal Declaration of Human Rights, which includes the right to education at all levels (Sunstein, 2004).

Since that time, while *opportunity* dominates the discourse of access in the United States, the *right* to an education has become a key element of global calls for social justice. The difference between a right and an opportunity has been central to critiques of the state and education (Freire, 1970) as well as feminist theory. Adrienne Rich expressed the distinction this way: "The first thing I want to say to you who are students is that you cannot afford to think of being here to receive an education; you will do much better to think of being here to claim one. One of the dictionary definitions of the verb 'to claim' is 'to take as the rightful owner; to assert in the face of possible contradiction.' To 'receive' is 'to come into possession of: to act as a receptacle or container for; to accept as authoritative or true'" (Rich, 1979, 231).

In the post-World War II period, the debate over the public good in higher education moved away from considerations of postsecondary education as a right or an entitlement. The debate has been fundamentally reframed around two issues: finance and access. While the finance question has obscured the public good conversation, the deliberation over access has returned it to the forefront of research and policy debates.

The Higher Education Act (HEA) of 1965 institutionalized the provision of national subsidies for postsecondary students. The availability of need-based grant aid and portable student loans dramatically restructured the relationship between the public good and public support for higher education. Prior to the HEA, public universities (and, to a lesser degree, private ones) generally offered low tuition and open access. The HEA marked the beginning of a shift in the nature and the amount of subsidies to higher education, so that what were essentially state-funded institutions have become institutions with multiple sources of revenue, albeit increasingly funded by individuals (Breneman, 1991; Geiger, 2004). The shift from a system that was predominately public and funded by the public to a system of public institutions increasingly funded by private sources also shifted the public claim on the university as a public good.

While the pattern of postsecondary subsidies was shifting, so too was the discourse used to define the missions of the university. Postsecondary institutions and the public conversation regarding higher education were increasingly based in human capital theory and drawn from the discourses of economics and commerce (Giroux, 2003; Marginson, 2004). By the early 1970s, the public policy and institutional debates no longer turned on the question, "Is the right to a higher education a public good?" The new question was epitomized in the title of a 1973 Carnegie Commission report—*Higher Education: Who Pays? Who Benefits? Who Should Pay?*

In contrast to the contest over finance, the public discourse and debates over postsecondary access in the post-WW II period have been driven by social and political concerns over equity. The struggles to desegregate postsecondary institutions in the early 1960s and the political contests over "Great Society" programs designed to open access and opportunity were based in both public good arguments and in claims for individual opportunity. Ironically, challenges to postsecondary access policies in the same period, as manifested in court challenges ranging from *Bakke v. Regents of the University of California* through *Grutter v. Bollinger*, also attempted to frame these contests as conflicts over individual rights and the common good (Chavez, 1998; Pusser, 2004). As the contest over postsecondary access has carried questions of rights, entitlements, and equity in higher education to the Supreme Court, one of the most influential and visible institutions of the state, it also has been a key driver in reviving the discussion of the public good and higher education.

ALTERNATIVE CONCEPTUALIZATIONS OF THE PUBLIC GOOD AND HIGHER EDUCATION

While the revival of interest in the public good and higher education is a positive development, research over the past decade has only begun to widen the scope of the question or draw on other domains of social science. Contemporary approaches within higher education have neglected an essential argument for conceptualizing higher education as a public good. To date, little attention has been turned to the role of the university as a public sphere and the concurrent role of the university as a site of contest in the broader political economy (Ambrozas, 1998; Giroux, 2003; Ordorika, 2003; Pusser, 2004).

Over the past two decades, critical theorists have argued for the centrality of the university as a producer of the public good on two primary dimensions: (1) the university as a site of essential knowledge production, where public and private resources are allocated to various courses of study and forms of research with significant impact on the wider society (Aronowitz, 2000; Marginson and Considine, 2000; Gumport, 2002; Slaughter and Rhoades, 2004); and (2) the university is seen as a site for the production of critical perspectives and for the development of autonomous citizens and leaders (Giroux, 2003). Each of these arguments has been raised in response to the rising application of neoliberal and corporate models of finance, governance, and organization in higher education (Kirp, 2003). In each case, the concern and the critiques are well grounded. They focus on the nature of university production—in the form of research products and educated students—under changing economic and political regimes. Under that paradigm, the university is seen as losing control over the production of such public goods as basic research and knowledge located at "a distance from the market" (Slaughter and Leslie, 1997), as well as the production of educated citizens with a critical perspective on such issues as diversity and economic stratification.

An essential concept that has occasionally surfaced at the margins of work on public good and higher education is the idea of the university itself as a public sphere, a space that is at once physical, symbolic, cultural, political, and semantic, not in relation to the state or the broader political economy but as a site of complex, autonomous contest in its own right. Henry Giroux, writing on higher education as a site for the production of critical thinkers, pointed to the importance of the university and the public sphere: "Fundamental to the rise of a vibrant democratic culture is the recognition that education must be treated as a public good—as a crucial site where students gain a public voice and come to grips with their own power as individual and social agents. . . . Reducing higher education to the handmaiden of corporate culture works against the critical social imperative of educating citizens who can sustain and develop inclusive democratic spheres" (Giroux, 2002, 182). The pursuit of a better understanding of the relationship of higher education to the public good turns attention to the university itself as one of those spheres.

Public Spheres

The critical social philosopher, Jurgen Habermas (1962, 1991), suggested that alongside the state and private interests, there exists a space, the public sphere, where public interaction, conversation, and deliberation can take place, and where the nature of the state and private interests can be debated and contested. Craig Calhoun has described Habermas's vision of the public sphere as "an institutional location for practical reason in public affairs and for the accompanying valid, if often deceptive, claims of formal democracy" (Calhoun, 1992, 1).

Nancy Fraser further refined the concept by placing the public sphere beyond the market economy and suggested that it is an arena of discursive, rather than economic, relations: "Here the public sphere connoted an ideal of unrestricted rational discussion of public matters. The discussion was to be open, and accessible to all, merely private interests were to be inadmissible, inequalities of status were to be bracketed, and discussants were to deliberate as peers. The result of such discussion would be public opinion in the strong sense of a consensus about the common good" (Fraser, 1992, 112–13). Fraser also points out that as well as being sites of open discourse and contest, public spheres are key arenas for the creation of social identities. Seyla Benhabib (1992) argues that since the American Revolution the scope of the public has increased, driven in part by contests and social movements emerging from public spheres. Key to the emergence of these contests is that within a public sphere there is no predefined agenda. She asserts: "The struggle over what gets included in the public agenda is itself a struggle for justice and freedom" (Benhabib, 1992, 79).

Higher Education as a Public Sphere

Fraser and other theorists maintain that in contemporary societies there are multiple public spheres, embodying different cultures, discourses, and values. Building on Fraser's argument, Ambrozas (1998) suggests that the university can be understood as one essential public sphere, where inclusiveness, discourse, identity development, knowledge production, and politics combine to enhance democracy.

For the most part, research and scholarship in higher education have not tended to treat the university as a public sphere, or to conceptualize the "public space" of the university as a key public good. In part, this can be attributed to a dearth of political-theoretical research in higher education (Ordorika, 2003) and the scarcity of work on education in political science (Orr, 2004). The vast majority of research in higher education treats university politics as an essentially endogenous process with administration and governance of external demands a process of interest articulation (Pusser, 2003). At the same time, the literature of higher education in the United States is replete with references to key political movements that shaped and were shaped by university activity. These efforts encompass the abolitionist movement, resistance to McCarthyism and the loyalty oaths, the free speech and civil rights movements, Vietnam-era activism, struggles over affirmative action, divestment from South Africa, contests over campus labor organization, and more recently animal rights and socially responsible manufacturing (Gitlin, 1987; Rhoads and Rhoades, 2005). A global perspective on social movements and higher education would add considerably more examples (Maldonado, 2002; Kurlansky, 2004).

In many of these contests, it was the interaction of the university as a site of history, culture, and symbolic importance in the broader political economy, with actors from within and beyond the physical borders of the campuses, that gave critical energy to the political struggles (Ordorika, 2003; Pusser, 2004; Rensburg, 1996). The university served as a place to bring together disparate actors for open conversation and collaboration in a public space, where critiques could be generated in pursuit of the public good. In short, the university served as a key public sphere.

It is important to note that the publics coming together in the university sphere have reflected many ideologies and social perspectives. A markedly different coalition of actors and interests shaped the Free Speech movement at UC Berkeley than the one that sparked the end of affirmative action at the same university and throughout the state of California in 1995 (Chavez, 1998; Pusser, 2004). In each case the university served as a site for the construction of discourse, symbols, and public political activity in pursuit of critical engagement, rather than private good or state authority.

Ambrozas (1998) suggests that the university became a more powerful public sphere in the aftermath of WW II, as institutions became more inclusive, with a proliferation of interests and a greater potential for linkages between politics and academe. Kurlansky (2004) documents the key role of the university in 1968 as a public sphere in the political lives of France, Mexico, the United States, and Czechoslovakia. He argues that the contests generated in each of those public spheres shaped other spheres in the moment and for generations to come. Case studies of campus activism are replete with references by key actors in one generation to the activities, conversations, and symbols of earlier campus contests (Ordorika, 2003; Kurlansky, 2004; Rhoads and Rhoades, 2005).

Building on Habermas, to understand the university as a public sphere also requires conceptualizing the university as a space where contest can take place outside the control of private or market interests and the state. This space exists despite the rapid increase in political-economic activity directed at the university by private and market interests (Bok, 2003; Geiger, 2004; Kirp, 2003; Slaughter and Rhoades, 2004).

Many unique attributes of public and private universities support the development of public spheres, and many have found support in the political arena through appeals to the public good. As one example, a number of both American and international universities have a charter status that gives authority over the institution to a public board of governors rather than to a state entity or to a private governance mechanism. Similarly, most public and private degree-granting universities have been organized as nonprofit institutions, operating under nonmarket or quasimarket conditions, with the support of a variety of public and private subsidies for that purpose (Winston, 1997).

Also, a number of the most fundamental activities carried out by public and private universities in the interest of the public good are organized in ways that diverge from many norms of state action or private interest. Universities have adopted codes of honor and behavior with considerable coercive and symbolic power that are quite distinct from those enforced beyond campus borders. Institutions of higher education design modes of interaction, physical spaces, residence life assignments, and other forms of social integration unique from those found in the surrounding communities. Universities also generally practice a form of financial redistribution through institutional fees and financial aid policies that could not easily be replicated in the broader society under prevailing political norms. In important ways, the university has exclusive dispensation to organize and operate outside of state and private norms in the interest of the common good on campus and the public good more generally. At the same time, the public spheres of the university are under constant challenge from the state and private interests. While Columbia University and the University of California served as essential public spheres for activism in 1968, Governors Rockefeller and Reagan (with the support of regents with significant business interests) endeavored to close down that same activist space by constraining the public sphere for engagement (Baldridge, 1971). The challenge to critical engagement is often at the center of campus activism and university politics and is central to understanding the challenge to preserving the university as a public sphere.

SUSTAINING A PUBLIC SPHERE THROUGH PUBLIC HIGHER EDUCATION

In order to better understand challenges to the public sphere through higher education, researchers and policy makers will need to consider new conceptualizations of three traditional arenas of higher education: (1) institutional autonomy; (2) the role of markets and private interests in university revenue generation and efforts at cost containment; and (3) political and legal challenges to critical engagement on campuses.

Autonomy and the Public Sphere

Autonomy is a key concept in higher education that is more often invoked in governance crises than theorized or studied in postsecondary research. The prevalent understandings of autonomy in higher education research have been significantly shaped by the pioneering and quite useful work of Berdahl (1971) on the relationship between states and higher education institutions. Much of the subsequent work has addressed aspects of that original conception, such as the importance to the faculty of autonomy from administrative intervention in tenure and curricular decisions (Kerr and Gade, 1989), or the appropriate degree of autonomy for boards of governors as they negotiate contested policy issues (Ingram, 1994; Pusser, 2004). Ken Mortimer and Colleen O'Brien Sathre expand on this topic in chapter 4.

While Berdahl and others have pointed to key constraints on effective organization and governance that flow from these tensions, contemporary research on autonomy can be enhanced through the application of emerging models for understanding universities as political institutions and as instruments in broader state and national political contests (Marginson and Considine, 2000; Ordorika, 2003; Pusser, 2004). The work of Rhoades (1998) on administrative challenges to faculty organization and professional expertise also offers considerable utility for future work on autonomy as both an individual and institutional issue in higher education. A public sphere depends on autonomy at many levels—individual, institutional, and social—to enable unfettered critical engagement to flourish. As an element in preserving a public sphere through higher education, autonomy needs to be understood as a guiding principle at the center of a multidimensional arena of contest.

New Forms of Revenue and the Public Sphere

Shifting patterns of revenue generation in higher education also present formidable challenges to preserving higher education as a public sphere. The rapid commercialization of university-based research and knowledge production, and the inherent challenges to norms of research and publication, has been widely documented (Aronowitz, 2000; Bok, 2003; Slaughter and Rhoades, 2004). In a similar fashion, a significant body of contemporary research points to shifting patterns of organizational resource allocation, governance, and authority that emerge from relative declines in state support and concurrent increases in tuition, donative income, and other private sources of revenue (Ehrenberg, 2000; Kirp, 2003; Newman and Couturier, 2001; Winston, 1999). Alongside new forms of revenue generation, efforts to reduce costs through the deployment of new technologies and shifts in the organization and compensation of academic labor will have significant impact on critical engagement and the public sphere through higher education (Levin, 2001; Tierney, 2004).

Political and Legal Challenges Shaping the Public Sphere

In a development that is not unrelated to changes in university revenue generation, the amount of political and legal activity directed at the organization, conduct, and governance of higher education has increased dramatically over the past two decades (Cook, 1998; Giroux and Giroux, 2004; Savage, 1999). Political and legal initiatives cover a wide range of issues, from efforts to increase funded research projects (Savage, 1999), efforts to end affirmative action (Pusser, 2004), interest group challenges to university curricula (Levine, 1996), efforts to ban the distribution of certain contraceptives in college pharmacies (Stepp, 2003), and congressional legislation to enforce limits on institutional costs (Burd, 2003). The increase in legal challenges to universities has been so dramatic that it was described by Olivas (2004) as a "torrent" that requires a "cottage industry of publications to track the thousands of cases each year" (258).

Contemporary political and legal challenges to higher education will significantly impact the public sphere in higher education, though how that will occur, and what the implications will be, is not entirely clear. Such challenges can either limit the space for critical engagement or open new avenues for productive contest and interaction. Given the pace of change in the political and legal environment for postsecondary institutions, attention will usefully be turned to broad models from political and legal theory that incorporate the role of higher education in the wider political economy. The role of university administration as a mediator of political and legal demands is another under-researched arena that offers great promise for better understanding the public sphere. By definition, the public sphere of higher education exists beyond the control of the university's administrative and governance mechanisms. This takes on additional import, given the rapid increase in institutional efforts to forge complex political-economic alliances with the state and private interests in the pursuit of greater economic, political, and legal legitimacy.

CONCLUSION

To ensure the public good derived from higher education as a public sphere, structural and procedural changes will be required in many aspects of the postsecondary arena. In essence, demands for control will need to give way to contest, collaboration, and consensus. Faculty members will need the freedom to promote critical engagement with sufficient autonomy from institutional, state, and private interests. Students will need institutional support for their role as critical actors in enacting and preserving the public sphere and the university. Institutional administrations will be challenged to protect the public sphere from state and private interventions as well as from institutional control.

Institutional actors and constituents of higher education will be particularly challenged to ensure the protection of the public sphere as a space for critical public discourse as higher education expands. Greater enrollments produce more elaborated institutional structures, power bases, and regulatory authority, and greater attention will need to be devoted to protecting the public sphere from the institution itself as well as the state and private interests. Given that the public sphere depends on critical engagement between those with equal status, broader postsecondary efforts to achieve equality throughout higher education will also support the public sphere. Just as a contest is necessary to ensure the space for a public sphere through higher education, a contest to achieve the equality necessary for effective critical engagement in the public sphere is also necessary.

Governing boards at every level will continue to play pivotal roles in sustaining a public sphere through higher education. Enacting and sustaining the public sphere presents challenges that touch on nearly all aspects of universities—coordination will remain essential to success. Trustees will need to understand the public sphere in higher education as a unique public good in order to allocate resources, create structures, and support policies that promote the university as a viable public sphere. Governance mechanisms that are dedicated to the preservation of the public sphere will also ensure that no single group controls the institution, a practice that is a time-honored tenet of responsible trusteeship.

Can a public good be preserved in higher education that is physical and fluid, discursive and symbolic, historical and mutable? Can it be privileged by the state, the institution, and private interests at the same time that it is beyond the control of the state, the institution, and private interests? To do so will require a new understanding of the public sphere in higher education and a renewed commitment to the critical engagement that sustains that public sphere and the public good in higher education.

REFERENCES

Ambrozas, D. 1998. The university as a public sphere. *Canadian Journal of Communication*, 23(1). http://www.cjc-online.ca/viewarticle.php?id=447.

Aronowitz, S. 2000. *The knowledge factory*. Boston: Beacon Press.

Baldridge, J. V. 1971. *Power and conflict in the university: Research in the sociology of complex organizations*. New York: J. Wiley.

Becker, G. 1964. *Human capital: A theoretical and empirical analysis with special reference to education*. New York: Columbia University Press.

Benhabib, S. 1992. Models of public space: Hannah Arendt, the liberal tradition, and Jurgen Habermas. In *Habermas and the public sphere*, ed. C. Calhoun, 73–98. Cambridge: MIT Press.

Berdahl, R. 1971. *Statewide coordination of higher education*. Washington, DC: American Council on Education.

Bok, D. 2003. *Universities in the marketplace*. Princeton, NJ: Princeton University Press.

Breneman, D.W. 1991. Guaranteed student loans: Great success or dismal failure? Indianapolis, IN: United Student Aid Fund.

———. 2003. Declining access: A potential—if slow-moving—train wreck. *National CROSSTALK* 11(2) (Spring).

Burd, S. 2003. High stakes on tuition. *Chronicle of Higher Education (May 2):* 34–35.

Calhoun, C. 1992. Introduction: Habermas and the public sphere. In *Habermas and the public sphere*, ed. C. Calhoun, 1–47. Cambridge: MIT Press.

Chavez, L. 1998. *The color bind*. Berkeley: University of California Press.

Cook, C. E. 1998. *Lobbying for higher education: How colleges and universities influence federal policy*. Nashville, TN: Vanderbilt University Press.

Cuban, L., and Shipps, D. 2000. *Reconstructing the connom good in education: Coping with intractable American Dilemmas*. Stanford, CA: Stanford University Press.

Douglass, J. A. 2000. *The California idea and American higher education: 1850 to the 1960 master plan*. Stanford, CA: Stanford University Press.

Ehrenberg, R. G. 2000. *Tuition rising: Why colleges cost so much.* Cambridge, MA: Harvard University Press.

Feller, I. 2000. Social contracts and the impact of matching fund requirements on American research universities. *Educational Evaluation and Policy Analysis* 22(1): 91–98.

Fraser, N. 1992. Rethinking the public sphere: A contribution to the critique of actually existing democracy. In *Habermas and the public sphere*, ed., C. Calhoun , 109–42. Cambridge: MIT Press.

Freire, P. 1970. *Pedagogy of the oppressed.* New York: Continuum Press.

Geiger, R. L. 2004. *Knowledge and money.* Stanford, CA: Stanford University Press.

Giroux, H. A. 2002. Neoliberalism, corporate culture, and the promise of higher education: The university as a democratic public sphere. *Harvard Educational Review* 72(4): 425–63.

———. 2003. Selling out higher education. *Policy Futures in Education* 1(1): 179–200.

Giroux, H. A., and S. S. Giroux. 2004. *Take back higher education: Race, youth, and the crisis of democracy in the post-civil rights era.* New York: Palgrave.

Gitlin, T. 1987. *The sixties: Years of hope, days of rage.* New York: Bantam.

Goldin, C., and L. Katz. 1998. *The shaping of higher education: The formative years in the United States, 1890–1940.* Working Paper 6537. Cambridge, MA: National Bureau of Economic Research.

Gumport, P. J. 2002. Universities and knowledge: Restructuring the city of intellect. In *The future of the city of intellect*, ed. S. Brint, 47–81. Stanford, CA: Stanford University Press.

Habermas, J. 1962. *The structural transformation of the public sphere.* Cambridge: MIT Press.

———. 1991. The public sphere. In *Rethinking popular culture*, ed. C. Mukerji and M. Schudson, 398–406. Berkeley: University of California Press.

———. 1996. *Between facts and norms: Contributions to a discourse theory of law and democracy.* Cambridge, MA: MIT Press.

Institute for Higher Education Policy (IHEP). 1998. *Reaping the benefits: Defining the public and private value of going to college.* Washington, DC: Author.

Ingram, R. 1994. *Effective Trusteeship: A guide for board members of independent colleges and universities.* Washington, DC: Association of Governing Boards.

Jefferson, T. 1812. *Letter to William Duane.* ME 13: 186, Library of Congress.

Kerr, C., and M. Gade. 1989. *The guardians: Boards of trustees of American colleges and universities.* Washington, DC: Association of Governing Boards.

Kirp, D. L. 2004. *Shakespeare, Einstein, and the bottom line.* Cambridge, MA: Harvard University Press.

Kurlansky, M. 2004. *1968: The year that rocked the world.* New York: Ballantine Books.

Levin, J. 2001. *Globalizing the community college: Strategies for change in the twenty-first century.* New York: Palgrave Macmillan.

Levine, L. 1996. *The opening of the American mind: Canons, culture, and history.* Boston: Beacon Press.

Maldonado, A. 2002. The National Autonomous University of Mexico: A continuing struggle. *International Higher Education* 28: 23–25.

Mansbridge, J. 1998. On the contested nature of the public good. In *Private action and the public good*, ed. W. W. Powell and E. S. Clemens, 3–19. New Haven, CT: Yale University Press.

Marginson, S. 1997. *Markets in education.* Melbourne: Allen and Unwin.

———. 2004. Competition and markets in higher education: A "glonacal" analysis. *Policy Futures in Education* 2(2): 175–244.

Marginson, S., and M. Considine. 2000. *The enterprise university.* Cambridge: Cambridge University Press.

Newman, F., and L. K. Couturier. 2001. The new competitive arena: Market forces invade the academy. *Change,* Sept./Oct., 10–17.

Olivas, M. A. 2004. The rise of nonlegal legal influences on higher education. In *Governing academia*, ed. R.G. Ehrenberg, 258–75. Ithaca, NY: Cornell University Press.

Ordorika, I. 2003. *Power and politics in university governance: Organization and change at the Universidad Nacional Autonoma de Mexico.* New York: Routledge Falmer.

Orr, M. 2004. Political science and educational research: An exploratory look at two political science journals. *Educational Researcher* 33(5): 1–6.

Powell, W. W., and E. S. Clemens, eds. 1998. *Private action and the public good.* New Haven, CT: Yale University Press.

Pusser, B. 2002. Higher education, the emerging market, and the public good. In *The knowledge economy and postsecondary education*, ed. P. Graham and N. Stacey, 105–26. Washington, DC: National Academy Press.

———. 2003. Beyond Baldridge: Extending the political model of higher education governance. *Educational Policy* 17(1): 121–40.

———. 2004. *Burning down the house: Politics, governance, and affirmative action at the University of California.* Albany: State University of New York Press.

Pusser, B., and D. Doane. 2001. Public purpose and private enterprise: The contemporary organization of secondary education. *Change, 33*, 18–22.

Rensburg, I. L. 1996. *Collective identity and public policy: From resistance to reconstruction in South Africa, 1986–1995.* Palo Alto, CA: Stanford University Press.

Rhoades, G. 1992. Beyond "the state": Interorganizational relations and state apparatus in postsecondary education. In *Higher education: Handbook of theory and research*, ed. J. C. Smart, 84–142). New York: Agathon.

————. 1998. *Managed professionals: Unionized faculty and restructuring academic labor.* Albany: State University of New York Press.

Rhoades, G., and R. A. Rhoads. 2002. The public discourse of U.S. graduate employee unions: Social movement identities, ideologies, and strategies. *Review of Higher Education* 26(2): 163–86.

Rich, A. 1979. *On lies, secrets, and silences, selected prose: 1966–1978.* New York: Norton.

Rudolph, F. 1965. *The American college and university.* New York: Vintage Books.

Savage, J. D. 1999. *Funding science in America: Congress, universities, and the politics of the academic pork barrel.* Cambridge: Cambridge University Press.

Slaughter, S. 1990. *The higher learning and high technology: Dynamics of higher education policy formation.* Albany: State University of New York Press.

Slaughter, S., and L. L. Leslie. 1997. *Academic capitalism: Politics, policies, and the entrepreneurial university.* Baltimore, MD: Johns Hopkins University Press.

Slaughter, S., and G. Rhoades. 2004. *Academic capitalism and the new economy.* Baltimore, MD: Johns Hopkins University Press.

Stepp, L. S. 2003. Pill ban gives birth to protest. *Washington Post, April 24*, p. C01.

Sunstein, C. R. 2004. *The second bill of rights.* New York: Basic Books.

Tierney, W. G. 2004. A perfect storm: Turbulence in higher education. In *Competing conceptions of academic governance*, ed.,W. G. Tierney, xv–xxxi. Baltimore, MD: Johns Hopkins University Press.

Turner, S., and B. Pusser. 2004. Nonprofit and for-profit governance in higher education. In G*overning academia*, ed. R. G. Ehrenberg, 235–57. Ithaca, NY: Cornell University Press.

Winston, G. 1997. Why can't a college be more like a firm? *Change*, Sept./Oct. 33–38.

————. 1999. Subsidies, hierarchy, and peers: The awkward economics of higher education. *Journal of Economic Perspectives* 13(1): 13–36.

Winston, G., J. C. Carbone, and E. G. Lewis. 1998. *What's been happening to higher education: A reference manual, 1986–87 to 1994–95.* Working Paper No. 47. Williamstown, MA: The Williams Project on the Economics of Higher Education.

2

Lost In Transition

Governing in a Time of Privatization

Karen M. Whitney

Volumes of literature have been written regarding the price students pay for college, many of them creating a widespread feeling that something is not quite right with higher education (Bowen, 1981; Callan, Finney, Bracco, and Doyle, 1997; Halstead, 1996; Harvey and Immerwahr, 1995; Trombley, 2003; Troutt, 1998). More critical accounts indicate that the problem of increasing college costs is not simply a matter of controlling expenditures but recognizing the states' declining support for higher education (Halstead, 1996; McKeown-Moak, 2000; Mortenson, 1998). In most cases, the discourse stops after describing funding shortfalls. Rarely are the consequences of these funding trends critically considered (Callan et al., 1997; Callan 2003; Gumport and Jennings, 1999; Mortenson, 1998). What has only recently emerged in the research literature, and a relationship that could be considered both cause and consequence, is the connection between state financing and state control of higher education (Gose, 2002; Selingo, 2003a).

State control of public higher education has been considered publicly much less often than state financing. Government regulation of higher education gained some prominence in 1996 and again in 2003. In both years, Republican lawmakers called for increased regulation of higher education in order to control costs through amendments to the Higher Education Act. In 1997, President Clinton appointed a group of educators and policy leaders to a National Commission on the Cost of Higher Education, which was responsible for evaluating national issues related to higher education costs (Troutt, 1998). The commission's report cited governmental regulation compliance as a major expense for institutions of higher learning. More recently, federal regulation of higher education has emerged as a way to respond to rising costs (Clayton, 2003).

State control of higher education is defined as the extent to which a state government controls or governs the financial and academic operations of its

29

public institutions (Volkwein, 1986; Whitney, 2003). Control should be viewed on a continuum with institutions operating in an environment of more or less control as compared to other institutions in other states. The higher the level of state control, the less autonomous the institution and the more dependent the institution is upon state review and approval for typical operations. State funding of higher education, in this chapter, is focused on the extent to which public institutions of higher learning can expect state funding in the future (Whitney, 2003). Therefore, the focus is not on how much funding is allocated by the state to the institution but, more importantly, on the state's sustained funding of public institutions over time.

Many higher education leaders continue to believe that declining state funding is cyclical, and that there will eventually be a return to greater state investment in higher education (Penley, 1997; Zemsky and Wegner, 1997). Conversely, a growing number of researchers suggest that the national decline in state appropriations for postsecondary education is not cyclical but, in fact, leads to the privatization of public colleges and universities (Callan and Finney, 1997; Gose, 2002; Gumport and Jennings, 1999). Privatization, in this chapter, is defined as the shifting of the proportion of public, state-appropriated funds to nonstate sources such as student tuition and fees, contracts for services and grants, and gifts as the principal institutional funding sources (Zemsky, Wegner, and Iannozzi, 1997; Whitney, 2003).

David Breneman, dean of the Curry School of Education at the University of Virginia, has questioned whether the privatization of public universities is a mistake or a model for the future. Breneman (1997) conceded that public institutions have negotiated more autonomy in light of diminished state funding, but he was skeptical that state funding could decline to a level that would actually lead to a de facto privatization of public institutions. However, James Duderstadt, former president of the University of Michigan, maintained that flagship universities might actually exchange state funding for greater autonomy in order to better pursue their missions (Gose, 2002). The University of Michigan has aggressively pursued private nongovernmental funds, transforming itself into a quasi-private institution of higher learning. Privatization is neither inherently good nor bad for public higher education, but it has an obvious impact on the governance of the institution. As public institutions become more privatized, who should govern?

Privatization challenges the historical arrangement of public higher education as managed by public bureaucracies. With the increasingly fragmented funding of higher education, the systems that lead and influence higher education also have become disjointed in their effort to advance the public good. As Brian Pusser noted in chapter 1, one way of conceptualizing the public good is as a classic economic dichotomy. A public good benefits the greater society or community more than an individual; a private good operates conversely, with benefits accruing to the individual more than the community. Such distinctions are critical in terms of funding. If a good is public, then the public should fund and control the enterprise. If it is private, then the individual should fund the cost of the activity. This perspective is an individualized orientation of public good.

Another perspective significant to this chapter is higher education's efforts to advance "the public good," which is the idea of educational leaders acting in the public's best interest. Public higher education is viewed as an economic, a social, and a cultural enterprise that impacts individuals and communities—locally, regionally, nationally, and globally. Howard Gardner's research regarding the nature of work defines "good work" as high quality and socially conscious (Gardner, Csikszentmihalyi, and Damon, 2002). Many would argue that public higher education has been both high quality and socially conscious. This perspective is an institutionalized orientation of public good.

Who governs and funds public higher education, and what specific systems are created to manage public institutions of higher learning in a time of privatization that defines the relationship between public higher education and the public good? Is public higher education a product that can be divided neatly according to beneficiary? Or is it a transcendent enterprise that acts on behalf of the students through the distribution of knowledge, scholarship, and creative activities such as teaching? If so, can it simultaneously act on behalf of multiple communities through the creation and application of knowledge and scholarship?

In order to help understand the complex relationships between state funding and control of public institutions of higher learning, a conceptual framework was developed (Whitney, 2003):

$$Control + Finance = Likelihood\ of\ Privatization$$

For higher education leaders, this area of inquiry provides a context for evaluating higher education administration, including issues of institutional mission and organizational structure. The relationship between public and private financing is a substantial policy issue for politicians as it relates to state spending priorities (Selingo, 2003a). Lawmakers annually consider how state tax dollars should be allocated to higher education in comparison to other state obligations, including K–12 education, prisons, transportation, and health care. Citizens may find this research area significant in response to the growing national anxiety over how to pay for higher education. Declining institutional sovereignty, increasing legislative regulation, and continuing public concern may be the consequences of what the National Commission on the

Cost of Higher Education (Troutt, 1998) cited as an "opaque relationship" between costs and prices that exists in higher education. Quite simply, individuals both inside and outside of higher education do not understand the connection between prices, costs, and subsidies, resulting in the privatization of public higher education. In order to further explore privatization, I have organized this chapter into three conceptual sections that consider privatization as an event, a process, and a continuum.

Privatization as an Event

For as long as public higher education has existed, events have illustrated a struggle over who pays and controls the practice. During the latter part of the nineteenth century and the early twentieth century, many conflicts ensued between state governments and public colleges and universities (Henderson, 1969; Shelburne, 1939). In 1895, Kansas established a public higher education system that was to be free to all who lived in the state. However, in order to fund the library, the regents charged a $5 fee, which students had to pay before they could use the facility. The Kansas attorney general filed a lawsuit against the board in an attempt to remove the fee. The court ruled in favor of the attorney general, indicating that the "regents have no power to raise a fund . . . unless expressly authorized to do so by law" (Shelburne, 1939, 87). In 1914, a similar situation occurred in Oklahoma, where a university charged a mandatory fee to students for use of university services, however the university prevailed in that case. Several years later, it was noted that funding of higher education was shifting from governments to individuals. For example, in 1927–1928, "a larger portion of the receipts was collected from students, private benefactions, and miscellaneous sources, while a percentage decrease was noted in funds from all public sources and endowment income" (Greenleaf, 1930, 260).

A concern in the 1950s was that public institutions were shifting from their historically populist structure toward a more privatized corporate structure, to the detriment of the essential mission of higher education (Carey, 1956). Carey noted that in the public's mind, there were certain "loosely drawn similarities between corporations and universities" (440). These similarities included viewing state taxpayers as stockholders, boards of trustees and regents as boards of corporate directors, university presidents as general managers, and students and parents as customers. Carey referred to this as a "corporation complex." He argued that the corporate paradigm would cause "the university to supplant some of its pedagogical objectives with business objectives, [and] probably there will be an overemphasis on economic profits at the expense of educational values" (441). In the corporate paradigm, numbers of students become more important than the creation and dissemination of knowledge. Carey predicted that the corporate complex would create a circular framework of "getting more students, to get more state funds to get more buildings to get more students, to get more funds" (441). In considering the corporate construct, Carey asked whether faculty were "state employees" or "appointees to an academic community" (443). He viewed the corporate "employee" paradigm as lacking flexibility and independence of thought, which might render faculty unable to conduct research or teach.

In 1946, President Truman established the President's Commission on Higher Education, which predicted that there would be an enormous demand for higher education by 1960. The report was considered unprecedented in that it aggressively outlined the importance of educating significant numbers of citizens as a prerequisite for maintaining democracy and ensuring a quality of life for the nation (Russell, 1949; Simpson, 1948). Governmental funding of higher education was an investment in human capital. Additional state and federal financing of higher education was necessary to advance economic, social, and national agendas. The Truman Commission Report further indicated that although it was unlikely that the cost of education could be reduced, the "proportion of costs borne by the individual" (Newburn, 1950, 178) must be reduced.

In 1998, fifty years after the Truman Commission, another national attempt to define who should pay for higher education was released in the National Commission on the Cost of Higher Education report, *Straight Talk about College Costs and Prices* (Troutt, 1998). The report was commissioned by President Clinton in 1996 to study the cost of higher education and find ways to make college more affordable (Burd, 1997). According to Burd, Republican congressional leaders were interested in considering whether student financial aid drove up the cost of college, whereas educators welcomed a review of college costs as an opportunity to discuss how government controls contributed to the cost of higher education.

According to the report, funding of public higher education originates from three major sources: government, students and families, and institutions themselves. Historically, the largest contributor to public higher education has been the state (Bowen, 1981). However, state contributions have declined over time, and in some cases student tuition and fees have become proportionally the larger funding source for institutional operations (Troutt, 1998). State appropriations have devolved to a secondary or tertiary contributor. Students fund higher education each semester through tuition and fees. Colleges and universities acquire an increasing amount of revenue from nonstate sources, including grants, outsourcing, and direct sale of services and goods (Breneman, 1997). The federal government has historically contributed the least to higher education in terms of direct operating funds but has chosen to affect higher

education through appropriations to students in the form of grants and loans
and to faculty for research and facilities (St. John, 1994).

One of the most important concepts related to how higher education was
organized and funded. This topic was extensively addressed in an expert paper
located in the appendix of the report. The paper, presented by Gordon Winston (1998), contained information that reviewed the economic structure of
the typical university in relation to the typical economic structure of a private
firm. Winston contended that the economic structure of a university operates
in a manner contrary to that of a private firm. The most significant difference
between higher education and the private sector, according to Winston, was
that all institutions of higher education sell their product (education) at a sub-
sidized price "far less than the average cost of its production" (Winston, 1998,
117). Winston advanced a critically important concept, that private firms price
their product based on the cost of the product plus profit, whereas higher education institutions set their price less than cost because of a student subsidy.
The following represents Winston's position:

Private Firm   Institution of Higher Learning
Price = Cost + Profit   Price + Subsidy = Cost (or Price = Cost – Subsidy)

Winston maintained that our entire society has developed what he called
an "intuition" about how organizations should operate based upon the economics of the private firm. Consequently, popular notions regarding the price
of higher education have assumed that the increased cost of attending college
was a function of increased cost or increased profit taking of some sort. As a
result of this belief, there have been political efforts to dissect and re-engineer
cost in order to ascertain how to reduce the price charged to students. However, in Winston's model, the increased price of public higher education may
also result from a decrease in student subsidy, such as a decrease in state support. In fact, the economics of higher education are counterintuitive to a business paradigm. This difference has been a major barrier to accurately
understanding the pricing of higher education.

The Truman Commission report focused on achieving enrollment expansion, whereas the National Cost Commission report focused on achieving cost
containment. Both commissions, in their time, ignited a national discussion
regarding college access, equity, cost, price, and subsidy, and both attempted to
learn from the past and prepare the country for future educational demands.
Since the founding of Harvard in 1643, institutions of higher learning in the
United States have grown from one in every colony to one in almost every
county, and from nine to more than 3,700 (NCES, 2003). Regardless of this
growth, issues of control and funding have pervaded the 360–year history of
higher education in the United States. I have presented a series of events that

provides examples intended to help explain how public higher education has become increasingly privatized over time. In order to further explore the control funding connection, I will focus on privatization as a process.

PRIVATIZATION AS A PROCESS

Economic, political, and bureaucratic processes have contributed to the privatization of public higher education. Although the country has a historically populist approach toward postsecondary education, the distribution of the cost of higher education has challenged student access (Brown and Gamber, 2002; Brubacher and Rudy, 1976; Lennington, 1996). "The cost of higher education to students," noted Lennington, "has a direct impact on access, so that increases in cost are understandably of great concern to students, parents, and education policy makers" (Lennington, 1996, 3). This approach toward higher education has resulted in a demographic profile of college students increasingly reflecting the demographic profile of our society. There has been a constant debate about whether declines in state subsidies will adversely affect access to higher education.

Economists looked at the relationship between direct fees (what the student pays) and taxation (what the community pays) in terms of balancing who should pay and how much. Who should pay is ideally connected to who benefits from higher education. If the individual benefits, then it could be seen as a private good and should be funded more by the individual. If society benefits, however, then it should be considered a public good and be funded by the community. If it is both a public and private good, then this prompts the question (Creedy, 1994, 91) "Under what circumstances would a majority of individuals be prepared to vote for a proportion of the cost of higher education per person to be met from tax revenue, given that the majority will not find it worthwhile to invest in education?" With the public's tendency to mistrust government, including higher education institutions, there is a perception that colleges and universities are wasting, or not optimally spending, public funds (Brown and Gamber, 2002). This suspicion questions the validity of a higher education. McPherson (1991) noted that productivity has not increased in higher education, because the "basic production functions" have remained unchanged. Faculty and administrators have few incentives to become more productive, because faculty are rewarded for "productivity in research and not in teaching, and administrators are rewarded for number of staff and programs managed with often little attention about their productivity or efficiency" (9).

For more than 100 years, public higher education in the United States has followed a political and bureaucratic policy, which is based on the concept of direct appropriations. Public institutions then charge students a low rate of tuition. "The resulting charges are . . . low relative to the cost of providing education services at these institutions, and low relative to charges by comparable private institutions," according to Fischer (1990, 44). Fischer outlined several factors that have shaped this public policy, including the following: (1) Higher education is a public good that should be free or very accessible; (2) A better-educated community is a benefit to society, thus public higher education deserves the same financial support that is allocated to public elementary or secondary education; (3) Higher education is an entitlement, as is public school education; (4) An affordable higher education is a way to keep talented people in a state or, with low-cost, out-of-state tuition, a way to recruit bright, college-oriented people to a state; and (5) Higher education is a way to promote equal opportunity for students from low-income families.

Changes in the historical patterns of governmental funding of higher education threaten future access to higher education (Halstead, 1993; McPherson and Schapiro, 2001). In the introduction to his report, *State Profiles: Financing Public Higher Education 1978–1993,* Halstead (1993) summarized the political situation that has continued into the twenty-first century:

> Governors and state legislators strive to allocate scarce revenues among competing public claims. Education officials seek to project and promote realistic budgets, which equitably and productively distribute appropriated support. Institutional administrators and faculty pursue academic excellence and competitive salaries. Students and parents desire a quality education at the lowest possible cost. And finally, taxpayers seek efficiently operated government services adequate to public needs. (10)

Who pays for higher education has steadily shifted away from government (the society) to the individual (the student). McPherson, Schapiro, and Winston (1997) determined that public institutions historically receive primary support from state appropriations and that these appropriations are in decline. They further indicated that "universities are going to have to gain an increased share of their revenues from other sources" (31). Callan (2003) not only confirmed that state support for public higher education has continued to decline but also predicts that further cuts in state support are likely.

Over time, students have paid significantly more for their education. From an annual survey of colleges, the College Board (2002) provided college cost trend data from 1971 to 2002. The College Board research indicated that, in constant dollars, students paid more than twice as much for their education in 2002 than they paid in 1971. The cost to attend public, four-year institutions increased from $1,577 a year in 1971–1972 to $4,081 a year in 2002–2003. The thirty-year study was consistent with a 1996 report conducted by the U.S. Department of Education, which indicated that in the 1960s, students attending public colleges and universities paid approximately 10 percent of the total cost of their education, compared to the 1970s, when they paid 33 percent of the cost. In the 1990s, students paid over 40 percent of the cost. Tuition and fees on the average grew 3.1 percent to 5.6 percent a year from 1980 to 1990 and increased an average of 3.9 percent a year from 1990 to 2000. However, median family income did not increase as fast (in constant dollars), which actually resulted in a loss in buying power (U.S. Department of Education, 1996; NCES, 2003).

Higher education researchers Kent Halstead (1998) and Thomas Mortenson (1999) found that the prices students pay have increased over time. However, when they took inflation into account, they found that institutional operating costs had not increased. The decline in the proportion of state appropriations to public higher education's total budget was the primary reason that the increases in the price students pay exceeded inflation (Halstead, 1993). States have historically paid the largest proportion of the cost of public higher education. However, this portion has declined over the past seventy-three years. Table 2.1 presents a pattern of funding by source from 1927 to 2000. Student contributions have increased, as other sources have decreased. Since student aid (i.e., loans, grants, etc.) is distributed to the student, these resources are considered part of the student source of funds.

Public institutions of higher learning in the twenty-first century have experienced reductions in state funding. Reductions can occur as a general redirection in state appropriated funds, or as defunding of specific items, such as maintenance, repair, or new construction. This pattern of "downward investment" also occurred in the early part of the 1980s and the 1990s (Mortenson, 2002). As a result of the reduction in state support, the price to students increased to offset the losses in state funding. This reduction in state support and increased price to students can be explained by the notion of higher education as a balance wheel. Hovey's (1999) concept described states using higher education as a way to balance state finances. When state funds are abundant, then states tend to allocate more funds to higher education. When state funds are short, then states disproportionately reduce the level of support to public higher education compared to other state-supported activities in order to balance their budgets. Legislators believe that public higher education makes a good balance wheel, because it has other funding sources it can turn to, such as tuition, to absorb cuts in state support. They also believe that public institutions have reserves and an ability to absorb short-term fiscal stress through such actions as increases in class sizes and/or teaching loads.

Public higher education is perceived to have more funding options than other state entities. According to Marcus, "Higher education is usually the biggest piece of the discretionary portion of a state's budget and is thus easiest

TABLE 2.1
Percentage Funding of Higher Education by Source: 1927–2000
Percent of Total Share (PTS)

	1927 PTS	1967 PTS	1996 PTS	2000 PTS
Student	18%	12%	22%	18%
Institution	20%	23%	27%	36%
State Government	54%	44%	40%	34%
Federal Government	8%	21%	10%	12%

Source: Greenleaf, 1930; NCES, 2003

to cut. Since education appears to have 'an independent source of revenue: tuition and fees,' it is all that more an attractive item to reduce" (1994, 11). As state fiscal support has declined, tuition and other fee incomes are an increasing source of revenue for many types of colleges and universities (U.S. Department of Education, 1996). Lennington (1996) observed that fees have significantly increased as an offset to the decline in tax subsidies.

Mortenson (2002) noted that in the state tax appropriations for THE fiscal year 2002–2003, states continued a renewed trend of reducing state support. Some years earlier he observed increases in state funding but cautioned that these increases did not reflect a renewed commitment to public higher education. Instead, they should be considered a result of increases in personal income and the general growth of the economy. Mortenson stated, "Over a longer period of time, these increases are nothing more than a modest pause in a trend of significant declines in state investment in higher education that began about FY 1980" (1998, 1). Appropriations of state tax funds for public higher education operating expenses per $1,000 of personal income were at their peak in 1979 at $11.22, while the 2002–2003 fiscal year state investment of $7.35 was at the lowest since 1967 (Mortenson, 2002). Public institutions of higher learning have changed their institutional structures as a result of the declines in state investment. Mortenson (1999) identified three primary approaches in response to the declines in state funding: (1) capacity: controlling enrollment with caps and increased admissions standards; (2) quality: reducing quality of instruction by increasing class size, paying below-market rates for faculty; and (3) affordability: passing on the reduction in state funds to students as price increases.

The other key element of the privatization process involves state regulation of public higher education. Since 1983, J. F. Volkwein has studied the relationships between institutional autonomy, state control (i.e., the lack of institutional autonomy), and the quality and productivity of public higher education. He notes that public higher education's "regulatory relationship with state governments forms a critical component of the external climate within which these institutions pursue their goals" (Volkwein, 1987, 120). Volkwein (1986) introduced two measures to determine the level of state control: fiscal flexibility and academic flexibility. *Fiscal flexibility* consisted of nine items: (1) lump sum versus line item budgeting; (2) institutional ability to shift funds among categories; (3) institutional ability to retain and control tuition revenues; (4) institutional ability to retain and control other revenues; (5) external ceilings for faculty positions; (6) external ceilings for other employee positions; (7) freedom from pre-audit of expenditures; (8) institutional ability to carry over year-end balances; and (9) institutional ability to issue own checks for payroll and purchases. *Academic flexibility* included an institution's ability to (1) define its own mission; (2) add new undergraduate programs; (3) add new graduate programs; (4) review/discontinue existing undergraduate programs; (5) review/discontinue existing graduate programs; and (6) add/discontinue departments.

Volkwein noted that these measures do not significantly vary across institutions within a state, therefore, the findings were aggregated by state and attributed to all institutions regardless of type. In a follow-up article, Volkwein and Malik (1997) reexamined the relationship between state regulation and institutional effectiveness. They found that academic flexibility and fiscal and administrative flexibility are independent components of campus autonomy. Their study examined changes between the original 1983 data and data collected in 1995. The authors found that "campuses in many states [had] gained increased flexibility in their academic, financial, and personnel transactions" (38). The authors noted that increased flexibility might have resulted as compensation for decreased state support to public institutions.

Recently, states have employed a variety of regulatory policies to control public institutions, including "imposing tuition freezes, reducing tuition levels, [and] placing restrictions on the rate of increase in tuition" (McKeown-Moak, 2000, 8). Additionally, performance-based funding has been under consideration in over half of the states. States also are considering other types of regulation, including "examining workload and productivity as a means of improving learning outcomes or decreasing expenditures" (16). I have provided examples of economic, political, and bureaucratic processes that have contributed to privatization. Finally, I consider the extent to which public colleges and universities are becoming increasingly privatized.

PRIVATIZATION AS A CONTINUUM

The causes, effects, and future consequences of the decline in state funding of public higher education could increasingly be considered along a continuum of de facto privatization of public higher education. Researchers and policy makers have created language to reflect levels of privatization in higher education. Institutional autonomy, independent-public, public-private, state supported, state-assisted, state-located, and deregulated are the various ways in which privatization has been described (Breneman and Finney, 1997; Callan et al., 1997; MacTaggart, 1998; Zemsky, Wegner, and Iannozi, 1997).

St. John (1994) presents an ideological framework to explain the variety of viewpoints regarding the funding (or lack of) higher education along a continuum. According to St. John, the dominant political belief system influences the ideology that shapes the direction of public policy. He categorizes belief systems into five categories: conservative, liberal, neoconservative, neoliberal, and neo-Marxist. The following summary outlines each ideological perspective connected to higher education funding (St. John, 1994, 6): (1) *Conservative:* Returns from public investment accrue primarily to individuals; (2) *Liberal:* Economic development and intergenerational equity provide bases for public investment; (3) *Neoconservative:* Student aid has no influence on access, institutions raise tuition to increase revenue from federal aid programs, institutions raise tuition to maximize revenue (greed) and because they are nonproductive, and poor academic achievement explains lower participation by African Americans; (4) *Neoliberal:* Institutions replace the loss of federal student aid dollars with their own aid dollars, reductions in state subsidies to institutions fuel tuition increases, and tax revenue returns provide a basis for public investment; and (5) *Neo-Marxist:* Low income and minority students are generally influenced by the entire cost controversy, and programs serving middle-class majors are more adversely influenced by budget decisions that serve elite professions.

Understanding the continuum of ideological perspectives contributes to an understanding of the political context that affects higher education fiscal policy. Ideological perspectives are the foundation from which political and educational leaders negotiate the cost, subsidy, and price of public higher education. The more conservative the ideology, the more reduced the government subsidy, which results in a higher price to the student.

St. John maintains that there is a crisis in higher education financing because of the (mis)perceptions of government spending, including the appropriations for public higher education. During the 1980s, higher education tuition rose sharply. This led to public criticism that increases in tuition must be caused by some form of mismanagement. In fact, actual federal and state support of higher education declined, enrollments decreased nationally, and institutions were still recovering from the effects of a period of high inflation in the late 1970s and the early 1980s. These economic factors were not commonly considered when explaining cost increases. Privatization can be viewed either as an opportunity or a catastrophe. James Duderstadt, former president of the University of Michigan, indicated that as a result of declining state support, flagship institutions might choose to trade state funding for greater autonomy in order to be successful (Gose, 2002). Pursuing other funding sources, such as private gifts, transferring new technologies from research to the marketplace, and setting tuition to market rates might be more productive than pursuing limited state appropriations.

State higher education policy and public institutions of higher learning's response to state policies has varied across the states. Examples of the variety of governmental policies included: (1) the conscious decision on the part of government to transfer to private management the responsibility for certain functions that had formerly been organized and carried out by public agencies; (2) the phenomenon that results from a government's inability to fund its agencies at previous levels, often implicitly transferring a greater degree of authority and initiative to individual agencies or institutions, while continuing to vest nominal control in government; (3) the initiative taken by public agencies and institutions to reduce cost by outsourcing functions and/or to increase revenues by raising the prices they charge for the services they deliver; and (4) the actions that proceed from a public perception that government itself has become cumbersome and inefficient, that taxation is excessive and tax dollars are not well spent, and that government should exert a smaller influence in public and private life (Zemsky, Wegner, and Iannozzi, 1997, 75).

One reason higher education has been prone to state defunding is its ability to generate funds from a wide range of sources. Most other state services and programs are unable to generate funds in the same manner. Higher education's ability to shift costs to students contributes to the cycle of reductions in state support (Roherty, 1997). According to Breneman and Finney, "If the share of funding by source had remained constant at 1980 levels, tuition could have been 30 percent lower than it was at the end of 1995" (1997, 37). Revenue generated by institutions from private nongovernmental sources has increased relative to state revenues (Gumport and Jennings, 1999). They expressed a concern that the more private sources support public institutions of higher learning, the more higher education will be portrayed as a private benefit as compared to a public good. They also found that "public and private institutions are beginning to depend on a more similar revenue mix" (Breneman and Finney, 1997, 13).

A consequence of the continued privatization of public higher education is the possibility of complete divestiture from the state. Mortenson (1999) describes the historical funding patterns of state investment in public higher education since 1975 and extends his analysis of state defunding to consider that state investment could decline to the point of reaching zero or no funding based on historical funding patterns. Mortenson projects the year that each state will stop funding higher education, using a simple regression formula.

Based on Mortenson's fiscal year 2000 national analysis, the median year that state funding of higher education nationwide will go to zero is 2054. According to Mortenson's 1999 calculations, Vermont would be the first to completely stop funding in 2015, while New Mexico would continue funding through 7119. Research I Universities and other "highly regarded public institutions may seek to 'privatize' in order to preserve what is most important to themselves" (Zemsky and Wegner, 1997, 63).

The transformation of sections of universities or entire institutions from public to private has been occurring across the country (Selingo, 2003a). Public institutions that have provided specialized programs, such as health sciences, technology, law, business, and art, have been some of the first to convert from public to some type of private institution of higher learning (Schmidt, 2002). In 1992, Oregon transformed the Oregon Health Sciences University from a public university to a state-assisted public corporation. Ten years later, Oregon was again considering transforming the Oregon Institute of Technology, a public institution of higher learning, into a completely private institution. Most recently, the governor of Massachusetts announced a plan to privatize three public colleges and to reorganize the University of Massachusetts-Amherst into an independent, public-private university (Selingo, 2003b). The University of Wisconsin system President Katharine Lyall has proposed that "the state turn over its 26 campuses to an independent authority" in order to more effectively manage the institutions (Selingo, 2003a).

In addition to institutional transformation, other less radical approaches are under consideration that could move public institutions toward privatization (Selingo, 2003a). Colorado considered a voucher system, whereby students, rather than state institutions, would directly receive state appropriations. Institutions in South Carolina have made public an interest in breaking away from the control of the state higher education coordinating agency in order to more effectively pursue public-private partnerships. According to Winston (1998), our society has developed an intuition about how universities and colleges should operate based upon the economics of the private firm. Consequently, popular notions regarding the price of higher education have assumed that tuition increases are a function of increased institutional costs, managed inefficiencies, or perhaps profit taking. There have been political efforts to dissect and re-engineer costs to ascertain how to reduce tuition increases. However, there is a great deal of evidence that suggests that increased prices of public higher education actually resulted from decreased student subsidies. In public higher education, this means decreased state support in the form of appropriations.

The likelihood of some four-year public institutions of higher learning redefining their relationship with state government by conceptualizing themselves as de facto private institutions seems likely (Whitney, 2003). Public institutions of higher learning and states have been willing to exchange autonomy and funding to achieve a mutually beneficial relationship. This exchange between state and institution may explain public institutional movement along a continuum of privatization expressed on a four-sector likelihood of privatization matrix designed to describe various combinations of the funding and control relationship.

Figure 2.1 presents state funding and control data from a study completed in 2003 of 369 public institutions of higher learning (Whitney, 2003). The funding or vertical axis presents a continuum of the extent to which each state government supports public higher education. The higher number represents greater funding. The horizontal axis presents a continuum of data that was the extent to which each state controlled higher education. The higher number represented greater autonomy (less control). The state funding-control relationships with public higher education included: (1) state agency relationships of high funding and low autonomy; (2) state-aided relationships of high funding and high autonomy; (3) state-located relationships of low funding and high autonomy; and (4) state-constrained relationships of low funding and low autonomy.

Within a privatization paradigm, fundamental elements of higher education, such as institutional facilities, repair, renovation, and new construction, would be reconsidered. In terms of new construction, a building's purpose, design, development, and specifications would be regulated according to its funding source. Facilities that do not receive any state appropriated funds have typically been regulated in the same manner as facilities completely funded by state appropriations. Under a privatization construct, the funding source would be the controlling source. As a result, in a privatized world, buildings funded by student fees, for example, might be reviewed and approved by students or alumni, not by legislators or their designees. If the state wanted to maintain control of the facilities, then it would fund the design, development, construction, and maintenance of the facilities.

Curriculum and teaching might provide another good example of the impact of privatization. Remedial courses, multicultural curricula, and distance programs have been state mandated. Issues of tenure and post-tenure review also have been state regulated. Currently, public institutions comply with all government mandates, whether funded or unfunded. In a privatized world, institutions of higher learning might only comply with funded mandates. Unfunded directives would be considered recommendations. Under a privatization model, privatized-public institutions, with greater institutional flexibility, could pursue research that might otherwise be currently prohibited by the state. Access to higher education services and programs, including admissions and financial aid policies, would change in a privatized learning organization. Past responses to government mandates regarding affirmative action and

Figure 2.1
Likelihood of Privatization Matrix by State

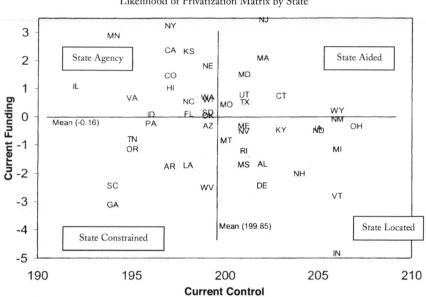

Note: Alaska is not shown in this figure because data were not available for past control.
Source: Adapted from Whitney, 2003.

admissions policy provide a good example of possible changes. In a privatized
environment, the institutions in these states might be less affected by these
government and legal restrictions and more able to utilize affirmative action
programs similar to those of private institutions.

CONCLUSION

Whether an event, a process, or a continuum, higher education administrators
should consider that privatization (as changes in state funding and control) has
changed the governing of public higher education. It is beyond the scope of
this chapter to determine whether privatization is a positive or negative for
public four-year colleges and universities. I demonstrate, however, that out of
an interest for institutional survival, public institutions of higher learning are
continually negotiating their relationship with state leaders. Institutions in
some states may negotiate for more autonomy in lieu of funding and ultimately
become public institutions in name only. Institutions in other states may substantially trade autonomy for continued state funding. Regardless of where

institutions fall on a continuum of privatization, all public four-year institutions of higher learning are more privatized now than in the past.

From a conservative philosophical standpoint, higher education is increasingly seen as benefiting individual students rather than society in general. It then follows that students should bear the greater proportion of the costs, and social support, through government subsidies, should decrease proportionately. However, if we are to be a society that values the comprehensive education of its citizens, then education would be a public good and should be publicly supported. As a result, higher education should seek public funds and accept public control.

Public colleges and universities have advanced local, state, national, and global public interests. As public institutions of higher learning become funded less by the state and more by other sources, redefining the public good appears inevitable. The push-pull relationship between various constituents, including the state and federal governments, the institution, students, and other stakeholders, has influenced how the leadership in public colleges and universities leverages teaching, research, and service to serve the public good. In light of public higher education becoming more privatized, the implications for governance are vast. In a few states, questions are now being asked about whether public colleges and universities should continue to be subject to the same levels of control and governing frameworks as in the past. During good and bad economic periods, state higher education funding has been subject to declining state support. The state has transitioned from a primary funding source to a major donor among many other major donors. As such, many higher education leaders may be faced with inevitable changes in how their institutions are governed—from public to private systems of control. These changing governing relationships increase the number of others who expect to be at the governing table, including students, alumni, corporate and industry leaders, and foundations. This finance and control debate will no doubt continue, and its long-term impact on public institutions of higher education could be profound.

REFERENCES

Bowen, H. R. 1981. *The costs of higher education: How much do colleges and universities spend per student and how much should they spend?* San Francisco: Jossey-Bass.

Breneman, D. W. 1997. The privatization of public universities: A mistake or a model for the future? *The Chronicle of Higher Education* (March 7): B4–B5.

Breneman, D. W., and J. E. Finney. (1997). The changing landscape: Higher education finance in the 1990s. In *Public and private financing of higher education: Shaping public policy for the future*, ed. P. Callan, J. E. Finney, K. R. Bracco, and W. R. Doyle, 30–59. Phoenix, AZ: American Council on Education-Oryx Press.

Brown, W. A., and C. Gamber, eds. 2002. Cost containment in higher education: Issues and recommendations. *ASHE-ERIC Higher Education Report* 28(5). San Francisco: Jossey-Bass.

Brubacher, J. S., and W. Rudy. 1976. *Higher education in transition.* 3rd ed. New York: Harper and Row.

Burd, S. 1997. A key Republican pushes for a congressional commission on college cost. *The Chronicle of Higher Education* (May 2): A37–A38.

Callan, P. 2003. A different kind of recession: College affordability in jeopardy. *National CROSSTALK* 11(1) (Winter). Retrieved January 3, 2006 from http://www.highereducation.org/reports/affordability_supplement/affordability_2.s html.

Callan, P., J. E. Finney, K. R. Bracco, and W. R. Doyle, eds. *Public and private financing of higher education: Shaping public policy for the future.* Phoenix, AZ: American Council on Education-Oryx Press.

Carey, J. C. 1956. University or corporation? *The Journal of Higher Education* 27(8): 440–44, 466.

Clayton, M. 2003. Backlash brews over rising cost of college. *The Christian Science Monitor.* (June 17). Retrieved October 27, 2004, from http://www.csmonitor.com/2003/0617/p15s01–lehl.html.

The College Board. 2002. *2002–2003 college costs: Keeping rising prices in perspective.* Retrieved October 20, 2004, from http://www.collegeboard.com.

Creedy, J. 1994. Financing higher education: Public choice and social welfare. *Fiscal Studies* 15(3): 87–108.

Fischer, F. J. 1990. State financing of higher education: A new look at an old problem. *Change* (January–February): 42–56.

Gardner, H., M. Csikszentmihalyi, and W. Damon. 2002. *Good work: When excellence and ethics meet.* New York: Basic Books.

Gose, B. 2002. The fall of the flagships. *The Chronicle of Higher Education* (July 5): A19.

Greenleaf, W. J. 1930. Financial support of colleges. *The Journal of Higher Education* 1(5): 254–60.

Gumport, P. J., and J. Jennings. 1999. *Financial challenges in public higher education: A trend analysis.* Technical Report NCPI-1320 for the U.S. Department of Education, Grant R309A60001. Stanford, CA: National Center for Postsecondary Improvement.

Halstead, K. 1993. *State profiles: Financing public higher education, 1978–1993 trend data.* Washington, DC: Research Associates of Washington, DC.

———. 1996. *State profiles: Financing public higher education, 1978–1996 trend data.* Washington, DC: Research Associates of Washington, DC.

———. 1998. *State profiles: Financing public higher education, 1998 rankings.* Washington, DC: Research Associates of Washington, DC.

Harvey, J., and J. Immerwahr. 1995. *The fragile coalition: Public support for higher education in the 1990s.* Washington, DC: American Council on Education.

Henderson, A. D. 1969. Control in higher education: Trends and issues. *The Journal of Higher Education* 40(1): 1–11.

Hovey, H. 1999. *State spending for higher education in the next decade.* The National Center for Public Policy and Higher Education. Retrieved October 20, 2004, from http://www.highereducation.org/reports/hovey/hovey1.shtm.

Lennington, R. L. (1996). *Managing higher education as a business.* Phoenix, AZ: American Council on Education-Oryx Press.

MacTaggart, T. J. 1998. *Seeking excellence through independence: Liberating colleges and universities from excessive regulation.* San Francisco: Jossey-Bass.

Marcus, L. 1994. A new way for states to fund higher education. *Planning For Higher Education* 23: 11–15.

McKeown-Moak, M. P. 2000. *Financing higher education in the new century: The second annual report from the states.* Denver, CO: State Higher Education Executive Officers.

McPherson, M. 1991. Paying for college: Rethinking the role of the states and the federal government. *Brookings Review* 9(3): 1–12.

McPherson, M., and M. Schapiro. 2001. Preparing for hard times shows wisdom, not pessimism. *The Chronicle of Higher Education* (April 20): B24.

McPherson, M., M. O. Schapiro, and G. C. Winston. 1997. *Paying the piper: Productivity, incentives, and financing in U.S. higher education.* Ann Arbor: University of Michigan Press.

Mortenson, T. 1998. *State tax fund appropriations for higher education, FY 1999.* Oskaloosa, IA: Postsecondary Education Opportunity.

———. 1999. *State tax fund appropriations for higher education, FY 2000.* Oskaloosa, IA: Postsecondary Education Opportunity: The Mortenson Research Seminar on Public Policy Analysis of Opportunity for Postsecondary Education (December).

———. 2002. *State tax fund appropriations for higher education, FY 2003.* Oskaloosa, IA: Postsecondary Education Opportunity: The Mortenson Research Seminar on Public Policy Analysis of Opportunity for Postsecondary Education (December).

National Center for Education Statistics (NCES). 2003. *Digest of Education Statistics.* Retrieved October 20, 2004, from http://nces.ed.gov/pubs2003/2003060c.pdf.

Newburn, H. K. 1950. The future of higher education. *The Journal of Higher Education* 21(4): 177–84.

Penley, Y. S. 1997. *Responding to fiscal stress: A case study of higher education in New York.* Unpublished dissertation, Arizona State University.

Roherty, B. M. 1997. The price of passive resistance in financing higher education. In *Public and private financing of higher education: Shaping public policy for the future*, ed. P. Callan, J. E. Finney, K. R. Bracco, and W. R. Doyle, 3–29. Phoenix, AZ: American Council on Education-Oryx Press.

Russell, J. D. 1949. Basic conclusions and recommendations of the President's Commission on Higher Education. *Journal of Educational Sociology* 22(8): 493–508.

Schmidt, P. 2002. State college in Oregon may take itself private. *The Chronicle of Higher Education* (January 25): A21.

Selingo, J. 2003a. The disappearing state in public higher education. *The Chronicle of Higher Education* (February 28): A22.

———. 2003b. Massachusetts governor proposes major higher education reorganization. *The Chronicle of Higher Education* (March 7): A24.

Shelburne, J. C. 1939. Fees in a public system. *The Journal of Higher Education* 10(2): 83–89.

Simpson, A. D. 1948. Financing higher education. *The Journal of Higher Education* 19(4): 194–202, 217–18.

St. John, E. P. 1994. *Prices, productivity, and investment: Assessing financial strategies in higher education*. Washington, DC: ASHE-ERIC Education Report.

Trombley, W. 2003. The rising price of higher education: College affordability in jeopardy. *National CROSSTALK* 11(1) (Winter). Retrieved January 3, 2006 from http://www.highereducation.org/crosstalk/ct0202/news0602-harshreal.shtml.

Troutt, W. E. 1998. *The report of the National Commission on the Cost of Higher Education: Straight Talk about college costs and prices*. Phoenix, AZ: American Council on Education-Oryx Press.

U. S. Department of Education. 1996. *Findings from the condition of education, 1995, No. 6: The cost of higher education*. NCES 96–769. Washington, DC: Author.

Volkwein, J. F. 1986. Campus autonomy and its relationship to measures of university quality. *The Journal of Higher Education* 57(5): 510–28.

———, ed. 1987. *State regulation and campus autonomy*. Vol. 3) New York: Agathon Press.

Volkwein, J. F., and S. Malik. 1997. State regulation and administrative flexibility at public universities. *Research in Higher Education* 38(1): 17–42.

Whitney, K. M. 2003. *The privatization of public higher education: The relationship between state control and state funding of public institutions of higher learning*. Unpublished doctoral dissertation, University of Texas at Austin.

Winston, G. C. 1998. College costs: Subsidies, intuition, and policy. In *The report of the National Commission on the Cost of Higher Education: Straight talk about college costs and prices*, ed. W. E. Troutt, 117–27. Phoenix, AZ: American Council on Education-Oryx Press.

Zemsky, R., and G. R. Wegner. 1997. Shaping the future. In *Public and private financing of higher education: Shaping public policy for the future*, ed. P. Callan, J. E. Finney, K. R. Bracco, and W. R. Doyle, 60–73. Phoenix, AZ: American Council on Education-Oryx Press.

Zemsky, R., G. R. Wegner, and M. Iannozzi. 1997. A perspective on privatization. In *Public and private financing of higher education: Shaping public policy for the future*, ed. P. Callan, J. E. Finney, K. R. Bracco, and W. R. Doyle, 74–78. Phoenix, AZ: American Council on Education-Oryx Press.

3

Rethinking State Governance
of Higher Education

Jane V. Wellman

State governing structures are relatively recent transplants in higher education, having grown up in the post-World War II era and since the 1960s in the majority of states. These creatures of government were grafted onto existing institutional governance structures, which were most highly evolved in the established public universities, and there modeled after private nonprofit governance. For this discussion, state governance is defined as the combination of governmental and institutional structures responsible for oversight of postsecondary education in a state. Governance is distinct from administration or management, as it is focused on the policy rather than operational levels or, in the language of the "reinventing government" movement, "steering, and not rowing" (Osborne and Plastrik, 1998). The key functions of governance are strategic planning and articulation of goals; financing; public communication and accountability to different stakeholders; and selection and performance review of management. The primary tools of governance are policy development, performance review, regulation, and finance. Of these, finance is by far the most influential.

In most states, state governance consists of the governor and legislature; the statewide coordinating or governing board; and the regulatory, communication, and other mechanisms for linking state government to institutions. About half of the states have statewide governing boards, while the rest either have coordinating boards or no statewide entity. Although the focus in this chapter is on state governance, it is instructive to look briefly at the literature on institutional governance, since this is the political and organizational gene pool from which state governance has evolved.

The literature on college and university governance is dominated by structural and organizational analyses that dwell on identifying different actors involved in aspects of governance and their roles and responsibilities. The literature is more descriptive than normative, in that it is largely devoted to functional characterizations of how the systems work than on how they *should* work. Despite much debate about language—parsing the meaning of "shared governance" is a favorite topic—there is not much to be construed from the literature that could pass for principles of good or effective governance.

Virtually all authors comment on the messiness of college and university governance; indeed, there is general consensus that some level of inefficiency (if not dysfunctionality) is inevitable. Cohen and March (1974) called the institutions "organized anarchies," overseen by often-embattled presidents whose job is to preside over decision processes that typically separate problems and solutions. Baldridge (1971) described governance in political terms, as a pluralistic system, "often fractured by conflicts along lines of disciplines, faculty subgroups, student subcultures, splits between administrators and faculties, and rifts between professional schools. The academic kingdom is torn apart in many ways, and there are few kings in the system who can enforce cooperation and unity" (107). Baldridge also emphasized the parallel (and therefore never intersecting) authority structures within university administration—separating academics from the bureaucrats. These two groups are characterized both by the basis of their authority and spheres of influence. Academic authority derives from expert knowledge and is thus durable and superior to bureaucratic authority, which depends on position and is temporary as well as political. The spheres of influence are also separate. Academic policy is typically delegated to the faculty who are members in the academic senate. The academics are responsible for decisions about curriculum, admissions, and graduation standards, and criteria for faculty appointment and review, and the bureaucrats for resources and institutional management. Presidents navigate between the senates and the governing boards, and the boards preside over all, as reflected in Litchfield (1959):

> There are few among us who regard the university as a total institution. It would be more accurate to say that we treat it as a miscellaneous collection of faculties, research institutes, museums, hospitals, laboratories and clinics. Indeed, it has become commonplace to observe that most of our large university organizations are held together by little more than a name, a lay board of trustees, an academically remote figure called a president, and a common concern for the power plant. (376)

F. M. Cornford (1923), in his classic satire on academic politics, outlined the core principles of academic governance and the reasons for the delineation of responsibility between the senate and the governing board:

> These principles are all deducible from the fundamental maxim, that the first necessity for a body of men engaged in the pursuit of learn-

ing is freedom from the burden of practical cares. It is impossible to enjoy the contemplation of truth if one is vexed and distracted by a sense of responsibility. Hence the wisdom of our ancestors devised a form of academic polity in which this sense is, so far as human imperfections will allow, reduced to the lowest degree. By vesting the sovereign authority in the . . . "Senate" our forefathers secured that the final decision should rest in a body which . . . has no corporate feeling whatever. . . . In the smaller bodies, called "Boards," we have succeeded only in minimizing the dangerous feeling, by the means of never allowing anyone to act without first consulting at least twenty other people who are accustomed to regard him with well-founded suspicion. (section V)

In the more than eighty years that have passed since Cornford's satire, academic governance has become even more complicated. Faculty capacity to control academic policy has obviously eroded, along with the thinning ranks of full-time tenured faculty. Boards have grown, resources have become more fragmented, unionization is more common, and professional managers often outlast presidents, board members, and even faculty. But despite these changes, there are enduring themes about what might constitute "best practices" in institutional governance that persist in the literature, as commonly held values that shape language and behavior today.

These themes include a commitment to lay governance that protects individual autonomy, respect for decentralization of control and shared governance with faculty, and support for boards that play a role of both bridge to external groups and buffer against political interference in academic decision making. Above all, governance is supposed to protect institutions from short-term political trends, ensure stability, and guard the institution from intellectual fads or inappropriate control of the institution by single-interest groups. By ensuring the stability and well-being of the institution, the state also ensures the ability of higher education to satisfy the public good. In this chapter, I consider the impact of political, economic, and social influences on state governance of postsecondary education. First I explore the purpose and design of state governance. I then define political and policy pressures on state governance, detailing how each is impacting postsecondary education in the states. After considering the response of state-level governance to these pressures, I conclude with consequences for the future of higher education if pressures on state governance are not effectively managed. I am guided throughout by the question of what role state governance performs (or should perform) in assisting postsecondary institutions to most effectively serve in the public interest.

PURPOSE AND DESIGN OF STATE GOVERNANCE

The literature on state postsecondary governance bears a strong resemblance to that of its genetic ancestors and is mostly characterized by structural analyses of power relationships between different actors. Previous literature is commonly more descriptive than normative and does not provide a good theoretical basis for identifying properties of successful governance. It also reflects a version of the same academic values from the literature on institutional governance, transformed to the state rather than the institutional level. In the state model, the state replaces the role of the administrator in the internal institutional model, responsible for finance and oversight, whereas the academic role is delegated to institutional management. The language of "shared governance" as a positive value is maintained, transformed at the state level to an expectation for consensus-driven decision making, involving the institutions and key interest groups in state policy matters.

In the state model, the state's primary interest is the efficient allocation of resources in support of broad public purposes. States are interested in investment in higher education for economic development, the broader public interest, and educational equity. The state is concerned with institutional quality and competitiveness in the broadest sense, access to state markets through institutional licensure in the private sector, and mission differentiation and program review in public institutions. State policy promotes institutional competition for students by providing state subsidies through vouchers in the student aid programs. Such policy also requires the state to become directly involved in the management and distribution of student aid (see ECS, 1997; Glenny, 1985; Richardson, Bracco, Callan, and Finney, 1998).

There is a strong preference in the literature for decentralized governance to protect institutions from political interference and "inappropriate" controls (a word that appears often, usually without being defined) and to respect the energy and integrity of institutional self-governance. State oversight should avoid intrusion into academic policy, particularly curriculum, terms of faculty appointment, admissions criteria, or degree requirements. The literature embraces the value of consensus and collaborative decision making in "shared governance" models that, at the state level, mean that authority is distributed among many state agencies, the governor and legislature, and institutional governing boards. But there is relatively little policy guidance that differentiates between state policy and institutional interests.

Perhaps as a result, most of the literature focuses on analyses of power distributions between the state and institutions over institutional control. The language and analytical frameworks describe a continuum between absolute institutional autonomy at one end and direct regulation by the state at the other. Statewide boards are classified according to their relative degrees of control over institutions whether governing or coordinating. The chief distinction between the two is that governing boards have central fiscal control, appoint the campus presidents, and have some regulatory authority over the campuses. There also are distinctions between institutional boards as to their degree of autonomy from the state, whether they enjoy constitutional status, corporate status, or statutory status. The statutory institution is governmentally no different than any other state agency, whereas institutions with constitutional status have autonomy from direct state control embedded in the constitution (ECS, 1997; Richardson et al., 1998).

The language differentiating "coordination" and "governance" suggests a greater distinction between the two than may in fact be the case. Such language also implies more institutional independence for "autonomous" public institutions than most of them have. As just one example, the constitutionally autonomous University of Michigan must negotiate tuition levels with the governor and state legislature, lest it have its budget reduced in punishment for excessive levels. Even in strong governing board states, there has never been much appetite for real centralization of power in a single agency, as state authority over tuition, state financial aid, capital outlay, private school licensure, and program review is typically dispersed between the governing board, a separate student aid authority, the governor, and the legislature.

State governance in most states is additionally separated between four-year and two-year institutions. And finally, all institutions are subject to regulatory controls that have nothing to do with academic policy—environmental regulations, health and safety, and labor and employment primary among them. At least in the research institutions that have the greatest autonomy in higher education, most institutional attention to external regulation stems from federal and state regulation that is not dictated by educational policy (Congressional Commission on College Costs, 1998)

Glenny, Berdahl, and Palola (1971) and McGuinness (1998) plaintively pointed out that the state's interests are, after all, legitimate, and that public policy capacity is needed to balance the interests of the institutions and the market with public concerns. Some thirty-five years ago, Glenny and others expressed the concern that unchecked decentralization and preference for competition advantaged the wealthiest and oldest institutions, to the disadvantage of community colleges in particular. McGuinness, writing more recently, argued that the state needs to focus essentially on boundary control to protect institutions from direct interference, stabilize decision making, protect campus presidents, and cope with public policy issues.

POLITICAL AND POLICY PRESSURES ON
STATE POSTSECONDARY GOVERNANCE

Positioned at the intersection between higher education and state government, state postsecondary entities must navigate between public policy and politics to be effective. This has become an almost insurmountable challenge in the current environment, because the political climate and public policy needs are pulling in entirely opposite directions in most states. At the public policy level, a changing labor force, demographic developments, and educational delivery trends are forcing greater need for policy-level attention to statewide and cross-sector interests than in previous generations. But the political pressures are moving away from public policy in preference for institutional and market-based solutions, accompanied by the rhetoric of accountability in the name of performance. So the political response to the policy problems in most states has been to deregulate and decentralize state governance rather than to rebuild or refocus it. This has created a vacuum of leadership at a policy level; if left unattended, the absence of leadership bodes ill for the future capacity of higher education to meet public as well as private interests. Before turning to a discussion of what can be done, some more details about the political and policy pressures are in order to highlight the nature of the dilemma currently facing state-level policy. The distinction between policy and politics is somewhat artificial, as the two merge at several levels. Politics is not always negative, nor the exclusive domain of elected officials. To the contrary, higher educational institutions are notorious for their own brand of politics.

Policy Pressures

At a public policy level, the major challenges facing postsecondary education are increased demand for college access, fueled by tight labor markets and growing populations; the deinstitutionalization of student learning; low levels of student academic achievement; and growing access and achievement gaps between racial and income groups. These collectively are pushing the current state policy agenda in new directions, away from a traditional focus on institutional oversight to issues of student flow across the K–16 continuum, the use of public resources to accomplish broad purposes, and the intersection between higher education and the economy.

Increasing Demand for College

Demand for some post-high school education has grown steadily over the past twenty years, fueled by the baby-boom echo, the economic necessity of postsecondary education, and tight labor markets. Nationwide, the percentage increase in enrollments in public postsecondary institutions since 2001 has outstripped that of the previous two decades (SHEEO, 2004). This truly phenomenal growth is all the more remarkable, given its parallel development with a time of budget cuts and tuition increases. Many public institutions are well beyond capacity limits and are cutting access by raising standards or rationing admissions. Growth is expected to continue through 2015, when declines in high school graduates are predicted for most states. Because of the mismatch between demand and capacity, state and institutional policy makers are scrambling to find new ways to distribute enrollments among existing institutions rather than to grow capacity on a permanent basis. This results in an increased emphasis on consortia arrangements and distance and distributed learning, in lieu of conventional, campus-based education.

The Deinstitutionalization of Student Learning and the Consequences for Quality Control

Student attendance patterns have changed within higher education, as has the "typical" student. Higher education has traditionally relied on institutional controls—requirements for student admissions, breadth and curriculum prerequisites to graduation—to assess and maintain student learning standards. However, changes in higher education mean that these controls now capture relatively small proportions of students who earn the bachelor's degree. For instance, 75 percent of students are "nontraditional" (a term that says something about the pace of language change in higher education), meaning they have one or more of the following characteristics: part-time enrollment, full-time employment, financial independence, married, or responsibility for dependents. Only 10 percent of college students attend fulltime and live on campus (Wolanin, 2003). Sixty percent of students who complete the baccalaureate degree obtain credits from more than one institution. Over 40 percent of students who transfer do so across state lines (Adelman, 1999).

Almost all college students now experience some part of their learning electronically, through supplementary, Internet-enhanced classroom instruction and enrollment in completely online courses. Online enrollments within accredited institutions are growing in excess of 20 percent a year. If current growth rates continue, by 2015, "virtual" student enrollments will almost equal the number of college and university students enrolled today (Seaman and Allen, 2003). These changes cumulatively erode the institution as the unit of analysis (in terms of quality controls, measures of institutional productivity, and funding) and place more pressure on finding ways to track students across institutions as well as states. This expansion of students creates more interest in national collaborations for data sharing and accountability. These changes also contribute to pressure on public policy makers to intervene in academic decisions about transfer of credit.

Achievement and Access Gaps

The system of higher education in the United States is internationally known for its diversity, the wide range of options available to students, and the quality of some of its best institutions. The American system also is known for producing some of the largest achievement gaps in the world, as measured by rates of degree attainment and time to degree. The computations of graduation rates and time to degree are problematic in many ways, but the undeniable fact is that the American system produces fewer graduates per enrollee than most other developed countries. According to National Center for Educational Statistics (NCES) data, nationwide the three-year associates' degree graduation rate of students in "two-year" institutions is just 27 percent, and the five-year graduation rate from baccalaureate institutions is 53 percent (NCES, 2004). Baccalaureate attainment rates for African American and Latino students are much lower, averaging 20 percent or more below their white and Asian counterparts. Despite the investment in billions of dollars in student aid in the last two decades, the proportion of students from low-income families attending postsecondary education has not materially improved. Family income—which correlates strongly with academic achievement—remains the single biggest predictor of college-level access and success. Two-thirds of the projected growth in students over the next decade will be low-income students, many the first in their families to attend college. Without material improvements in retention and graduation rates, these access gaps spell real trouble for the future national production of baccalaureates.

Political Pressures

Whereas the policy pressures are pointing toward greater statewide cross-institutional capacity, the political environment is pushing in a somewhat different direction. The predominant political themes are tax policies designed to shrink the public sector, the governmental accountability movement, including K–12 reform, the growing influence of proprietary institutions, and greater politicization of governing boards. These forces combine to spell out an agenda of simultaneous privatization of finance and greater centralization of academic policy.

State Funding and Decision-Making Constraints

Some of the most important political forces affecting state postsecondary gov
ernance have occurred in the broad arena of government policy and are not
confined to postsecondary education. The most profound and far-reaching
influences have been the changes in tax policy, which have altered the face of
public finance, including in higher education. Beginning with the Proposition
13 tax revolts in the 1980s and extending to the Reagan-Bush agenda at the
federal level, the last two decades of the twentieth century were defined by
increasing populism, public mistrust of government and institutional decision
making, and a series of tax-cutting initiatives designed to shrink the size of
public institutions.

State policy capacity has been further diluted in many states through a succession of initiatives and referendums to place limits on revenues and spending
directly into the state constitution. California, Oregon, and Colorado all have
constitutional limitations on revenue and expenditure growth, Colorado's
TABOR (Taxpayers' Bill of Rights) amendment being the most recent and
arguably the most extreme. Several states also have passed spending guarantees
designed to protect funds for K–12 education, such as California's Proposition
98 and Florida's class size reduction initiative. These restrictions combine with
non-negotiable funding requirements such as Medicaid, the fastest-growing
area of state funding, where cost escalation and population growth have fueled
increases in excess of 11 percent a year since 2000. Medicaid expenditures now
exceed 20 percent of all state spending (NASBO, 2003).

The changed funding situation has been particularly evident in public
higher education, which is financed from the shrinking discretionary portion
of budgets in every state. The erosion in state funding for higher education
began in the 1990s, as states incrementally reduced the proportion of state
funding going to higher education and allowed institutions to partially replace
lost state revenue through tuition increases. The squeeze on finances has put
great pressure on the distribution system for student financial aid, which is
now the primary vehicle for distributing government subsidies to institutions
as direct institutional appropriations are waning. And while there are some
who advocate on economic grounds for a student-voucher-based distribution
system, it is safe to say that the reason for the shift in higher education has not
been higher education finance or policy decisions but a reaction to tax policy.
But whatever the cause, decreased funding is another factor contributing to a
change from a focus on institutions as state policy to students.

Both of the major political parties have embraced the notion of shrinking
the size of government as well as limiting its regulatory reach. The "reinventing government" movement influences decision making at both the state and

federal levels. Virtually every policy arena—from the environment to public welfare—has been subject to policy initiatives claiming to increase performance at reduced cost, focus on goals and performance indicators, leverage private providers in lieu of government finance, and substitute incentive or performance-based funding for old formulas. In education, the accountability movement is most visible in the K–12 school reform movement, which has been growing in momentum since the "Nation at Risk" report sounded the call of alarm about deteriorating educational achievement in relation to national economic prosperity. The movement has coalesced in a greater nationalization of standards in K–12 education than at any time in our country's history, most recently in the "No Child Left Behind" act. The law has created new tensions over K–12 governance, as the federal government, local school boards, and state officials are still sorting out roles and responsibilities for what has historically been a locally governed system. But despite these tensions, the momentum from the K–12 standards movement is carrying over to higher education through calls from public policy makers for greater accountability for student learning in higher education. Virtually every state has created some type of an accountability system as a result, including direct assessments of student learning in many states (National Governors Association, 2005; Wellman, 2001).

Rising Political Influence from Proprietary Institutions

The last decade has seen the proprietary sector come into its own within higher education. Traditionally shunned by the nonprofit and public institutions as inferior trade schools, many of these institutions have cleaned up their act and have emerged as major educational providers (and political players) at the state and national levels. The default rate scandals of the 1990s led to changes in state and federal regulations as well as accreditation standards, which had the effect of shutting down several hundred of the most marginal certificate and training schools. One of the largest private institutions in the country is now the for-profit University of Phoenix, with nationwide enrollments in excess of 100,000. There are many others—DeVry University, Jones International University, and Argosy University are all regionally accredited, degree-granting institutions. Most specialize in professional education in a few fields and cater to older students looking for skill development and job training.

The degree-granting proprietary sector has been particularly successful at the federal legislative and regulatory levels by encouraging changes in financial, administrative, and regulatory requirements for participation in the student aid programs. Like their nonprofit counterparts in the more venerable independent higher education sector, for-profit institutions have promoted a public policy agenda to shift higher education finance from subsidizing institutions to funding students, through voucher-based student aid distribution systems. For-profit institutions also have aggressively promoted a public policy agenda of greater accountability for all institutions that receive public funding through greater transparency of institutional outcomes, including measures of student learning achievement (Career College Association, 2004).

Knowing that it was poorly positioned to compete on the basis of institutional reputation, the proprietary sector made a strategic decision to enhance its competitive position by pushing public policies that base funding and access to markets on objective measures of institutional performance, through student learning results. For-profit institutions have marketed themselves as being capable of delivering customer-centered, on-demand education designed to meet student and employer needs, at reasonable prices. Several proprietary institutions use distance-mediated learning to cut costs, which has required them to pioneer new assessments of learning results to demonstrate quality to accreditors.

But in addition to advertising a different educational delivery system, for-profit institutions are marketing a cost structure made possible because of a unique internal governance model, adapted from the for-profit business model rather than an academic one. In for-profit institutions, curriculum is standardized. Decisions about curriculum and learning materials (textbooks and technology assistance) are typically made at a policy level, in consultation with, but not wholly delegated to, faculty. The majority of faculty are part time, and those who are full time typically have job security through renewable multiyear contracts rather than tenure. Learning goals are set by management, as part of their business plans, based on market analysis of employee demand and student demographics. Professional roles traditionally held by faculty in nonprofit and public institutions (curriculum development, course research, and student evaluation) are "unbundled" and shared between faculty and administrative professionals. Accountability metrics, or the evaluation of teaching effectiveness against goals, are built into course design at a corporate level.

Politicization of Governing Boards

The capacity of public governing bodies to serve as neutral defenders of the public trust depends heavily on the quality and stability of the political appointment process to the boards. Public institutional governing boards have always been subject to the external political dynamics of public appointments. But the firewall separating institutional governance from direct external pressure is more singed than ever due to the political agenda of activist groups seeking to shape higher education policy through influences on governing boards. In addition to isolated instances of visible political influences on boards, a national movement has developed that is designed to use college trustees as the point of access to influence institutional academic policy. Several groups have embraced this agenda at the national level, notably the National Association of Scholars, the Association of College Trustees and Alumni (ACTA), and different philanthropic groups organized through the National Committee for Responsive Philanthropy (see, e.g., NCRP, 1997). Their agenda is to restore academic accountability in higher education by encouraging governing boards to engage in activist oversight of academic quality.

The ACTA agenda explicitly embraces the cultivation and recruitment of trustees as its point of entry into academic policy by fostering alumni groups in private institutions and influencing the gubernatorial appointment process in public institutions. The ACTA and its members have been successful in working with several governors (Michigan, New York, Virginia, Florida, and California) to promote appointments of individuals to boards that pursue agendas to roll back affirmative action, increase merit as a criteria for funding, step up curriculum oversight, and guard against political correctness in the faculty tenure process. One of its rallying cries has been to bemoan the poor workforce and intellectual skills of recent college graduates, brought about by the degradations of standards in higher education resulting from weak or nonexistent standards for admissions and curriculum. According to the ACTA (n.d.), "Too many college students graduate with only high school level skills, a result of a watered down curriculum that has reduced the once nutritious cooked meal into a cafeteria of snacks and desserts."

Such organizations also have been active at the federal policy level by encouraging congressional oversight hearings to address what they call "intellectual diversity" or the alleged intolerance of conservatives on American college campuses. "In the past, systematic threats to academic freedom have been external. Today, however, the threat to academic freedom comes from within. The barbarians are not at the gates, they are inside the walls" (ACTA, n.d.). They have argued to remove accreditation as a criterion for receiving federal funds on the grounds that accreditors promote political correctness within higher education and weaken higher education accountability. Such organizations also have been successful in attracting favorable national media attention regarding their agenda—one example is the nationally read *The Wall Street Journal*, which editorialized in favor of gubernatorial influence on activist trustees (In Trustees We Trust, 2003).

THE GOVERNANCE RESPONSE: RESTRUCTURING AND PRIVATIZATION

Pressures for the restructuring of state-level governance began to accumulate at the end of the 1980s and 1990s, when the growth in enrollment demand and tight resources caused the majority of states to engage in major planning initiatives for higher education. Between 1983 and 1995, McGuinness (1998) reported at least thirty-three statewide special study commissions, state planning initiatives, or blue ribbon committees on higher education. In addition to traditional foci on access and system capacity, these efforts increasingly moved into the territory of academic quality by asking about evidence of quality for teaching and learning across the entire educational pipeline. Building "seamless" systems linking K–12 to higher education was a common theme, as was expanding access through distance learning.

During the 1990s, several states made modest moves toward the deregulation of postsecondary governance by loosening state regulations of higher education in favor of greater institutional autonomy. This happened most dramatically in New Jersey, where the statewide board and a host of regulations were eliminated, to be replaced by a coordinating board and greater institutional autonomy. Some form of less dramatic deregulation occurred in many other states, including Texas, Connecticut, California, Maryland, Georgia, Wisconsin, Oregon, and Florida. Transactional regulatory controls were relaxed or abolished, and many states turned away from formula funding to goal- or performance-based finance. Four-year public institutions, typically more heavily regulated than the flagship institutions, were given greater autonomy (in Georgia, California, Maryland, and Florida, for example) and also were given expanded opportunities to compete in graduate education, including at the doctoral level. Ties between K–12 and higher education were strengthened through stronger coordinating linkages designed to oversee better cross-sector student flow. During the 1990s, thirty-nine states redesigned their data collection systems to strengthen their capacity to look at student flow across institutions through student unit-record systems.

The path toward decentralization accelerated dramatically at the beginning of the twenty-first century, when the economy bottomed out, and the long-predicted crunch between excess student demand and inadequate resources became a reality. Since 2001, state appropriations for higher education have declined in forty-one of the fifty states, a loss, nationwide, of over $2.5 billion (Palmer, 2004). California, Colorado, Oregon, Massachusetts, Missouri, Maryland, and Oklahoma all saw budget declines greater than 10 percent. Institutions have increased tuition dramatically to offset the reductions. Despite the steep increases, the new tuition revenue has not been sufficient to offset losses in state funds. The result is that undesignated general funds (e.g., funds not earmarked for certain purposes by the donors, from the combination of general funds and tuition revenues) have been declining per student. The combination of funding declines and tuition increases has come at precisely the time that high school graduations are reaching their expected peak. In California alone, enrollments have been cut by an estimated 200,000, and qualified students are being denied access to higher education for the first time since the master plan was put into place (Smith, 2004).

The financial meltdown has accelerated attention to governance and the relationship between the state and public institutions. Unanswered questions remain about the proper role and reach of state postsecondary coordination and governance. At issue is the purpose and definition of public institutions in a time of privatization of finance, and the clarification of the state interest in a system combining public and private purposes. These issues are documented extensively in Neal Johnson's (2004) *State Governance Action Annual 2004*, prepared for the Association of Governing Boards, and have been commented on by David Breneman (2004) and others (se, e.g., Johnson, 2004), and thus will be touched upon only briefly here:

Virginia: The presidents of the three most selective public institutions—the University of Virginia, the College of William and Mary, and Virginia Tech—launched an initiative to transform the institutions from their historic status as public universities to a new status of "commonwealth chartered" universities. As initially proposed, the chartered universities would be political subdivisions of the Commonwealth but no longer state agencies. The institutions would be exempted from state capital outlay, procurement, personnel, and grievance procedures and would have bond authority without being subject to legislative approval. They would have authority to set tuition and fees without approval by the governor or legislature. The proposal, enacted as law in 2005, was amended to make the promise of institutional autonomy essentially contingent upon the successful completion of institutional performance contracts with the state, somewhat vaguely defined to mean meeting targets for enrollment, transfer, and regional employment needs. Whether the *quid pro quos* are successful will depend on the willingness of future legislators (and governors) to maintain the terms of agreements. Since much of the legislation is negotiated by term-limited Governor Mark Warner, that remains to be seen.

Colorado: Colorado voters passed, in 1992, a constitutional amendment known as TABOR, a tax, spending, and fee limitations initiative, that mandates refunds to voters when revenues from either taxes or fees increase beyond indexed inflation and population growth. State general funding for the University of Colorado has declined to around 10 percent of total funding. Yet under the TABOR, the university cannot increase tuitions to make up the difference. To rescue higher education from the TABOR restrictions, the state has recently enacted legislation (SB189) to change the basis for financing higher education. Under the new law, institutions are designated as state enterprises, removing them from constitutional revenue limits and thereby giving institutions greater latitude to increase tuition. Resident undergraduate students will receive a stipend of $2,400 a year to attend any Colorado public institution. Pell Grant-eligible residents who attend private institutions can receive $1,200 a year. Allocations for other subsidies—including departmental research, public service, and academic support—are to be provided based on accountability measures that have yet to be defined. There will be much interest in seeing how the fine print ultimately is written on what is clearly the most aggressive, and potentially far-reaching, change in higher education finance in the last fifty years.

Washington State: The state has considered legislation to open up state funding to private nonprofit and proprietary institutions and also to use competition and alternative delivery systems to stimulate institutions to find new ways to meet rising student demand, despite state funding constraints. The private college initiative, sponsored by the private, nonprofit college association, would have allowed state funds to be used in private colleges and universities to alleviate capacity shortages in public colleges for high demand and high need programs such as nursing, teaching, and business. Governor Gary Locke vetoed the bill, but the issue is expected to resurface as the state struggles to find ways to meet demand without being able to expand capacity in the public sector. The state also is considering using performance contracts to stimulate competition between the public institutions by permitting them to bid on state-funded contracts to provide services at a lower cost than would otherwise be provided through the normal appropriations process.

A changing relationship between the institutions and state government is only one manifestation of the shifts in governance with implications for the public interest. Similar shifts are occurring on the statewide governance side, manifested most strongly in reorganization of the state higher education governing and coordinating boards. A systematic study of changes in state agency governance over the last five years has not been done, but a brief scan of the landscape shows signs of a pattern of downsizing, reorganization, and change. The specifics differ, but the theme is consistently one of deregulation and decentralization, to reduce capacity for statewide oversight and planning in favor of greater institutional autonomy.

The most dramatic, and public, has been wrought in the Florida Board of Regents for Higher Education, which has been restructured two times in the last five years, eliminating the Board of Regents and providing each of the four-year colleges with an independent governing board. The first iteration created a new K–20 board, with oversight and planning responsibility across the educational spectrum. This was superseded with the passage of an initiative, sponsored by Senator Robert Graham and opposed by Governor Jeb Bush, to create a statewide Board of Governors. Meanwhile, the Florida Legislature has become more active in educational policy, through accountability legislation requiring direct reporting from the institutions to the Office of the Legislative Auditor General (Johnson, 2004). And the coup de grace was administered in 2005, when the former Center for Educational Policy Research and Improvement, the state policy office, was finally abolished altogether. While some data collection and analysis capacity have been shifted to the Legislature's Auditor General's office, the long-range planning, policy, and fiscal analysis capacity for this fast-growing state has completely disappeared.

The charter for state governance also has been changed in a number of states to remove budgetary and regulatory control from the state agency and shift authority to the institutions. Some of this is below the radar screen, carried out through attrition in personnel, budget cuts, and modest changes in scope and authority. Some states that fall into this category include Massachusetts, Maryland, South Carolina, Kentucky, Illinois, Minnesota, Nevada, Texas, Oregon, Washington, Arizona, and California. New York, once the leader in statewide regulation of higher education, has de facto eliminated state policy and planning capacity from the State Board of Higher Education and maintains statewide functions in higher education that are primarily focused on the administration of financial aid and licensure of private schools. Pennsylvania has a similar story, with the exception that it never had much of a statewide capacity for postsecondary policy.

A recent review of state governance in South Carolina, done by the National Center for Higher Education Management Systems, with the Association of Governing Boards, concluded that the statewide coordinating agency had so lost its viability that it should be abolished, and a new entity established outside of state government (Breneman, 2004). California, the state with one-year enrollment losses of 200,000 students, is on its third executive director for the California Postsecondary Education Commission in as many years. Whether that agency will be eliminated (as has been proposed in several budget sessions), restructured, or simply left to twist in the wind is unknown. Meanwhile, the California Legislature is putting the finishing touches on a new statewide accountability system, reporting directly to the legislature (Alpert and Scott, 2004).

Consequences for the Future

There has never been much of a consensus about the importance of state postsecondary governance, and some would argue that the erosion of state influence over postsecondary education is a positive development. Many college presidents have been actively seeking greater institutional independence from state control, arguing that autonomy is justified since reduced state funding means that the state is no longer the majority stockholder in the enterprise. Not all public institutions have benefited equally from decentralization, as legislatures are loath to abandon tuition setting, categorical program controls, and budgetary restrictions (see, e.g., Smith, 2004). Thus these institutions are left to struggle with greater student demand and constrained resources while remaining under the yoke of regulatory control.

But the evidence is accumulating that neither the state nor the institutional side of the public governance equation is doing a very capable job of promoting the public interest in higher education or sustaining the core principles of effective governance. Despite continued strength in some sectors and in many institutions, aggregate performance across all of higher education (the topic that should be front and center as a state policy priority) is clearly declining. In the last decade, the United States has lost its traditional international dominance in higher education and has sunk to sixteenth among the twenty Organization for Economic Cooperation and Development (OECD) nations in terms of college attendance and degree completion (OECD, 2004). In every other industrialized nation, national policies have been pursued to increase investment in education, a necessary component of ensuring high skills in the international marketplace. The United States, alone among the major industrialized nations, exhibits declining educational achievement levels. Part of this phenomenon is undoubtedly attributed to the declining affordability of college in the United States. Prospects for a return to the days of heavy state subsidies for postsecondary education are somewhere between slim and none. Absent a dramatic change in state tax policies, or serious cost control in other state-funded programs, forty-six of the fifty states are expected to have structural budget deficits requiring major funding reductions in higher education funding by 2013 (NCHEMS, 2005).

Along with the elimination of state-agency controls over institutional business, there has been an erosion of the always fragile capacity of state government to set a broad policy agenda for higher education. Such an agenda would ensure that state requirements for skill development, income growth, and social equity are met. This capacity may not have mattered in a different era, when a reasonable balance between supply and demand, generous levels of public support for institutions, and broad public support for institutional autonomy existed. But the crunch between capacity and need is now acute in almost every state, and skyrocketing tuition is the cause for greater political attention to institutional performance in the name of "accountability." These factors invite a greater degree of direct political intervention into the historically protected areas of academic policy, particularly admissions and curriculum.

Instead of serving broad social purposes, higher education is seen in utilitarian and economic terms, as the gateway to employment. The model of the market-defined academic product is evidently so powerful that it is sweeping away more abstract notions of public purpose and broad social outcomes as worth defending for higher education. Academic freedom is perceived as protectionism of the privileges of insiders, not as a tool for broader social purposes. Institutional stability is a sign of stodginess. Adaptability to changing market conditions is applauded. Underlying much of this is an evident inability to craft governance models that sufficiently distinguish between broad statewide and institutional interests.

Clearly, this is not a set of circumstances with a single cause with simple solutions. The governance frameworks within higher education have developed over centuries, and the values, language, and behaviors associated with them are part of the social culture of the academy. Behavior and language are difficult to change. At the state level, no amount of exhortation about the importance of the "public interest" will convince people that a call for better state governance is not really a call for a return to state bureaucrats bent on micromanaging every aspect of the academic enterprise. State policy makers will remain convinced that institutional efforts to secure tuition independence and greater deregulation are really no more than thinly disguised efforts to abandon the public interest entirely in pursuit of agendas of institutional prestige.

The legislative impulse to play politics with institutions is a by-product of life with elected officials. But the potential social and economic consequences of continued drift in public governance for higher education are huge. What is at stake is the future capacity of the country to ensure that the next generation of students has at least as much access to high-quality education as the last generation in educational institutions that protect freedom of inquiry from partisan political intrusion. Some modest attempts to steer this conversation in a more constructive direction are therefore worthwhile. A few suggestions about places to start are offered next.

1. *Understand the language.* The language of governance—governing versus coordinating, institutional versus state, public versus private—contributes to confusion and stalemate in the conversation. Such language is unduly oppositional, implying sharper distinctions between one side and the other than have ever existed. There is a difference between governance and coordination, but not that great a difference. Similarly, institutional interests are not categorically anti-state, and the state is not anti-institutional. The fiscal differences between public and nonprofit private institutions are eroding, but we do not have a good way to talk about that. The accountability model in proprietary education is achieved because these institutional interests are primarily individual and economic rather than social. Yet the models and the lan-

guage in state governance have not transformed to match the current realities.

2. *Clarify the audience for statewide governance.* Another issue that requires original thought is the problem of audience for statewide governance in post-secondary education. The object of statewide governance is state policy, and the audience needs to be state policy makers: the legislature, the governor, the business and philanthropic communities, and other agencies of state government. Statewide governance should not be a watered-down, distorted version of institutional governance, with a primary purpose to add another layer of oversight onto institutions. Finding and keeping the public policy audience can be challenging in the current political arena, but such efforts are central to maintaining a statewide policy capacity for postsecondary education.

3. *Take advantage of the accountability discussion.* The accountability movement provides an opportunity for higher education leaders at both the state and institutional levels to craft a different approach to governance in a task-oriented and specific way, without getting bogged down in abstract conversations about power that are likely to go nowhere. Rather than try to beat back the proprietary and K–12 models, leaders can take the opportunity to proactively define the terms under which they want to hold themselves accountable—for fiscal as well as academic performance. An accountability agenda can be the vehicle for discussions about differentiation of roles between the statewide and institutional levels in clear terminology that translates well to external political and business as well as institutional audiences.

4. *Understand the market analysis.* One of the acknowledged roles for state government is to use state regulation, including financing policies, to balance and correct for market strengths and weaknesses. Too much of the current debate about privatization and market is rhetorical, with little precision as to the types of performance most likely to benefit from market-based strategies. Recent research about the effects of competition among selective private institutions shows that competition for students tends to increase prices rather than lower them (Winston, 2000). State policy leaders need better information about institutional responses to competition to make judgments about how best to target increasingly precious state subsidies on priorities that will not fare well in a competitive model.

5. *Build better bridges.* Governing boards are designed to be buffers *and* bridges. There is a great deal of variation between institutional governing boards in the degree to which the members of the board are expected to play a serious and publicly visible role in overseeing institutional performance. Many faculty (and some presidents) are socialized to view governing boards the way some people view children—better seen than heard from, and potentially dangerous if given access to the wrong tools. But governing boards must have more visible roles in institutional oversight, of quality *and* cost, particularly if the values of academic freedom are to be protected and legislatures are

to be kept away from institutional micromanagement. The economic importance of higher education has put great stakes on issues of who gets into higher education, what they learn, and who teaches it. These are legitimate topics of public policy, yet the democracy will be better served over the long run if the decisions about them are made within the academy. To protect this privilege will require much more attention to visible public oversight and communication on the part of public governing boards.

REFERENCES

Adelman, C. 1999. *Answers in the tool box: Academic intensity, attendance patterns, and bachelor's degree attainment*. Washington, DC: U.S. Department of Education.

Alpert, D., and J. Scott. 2004. *SB 1331, as introduced: California postsecondary education accountability act of 2004*. State of California Senate. Retrieved September 7, 2004, from http://www.info.sen.ca.gov/pub/bill/sen/sb_1301–1350/sb_1331_bill_20040218_introduced.html.

American Council of Trustees and Alumni (ACTA). n.d. *Issues: Accountability*. Retrieved May 1, 2004, from http://www.goacta.org/issues/accountability.html.

Baldridge, J. V. 1971. *Power and conflict in the university*. New York: John Wiley and Sons.

Breneman, D. W. 2004. *Can a new bargain be struck between states and public higher education?* Washington, DC: Association of Governing Boards.

Career College Association. 2004. Legislative and regulatory agenda. *2003–2004 Annual Report*. Washington, DC: Author.

Cohen, M. D., and J. G. March. 1974. *Leadership and ambiguity*. Princeton, NJ: McGraw-Hill.

Congressional Commission on College Costs. 1998. *Straight talk about college costs and prices*. Phoenix, AZ: Oryx Press.

Cornford, F. M. 1923. *Microcosmographica academica: Being a guide for the young academic politician*. Cambridge, England: Bowes and Bowes.

Education Commission of the States (ECS). 1997. *State postsecondary education structures sourcebook: State coordinating and governing boards*. Denver, CO: Author.

Glenny, L. A. 1985. *State coordination of higher education: The modern concept*. Denver, CO: State Higher Education Executive Officers.

Glenny, L. A., R. O. Berdahl, and E. G. Palola. 1971. *Coordinating higher education for the 70s: The multicampus and statewide guidelines for practice*. Berkeley, CA: Center for Research and Development in Higher Education.

Johnson, N. 2004. *State governance action annual 2004*. Washington, DC: Association of Governing Boards.

Litchfield, E. H. 1959. The university: A congeries or an organic whole? *AAUP Bulletin* 45: 375–76.

McGuinness, A. 1998. The states and higher education. In *American higher education in the 21st century: Social, political, and economic challenges*, ed. P. Altbach, R.O. Berdahl, and P.J. Gumport, 183–215. Baltimore, MD: Johns Hopkins University Press.

National Association of State Budget Officers (NASBO). 2003. *State expenditure report*. Washington, DC: Author.

National Center for Educational Statistics (NCES). 2004. *The condition of education 2004*. Washington, DC: U.S. Department of Education.

National Center for Higher Education Management Systems (NCHEMS). 2005. State fiscal outlooks from 2005 to 2013: Implications for higher education. *NCHEMS News* (June). Retrieved January 3, 2006, from http://www.nchems.org/News/NCHEMS%20News%20June2005.pdf.

National Committee for Responsive Philanthropy (NCRP). 1997. *Moving a public policy agenda: The strategic philanthropy of conservative foundations* (July). Retrieved May 1, 2004, from: http://www.mediatransparency.org/movement.htm.

National Governors Association (NGA). Center for Best Practices. 2005. *Assessing student learning in state higher education*. Washington, DC: National Governors Association.

Newman, F. 1987. *Choosing quality: Reducing conflict between the state and the university*. Denver, CO: Education Commission of the States.

Organization for Economic Cooperation and Development (OECD). 2004. *Education at a glance: OECD indicators 2004*. Paris: Author.

Osborne, D., and P. Plastrik. 1998. *Banishing bureaucracy: The five strategies for reinventing government*. New York: Penguin Books.

Palmer, J. C., ed. 2004. An annual compilation of data on state tax appropriations for the general operation of higher education. *Grapevine*. Retrieved September 1, 2004, from http://coe.ilstu.edu/grapevine/50state.htm.

Richardson, R., K. R. Bracco, P. Callan, and J. Finney. 1998. *Designing state higher education systems for a new century*. Westport, CT: American Council on Education/Oryx Press.

Seaman, J., and E. Allen. 2003. *Sizing the opportunity: The quality and extent of on-line education in the U.S., 2002 and 2003*. Needham, MA: The Sloan Consortium.

Smith, M. S. 2004. Getting an education in California: Class dismissed. *Sacramento Bee*, March 28, E3.

State Higher Education Executive Officers (SHEEO). 2004. *State higher education finance: FY 2003*. Denver, CO: Author.

In Trustees We Trust: It's time higher education got some effective oversight. 2003. *The Wall Street Journal*, August 1, editorial.

Wellman, J. V. 2001. Assessing state accountability systems. *Change* 33(2): 48–49.

Winston, G. C. 2000. *The positional arms race in higher education.* Discussion paper. Williams Project on the Economics of Higher Education. Williamstown, MA: Williams College.

Wolanin, T., ed. 2003. *Re-authorizing the higher education act: Issues and options.* Washington, DC: The Institute for Higher Education Policy.

4

Be Mission Centered, Market Smart, and Politically Savvy

The Art of Governance

Kenneth P. Mortimer
and Colleen O' Brien Sathre

The most important governance challenge facing boards, administrators, and faculty in colleges and universities is staying focused on basic/core missions while adapting to an increasingly volatile set of market forces. These influences affect how and with what success higher education achieves its fundamental goals. Success in meeting these challenges will require a higher degree of political awareness than is apparent in contemporary debates about governance. Martin, Samuels, and associates (1997) make the point well:

> We note that the central challenge for those now holding a provost-ship or deanship is to understand how to define and then implement academic leadership on campus in a climate of changing faculty priorities, declining institutional resources, fickle student consumer preferences, and eroding public confidence. (8)

We would add boards and all who claim a right to share in governance to those who are faced with the perils of academic leadership, described above.

The dynamics of defining and implementing an agenda are the essence of governance. The traditional concept of governance, oriented in bureaucratic and collegial models, works best for routine issues such as hiring and rewarding faculty; recruiting, enrolling, and educating students; hiring and training staff; conducting research; and providing the community with a variety of services. These models are less useful in understanding how institutions cope with tough choices, such as program closure, resource allocation, and those issues where open conflict is the norm. The health of academic governance depends on how these exceptional issues are decided, and it is on these issues that political skills trump those required to operate in either a bureaucratic or collegial atmosphere. Understanding the context of institutional change ultimately fosters a stronger portrait of the university as a social institution capable of serving the public good. The concept of the public good is continually negotiable, as are the institutional behaviors put forth to achieve this mission. "Colleges and universities have vague, ambiguous goals," concluded Baldridge, Curtis, Ecker, and Riley (1977, 30). "They must build decision processes to grapple with a higher degree of uncertainty and conflict."

This chapter uses the case of closing a professional school at an anonymous public research university (identified here by a pseudonym) to illustrate the decision-making process and interaction between governing boards, administrators, faculty, and the public. In essence, the school closure required agreement on a substantial change in institutional structure, resource allocation, and indirectly, the clarification of the institution's educational and social mission. We argue that an important and not a well-acknowledged feature of academic governance is that universities operate more like political than collegial or bureaucratic entities when issues of this magnitude are at stake. In this case study, we explore the institutional decision-making behavior and how that behavior is connected to the university mission.

The details of the case are followed by an analysis of the dynamics, specifically related to shared governance and the concept of the public good. We then discuss other relevant factors, including external influences that challenge the relevance of internal governance traditions; the dynamics of power and influence in a shared governance environment; and how these politics of influence play out when faculty/campus senates coexist with a faculty union. This chapter concludes with a discussion of how significant issues can be better understood, governance can be more effective, and the concept of the public good can be more clearly framed if the canons of politics are taken into account.

THE SCHOOL CLOSURE CASE

At their last meeting of the 2000 academic year, the governing board at Glenhaven University voted to approve the administration's reorganization proposal to fold what was then a freestanding professional school into another school as a program with a narrowed scope of offerings. This action was the culmination of events traceable to accreditation concerns that had persisted for twenty years. Four years earlier, the professional accreditation site team visited Glenhaven and observed that, except for the direness of the resource picture, the problems they identified were the same as those identified in three previous accreditation reviews. This site team's concerns culminated in the decision of the professional accrediting body to place the school on probation. Following another site visit in 1999, the accrediting body informed Glenhaven officials that the probationary accreditation status of the school would be revoked one year later. The accrediting body established that revocation date so that students then enrolled could complete their degree requirements or make other arrangements.

The accrediting body's decision was based on concerns such as organizational and administrative shortcomings; the absence of a permanent dean for seven years; inadequate school resources, especially faculty; the absence of viable concentrations of programs; the lack of an active research program; and a faculty complement that lacked the breadth and depth of expertise needed to achieve the school's mission, goals, and objectives in graduate education and research. In general, Glenhaven administrators, faculty, and trustees did not dispute the findings of the accrediting body. There was little debate about the need to take corrective action and improve the quality of the school's program. But there was considerable disagreement between some Glenhaven faculty, the campus administration, and the public about the steps needed to achieve this outcome. The severity of the concerns suggested to some the need for a major overhaul of the structure and components of the program; others perceived that the solution lay in improving the existing structure.

From the campus administration's perspective, corrective action had to take place in the context of Glenhaven's eroding budget and internal and external assessments of multiple deficiencies in this school. During the previous decade, the university system had experienced major reductions to its general funding base, losing roughly 11 percent of its state support—the largest percentage loss for any state university system during that period. Given the severity of the university's fiscal situation and the reality of a dysfunctional school, the administration's preference was to discontinue the school's status as a distinct, freestanding unit and move the program into another school. By advocating this course, the administration made it clear that it was not willing to invest resources to maintain a school structure for an entity that for some time had not functioned in a manner consistent with the school's mission and goals, especially when Glenhaven's highest-priority academic programs were not escaping cuts. The move would require a reduction in the scope of the program and elimination of the professional doctoral degree.

Leaders of the professional school, on the other hand, took the view that the revocation of accreditation was a direct result of the administration's actions or inaction. From this perspective, the solution was to appoint a permanent dean, restore funding to the school, exempt the school from future budget cuts, and commit to retaining an accredited school. A campus faculty senate resolution supported the maintenance of an accredited school. By the time of the 1999 accreditation revocation decision, it also was becoming increasingly clear that pursuing a merger would require the appointment of a different interim dean to help with the planning for such a move. The administration pressed the serving interim dean for a commitment to lead this planning effort. However, he responded that he did not know the parameters of the planned program and would not commit to its leadership.

When the future of the school was placed on the Glenhaven governing board's July 1999 agenda, the controversies about how to best fix the situation and the future of the serving interim dean spilled over into the realm of the trustees. At the board's request, this session of the governing board became an informational briefing. The session opened with an announcement by the president that he would appoint a task force to provide the trustees with an independent report on the facts relating to the school and alternatives as to its future. The administration presented additional information and addressed the misperception that the university would terminate the entire program; administrators were committed to preserving generic master's programs while reducing their scope. For the remainder of the session, the board heard contradictory and often emotional testimony from approximately twenty individuals connected to the university—students, faculty, staff, and professionals in the community.

About this time, statements circulating on campus about the accrediting body's actions added to the confusion and unrest. As a result of various rumors, the Glenhaven administration contacted the accrediting body and clarified several issues. First, the revocation decision was final and, except for a possible procedural appeal, would not be reconsidered. In addition, there was no truth to the allegation that the accrediting body would no longer work with the administration and wished to work directly with the trustees. Also, public exploration of the option of accreditation as a program would not cause an instant loss of the school's current accreditation status.

Following the July 1999 meeting and at the insistence of the board's chair, the president appointed an impartial task force of highly respected community leaders to evaluate the costs and benefits of maintaining a reputable, accredited school. Their specific charge was to assess state and community needs, ascertain the facts, assess national trends, evaluate alternatives to a separate school, and report to the board at its September meeting.

As the task force undertook its work, the debate about the future of the school raged on. Immense pressure was brought to bear on the administration and members of the board. A hunger strike was staged on the lawn of the main administration building; community leaders and politicians, including congressional office holders, criticized the administration and spoke in favor of the school, and the local television and print media gave the matter considerable visibility in lead stories, articles, and editorials. In September 1999, the task force reported that it had reviewed three accreditation site visit reports; two internal university reviews of the school; financial, student, and institutional data; and a wealth of information from interested parties. The task force members also held a public meeting.

The major findings of the task force were these   that there was a need for this program in the state, and that the university should offer a quality response to this need. There was continuing demand for graduates of this program, and the school's continuing education and service efforts were effective. But the school needed to strengthen its research component. (Data showed several years when no research awards were received, and all current research awards were scheduled to end within a month. Several current training awards had a longer time frame.)

Ultimately the task force reported two options. The preferred option was to retain and rebuild the school and seek its reaccreditdation. If the necessary resources were not available and deficiencies cited by the accrediting body could not be met by early summer of the following year, then the task force recommended the second option: transitioning the program into another school and redefining its focus. Following further discussion and emotional testimony from concerned individuals, the Glenhaven board accepted the recommendation to pursue the second option—to close the school and locate its master's program in another school. Over the following year, the school remained in place as an accredited entity, a new interim dean was appointed, currently enrolled students were assisted in completing their degrees, and the administration finalized the reorganization proposal. In July 2000, one month after the final revocation of accreditation, the governing board took final action to approve the proposed merger. Today the school no longer exists as a separate unit within the university. The professional doctorate was eliminated, and master's programs in the field are now offered through a restructured department in another school.

CASE DYNAMICS

The closing of this school illustrates the dynamics of interactions among trustees, campus administrators, and the faculty in cases where tough and/or unpopular choices have to be made. When such issues are involved, traditional paths of governance are questioned, information becomes a political resource used to the advantage of the parties, and external interests are courted for their support. The decision-making process was intense, emotional, and complex, which was evidence of the lengthy history of the school as part of the institutional structure and the involvement of community members who felt vested in the school. Each party held a unique concept for what the program should involve and ultimately what role Glenhaven should play in service to the community. While a basic principle of institutional processes is related to the "inseparability of organization and environment" (Chaffee, 1985, 89), such complexity fosters an uncertain path toward collaborative decisions.

Glenhaven trustees debated whether they should support the administration, as well as whether the specific decision was a wise one. If they chose to reject the administration's recommendation, then they were likely to weaken the administration's ability to make hard choices. If they supported the administration, but it was not a decision in the best interests of the state, then the trustees were not fulfilling their obligation to protect the public interest and serve the public good. And finally, since the Glenhaven trustees were not experts in the subject matter at stake, whose data could they trust? In public meetings, program advocates made claims of dire results if the school closed—grants would be lost, students would go elsewhere, and the overall reputation of the university would suffer. Most of these claims were disputed by the administration, but the board wondered how the conflicting information could be reconciled. Who was telling the truth here? Considering the competing demands and opinions, which decision was best for the university?

The Glenhaven administration was not willing to commit the funds necessary to sustain the school's programmatic scope under the leadership of a faculty it deemed to be less than stellar. Administrators doubted that a faculty previously focused on training rather than research could be reoriented to accomplish the research mission of a graduate professional school. The accreditation team was clear—the faculty, as a whole, had not met the accreditation standard in this regard. Yet Glenhaven's faculty and school leaders believed that all of these problems were resource driven and could be corrected by an infusion of funds (roughly $700,000 to $1 million), hiring a permanent dean, and exempting the school from further cuts to the university's budget, should they come. But the institution suffered from budget cuts and the loss of financial support across the university. For almost a decade, it had suffered from a declining allocation of funds from the legislature. Resource, funding, staffing, and research concerns all underlined the larger question: Through what means could Glenhaven most effectively fulfill its educational mission and serve the public good?

Some individual trustees were clearly under intense pressure from acquaintances on the faculty and in the professional community who supported the school. These community and faculty advocates were vocal and insistent that the loss of the professional school as a freestanding entity would be a major blow to Glenhaven, the identity and prestige of the faculty, and practicing professionals in the state. Community supporters of the school maintained that the inability to grant the professional doctorate would be damaging to the overall region; they also argued that it was the role of the institution to responsively serve the needs of the public. According to these advocates, the board should reject the administration's proposed action and force it to commit the funds to reaccredit the school. Whatever the board decided, it had to operate in "the sunshine," and individual trustees would have to vote on the matter in a public meeting with the television cameras rolling. External expectations and the traditions of shared governance clash when issues like this one are at stake.

SHARED GOVERNANCE

The internal debate about shared governance is rooted in a set of values about legitimate behavior in the academy. These values support a view that authority and power need to be distributed in ways that ensure that those who have the relevant expertise and competence are in decisive roles. In addition, those who are concerned about the issues, those whose cooperation is necessary to implement decisions, and those whose cash is needed to fund the decisions all have legitimate claims to participate. These four claims—competence, concerns, cooperation, and cash, "the four Cs of shared governance"—lead to confusion and disagreements when it comes to actually "sharing authority" and making a difficult decision. As illustrated through this case study, shared governance occurs within a specific cultural, historical, and contextual environment. Institutional structures are fragmented, with students, faculty, administration, and the public all impacting the decision-making process. This pluralistic framework includes a variety of stakeholders often holding conflicting values (Baldridge, Curtis, Ecker, and Riley, 1977). At Glenhaven, the decision to close a freestanding school occurred within a context of long-term budget cuts, regional economic turmoil, and the consequences of fiscal uncertainty and difficult administrative choices.

Balancing and integrating these legitimacy claims for participation in decision making are a major litmus test of effective governance. Within the academy the list of legitimate activities is extremely long, and almost any activity that serves a client may be considered legitimate (Julius, Baldridge, and Pfeffer, 1999). This environment presents a challenge when making decisions that reflect institutional priorities. Which priorities should prevail when there is little agreement among the claimants about whose claim takes precedence? In Glenhaven University, should the school structure remain a top institutional priority, despite a shrinking funding base and serious school deficiencies? In terms of public good, through what structural format could the institution best provide an engaging and appropriate curriculum? Curricula and degree programs must be appropriate to the needs of society and delivered in an efficient, productive manner. As Gumport and Pusser noted, "The attention to the magnitude and nature of costs in higher education has forced [a] focus on two fundamental questions: 'Are we doing things right?' and 'Are we doing the right things?'" (1997, 9).

Before we answer these questions, we will consider the changes in the external environment of the modern university and discuss how they may clash with some of the traditional ideals, processes, and practices of academic governance. As Brian Pusser noted in chapter 1, colleges and universities serve a dual function, both as a self-contained community of complex interaction and as part of a broader social economy. In this case study, external influences played a crucial role in shaping the institutional decision-making process.

EXTERNAL INFLUENCES

There is a growing consensus that important changes to the academy are those that are external to it. "Institutions are certainly influenced by powerful, external factors such as demographic, economic, and political conditions," noted Tierney (1988, 3). A number of observers have reported on these events; they should always be considered when discussing more effective internal governance processes (Association of Governing Boards of Universities and Colleges, 1998; Kerr, 1999; Newman and Couturier, 2001). In the case study presented, the program closure resulted from a long-term interaction of internal and external factors—reduced state funding and institutional fiscal constraints, as examples.

At least seven major forces impact the governance of higher education. The institutional response to these demands must be considered in light of the specific contextual and cultural factors. The first four of the following are particularly relevant; we briefly discuss them in the context of the case study presented in this chapter.

- the rising importance of market forces
- the demands for accountability
- the increasing volatility of state- and system-level actions
- the integration of the university into the larger society
- the changing nature of student populations
- the globalization of science and technology
- the increased importance of educational technology

Market Forces

Market forces have always been with us, of course. But the cumulative effect of heightened competition for prestige, students, and money gives them their current power. To some extent, market forces have replaced public policy as a means of expressing public needs. The task for the academy is not to choose between market forces and state regulations (such as assigned roles and rules about the funding, operation, and scope of each institution) as the driver of policy but to balance the two (Newman and Couturier, 2001).

Market forces will not diminish. Higher education's evolution toward an enterprise heavily influenced by market forces will continue whether or not public policy makers and academic leaders are capable of dealing with those forces (Newman and Couturier, 2001). The school closure case at Glenhaven illustrates the divide that can exist between an institution and a community consumed with a debate about the structure for delivering a program, the external reality of fewer public funds assigned to higher education, a legitimate state need for a quality program (not necessarily a school), and increasing competition requiring the focused use of resources.

Accountability

The pressures for accountability in 2004 are different from the traditional demands for increased efficiency experienced in the 1980s and 1990s. Awarding degrees is no longer an adequate assurance of quality; it is a provider-centric view of quality and no longer fits current realities.

> When almost two-thirds of the students who graduate from colleges attend multiple institutions, restricting quality-assurance mechanisms to the individual "nodes" in the chain of instruction—rather than focusing on the collective experience and its consequences—misses key aspects of the quality-assurance problem as a whole. These problems are exacerbated by the growing inability of the degree (and particularly the baccalaureate degree) to certify a common standard of attainment. (Jones, Ewell, and McGuinness, 1998, 14–15)

These pressures for accountability result in pleas for performance based on results, not effort, and, together with market forces, had a strong influence on the Glenhaven administration in the closure case. The school was not research active and did not meet the market test for research funds and "cutting-edge" performance in the administration's view. These forces of change in the external environment are even more crucial when state and multi-campus policy developments are considered. Due to long-term cuts in state funding and the economic turmoil of the region, Glenhaven administrators focused on programs they felt were meeting the institutional mission and goals rather than to continue funding a dysfunctional structure.

Volatility in State-Level Governance

The changes in state government policies and practices for higher education require constant monitoring by institutional actors. According to experienced observers, fundamental shifts are under way and point to a renegotiation of the social contract between higher education and state government (Breneman, 2004; Longanecker, 2004; McGuinness, 2003; Wellman, 2004). These shifts include

- a shift from a focus on providers (institutions) to a focus on clients (learners);
- a shift from centralized regulation and control to decentralized management and the use of incentives, performance funding, and consumer information;
- a shift from institutional subsidies to competitive awards;
- a shift from accountability focused on institutional performance to accountability for the educational attainment of the state's population and the competitiveness of the state's economy;
- the increasing influence of alternative, for-profit institutions; and
- the increased politicization of governing boards.

These shifts can be accompanied by mixed signals. Some of the volatility in the school closure case was the result of government leaders who expressed opposite points of view. Some said privately that the university should have acted sooner; others argued publicly that the university should retain the school structure. Regardless, such indecision occurred amidst severe budgetary cuts in state funding to Glenhaven.

The University and Society

Finally, the overall direction and cumulative effects of the market and accountability pressures lead to further integration of the university into society. Clark Kerr (1999) has observed the following:

> In the 1960's, I talked about the multiversity, but if I were writing today, I might use the term "integrated university." Integrated into society. Integrated into the military efforts of the nation. Integrated into health care and the legal system. I talked about how we were reaching out in many ways, but society was also moving in on us. Higher education now faces the challenge of being less of an inde-

pendent force and being integrated more into elements of society than ever before. (19)

Glenhaven University and its academic programs serve a significant role in service to society, as evidenced by the community leaders and professionals who protested any change in academic structure. While the closing of a professional school at Glenhaven was directly the result of long-term accreditation problems, the closure also was the result of social pressures, political actions, and community influences. Supporters of the school saw its role as bettering society by providing well-trained and resourceful professionals. The need for the school was great, they maintained, given the economic turmoil of the region. Administrators and others who advocated for merging the school responded that institutional resources were not available for the school to adequately serve this function.

The integration into society means universities can no longer be self-contained entities. Engagement means opening institutions to external influences while insisting that the world beyond the campus respect the imperatives of the university (Kellogg Commission, 1999). Maintaining such duality is difficult, if not impossible. Engagement can reduce the amount of autonomy enjoyed by institutions and professors in the areas of research and development, curricula, and access (Slaughter and Leslie, 1997). Engagement also can provide the opportunity for higher education to use its governance of areas such as the curricula and program administration to bring its considerable resources to bear on societal problems. The challenge is to adapt internal governance processes to deal with the changed nature of the university's external environment while remaining responsive to the institutional mission. The institutional mission should be clear and well understood by all institutional stakeholders and encourage decisions that are consistent with public needs and the institutional agenda. This admonition to be "mission centered, market smart, and politically savvy" is easier said than done and requires a consideration of the role of power and influence in shared governance.

DYNAMICS OF POWER AND INFLUENCE

The issues that grow out of the school closure case at Glenhaven University illustrate the dilemmas in shared governance and are familiar to students of academic governance:

- *On what issues* should authority be shared?
- *Who should participate* in the sharing?

- *At what level* of the organization can the sharing be most effective?
- *At what stage* of the decision-making process can the sharing be most effective?

At Glenhaven, the formal authority to close the school resided with the governing board. But program faculty, administrators, students, and alumni, as well as campus administrators, community leaders, political office holders, and others, claimed a right to participate in the decision-making process and influence the outcome. In so doing, some participants crossed multiple stages of decision making in an effort to take their concerns to higher levels of authority. They thereby illustrated the point that the opportunity to be consulted about a recommendation and the timing of that consultation are central to the debate about effective shared governance. Their involvement also demonstrated that perceptions of institutional mission and the public good vary and are influenced by a host of individual factors.

The stages of decision making—initiation, consultation, recommendation, review, choice, and veto—have implications for shared governance and power relations (Mortimer and McConnell, 1978). The crucial question is one of timing. In the school closure case, the Glenhaven administration was criticized for targeting a school and then failing to "pull the trigger." This delay on the part of the administration speaks to the reality that a decision by itself changes nothing (Pfeffer, 1992). For most issues, including the school closure case, knowing what to do is not the problem. Many know what to do or what they ought to do but are stymied about how to get it done.

The school closure case illustrates that participants opposed to a likely outcome have nothing to lose by an extended decision-making process. Because they are operating in shared governance environments, administrators and governing boards will allow more time, hold more meetings, and conduct additional reviews that have the effect of dragging out a decision. All are aware that the use of force, or reliance on the formal authority of one's office or position, is criticized as inconsistent with the culture and/or ideology of shared governance. Decisions to close or merge entire colleges are among the most controversial on a university campus (Eckel, 2000). These types of decisions test the political savvy of governance practitioners and their responsiveness to mission-centered and market-smart imperatives. It is not, concluded Eckel, "a decision simply about the curriculum for the faculty, about institutional strategy for trustees, or about the institution's financial well-being for administrators" (2000, 18). Instead, program closures affect how individuals perceive the institution and their role within its structure; this conflict occurs amidst the inherent power structure within the organization (Pfeffer, 1992). Perhaps the best example of how the confluence of external forces and the dynamics of power and influence have resulted in a move to more politically oriented internal governance practices is the rise of faculty unions.

FACULTY UNIONS

The most recent data indicate that over 1,000 of the country's 3,500 or so college and university campuses have faculty unions. Approximately 250,000 to 300,000 (about 25 to 40 percent) faculty members are covered by union contracts. At Glenhaven University, the site of our case study, a faculty union exists alongside a campus senate. Both organizations were involved in the school closure case and were concerned with issues of procedure, faculty rights, and due process. The existence of faculty unions or similarly organized bargaining units adds another layer to the complex interaction of institutional stakeholders. Over thirty years of research, commentary, and experience will lead one to assert that the dynamics of campus power and influence are modified substantially under conditions of unionization (Maitland and Rhoades, 2001; Rhoades, 1998). The reader will have to determine whether these modifications are desirable or not. For example, union leaders at the state, system, and local levels often have better political "intelligence" than campus administrators. In general, system-level unions and administrators have better access to state governmental leaders (e.g., governors and legislators) than do campus administrators and faculty. This differential access to the political dynamics of state government may threaten the credibility of campus leaders.

In recent years, the unionization of graduate assistants consumed a great deal of energy at public research universities such as Washington, Michigan, and Wisconsin. Certain demographics are important when one seeks to assess the influence of unions on campus governance. In general, for example, unionization tends to be situated in institutions (including community colleges, comprehensive state universities, and non-selective private colleges) where the traditions of strong faculty participation do not have long historical roots. Large, multi-campus unions exist in at least ten states. Here many of the negotiations involve a system-wide union and either the system-wide board or an agency of state government.

What are the dynamics of campus governance when senates and unions coexist? There are strong and varied views about whether senates and unions are complementary or competitive. Some of the rhetoric is strong as well. For example, the views of some presidents and boards that try to persuade faculty *not* to vote for unions in a pending election illustrate this diversity of opinions. One university president (Smallwood, 2004) said the following:

These data lead me to the conclusion that a strong system of shared
governance is the best method of achieving and maintaining the faculty rights and privileges which are so important. . . . Further, I
believe faculty bargaining units are inimical to the growth of shared
governance. (A10)

This view—that bargaining is inconsistent with strong systems of shared
governance—has been repeated in several elections where there have been
attempts to persuade the faculty to vote for no representation. On the other
side of the argument, a joint statement from the higher education arms of the
American Federation of Teachers and the National Education Association
(AFT/NEA), "The Truth about Unions and Shared Governance," argued that
the fact of unions and collective bargaining does not and should not replace
effective shared governance. According to the AFT/NEA, unions complement rather than compete with other forms of shared governance—"the asser-
tion that unions undermine shared governance is completely false" (n.d., 6).

How do senates and unions coexist? The research, published commentary,
and our experience offer some guidance. First, it is not known how influential
senates were before collective bargaining at a given institution. In cases where
unionization was a response to statewide politics, such as in New York, Pennsylvania, and Hawaii, this question probably cannot be answered empirically.
Second, there is likely to be a substantial overlap in the faculty leadership of a
union and a senate (Kaplan, 2004). In many cases, the leadership of the faculty
moves freely between positions in the senate and the union. It is not uncom-
mon for members of the faculty bargaining team also to be members of the
senate executive committee. Patterns of political leadership among faculty
seem to reflect the axiom that there is a limited amount of "governance energy"
in the academic polity. Overlapping faculty leadership makes it difficult for
campus administrators to maintain clear delineations between issues to be
resolved with the union and those to be resolved with the senate. To the extent
that relations with the union are adversarial, they tend to impact the tenor of
relations with the senate. Clearly, senate activity on mandatory bargaining
issues ceases.

Third, if unionization accompanies a high degree of intra-faculty conflict,
or if the relations between the union and administration are highly adversarial, then senates will have difficulty being effective. In these situations, trust
and legitimacy are low, and forms of shared governance become an issue.
Fourth, the broader the bargaining unit, the more likely it is that senate influence is weak. If the senate cannot represent stakeholders who are members of
the bargaining unit, such as part timers, lecturers, and so on, then its legitimate
claim to represent the campus is questionable, as are its claims for jurisdiction.
At Glenhaven University, the faculty were represented by a union for almost

thirty years. There appeared to be a well-established set of assumptions that, on at least some issues, the administration and board were adversaries of the faculty rather than colleagues. The campus atmosphere included a history of adversarial negotiations, controversial grievances, visible lawsuits, and a well-developed infrastructure to handle adversarial confrontation. It was common for the union to criticize the administration and board for not being strong advocates for faculty interests.

THE BIG ISSUES

Closing or merging a school in a public research university is a big issue, and on such issues traditional governance processes become problematic. Market forces are results driven, not process oriented, and often clash with the value-laden nature of shared governance. Universities are challenged to clearly define and gain consensus on such concepts as the institutional mission and its role in serving the public good. The problems that arise from the focus on the big issues and attempts to adapt internal governance processes and values to external pressure are the most pressing dilemmas facing boards, administrators, and faculty. These dilemmas will be enlightened by the following observations.

Politics and the Big Issues

Political values and principles trump those of the collegium and bureaucracy on big-issue matters. While defining a "big issue" is an art form, there are obvious examples such as program closure, approaches to collective bargaining, and the sanctity of tenure. These issues are further complicated by the multiple arenas of political action that occur within and in relation to the university. Pusser and Ordorika maintain that "public universities and their governing boards are political institutions [and] public post-secondary policy making is political action" (2001, 149). Political systems have at least the following four characteristics:

- Conflict is normal.
- Goals are ambiguous and contested.
- Participation in governance is fluid.
- Decisions are not finally made—instead, they flow.

The Center for Higher Education Policy Analysis (CHEPA) (2003) and others have reported that there is great support for shared governance among internal actors in universities, but there are significant differences in what the term actually means. Some believe it requires consultation, others believe it simply requires that information flow freely, while still others believe it requires that final authority be granted to a specific set of participants. Further, in most institutions, the relative priority to be given to the balance of teaching, research, and/or service or the priority to be given to various academic programs is contested. Most participants agree about teaching, research, and service as *goals* and that an institution must set priorities. Yet in reality, collective institutional decisions are difficult, if not impossible, to create. In the case study in this chapter, the campus senate and faculty union were in a position to offer opinions about the work of fellow faculty; administrators were accused of negligence by community members; and the trustees were charged with mediating the divide. The decision-making process may have been shared, but it was also highly contentious and emotionally draining for the participants.

The implementation of such matters, where goals are contested and conflict is normal, is at the heart of governance. We will return to this discussion in our concluding observations about politics and the art of governance.

Administrators and the Big Issues

Administrators are often caught in the demand for institutional efficiency and accountability, which results from the conflict between the external influences on the university and its internal traditions. They are advised by consultants and other experts on governance to concentrate the attention of boards and other institutional stakeholders on the big issues, those of strategic importance to implementing the university's mission. Yet *implementing* strategic objectives receives insufficient attention when considering whether such objectives are realistic. For example, strategic plans seldom are linked to the financial requirements to implement them. It is clear that all parties at Glenhaven agreed that the status quo was unacceptable. The professional accrediting body, the board, the administration, and the school faculty all agreed that the matter had languished too long and that something had to be done. However, there was little agreement about *what* should be done. The dilemma for the administration was the same as that pointed out by Pfeffer (1992): nothing happens once a decision is made unless someone is prepared to implement it. Making the decision is only one stage of the process. How can difficult decisions be implemented in a timely and an efficient way? The Glenhaven administration had the authority to phase out admissions to degree programs offered by the school and to do this independent of board action. However, the authority to close a program and/or change the organization chart by closing a school rested with the board. The decision proposed by the administration avoided the necessity to spend an estimated $1 million. The dilemma at issue in this case was how to *implement* the decision—how to get the board's approval in the face of fierce faculty-student opposition.

Faculty and the Big Issues

Faculty have traditionally been charged with primary responsibility for educational policy of dealing with issues of curriculum, research, and faculty status. These areas are regarded as the faculty's particular domain of expertise. When big issues are on the table, competency and expertise become secondary to competing interest groups that hold conflicting goals. Those Glenhaven faculty most affected by the school closure fiercely opposed the board's action. Some saw it as an unwise decision in view of community and national needs, others saw it as a matter of professional self-identity and prestige, and still others were concerned about the possibility of job loss. School faculty mobilized students, alumni, and community stakeholders in an effort to forestall the closure. In political systems, such resort to external stakeholders is legitimate. At Glenhaven, the involvement of external parties was a major factor in the board's initial reluctance to accept the administration's recommendation.

Opposition to closing the school was not as severe from either the Glenhaven campus senate or the system-wide faculty union. The campus senate was concerned about whether proper procedures were followed, and it urged the administration to find a way to continue the school. The union was assured by the administration that no tenured or tenure-track faculty would lose their jobs because of the reorganization. The union, of course, reserved its right to grieve and eventually to arbitrate any breach of its contract and/or faculty rights and responsibilities.

Boards and the Big Issues

Public boards are typically chosen through a political process—usually by gubernatorial appointment and senate confirmation but sometimes by popular election. Their role is deceptively straightforward: to provide oversight of the institution, to represent the public interest in the institution, and to mediate external influences on institutional behavior (Duryea and Williams, 2000). Significant sources are available to help identify the characteristics of effective boards (Ingram, 1997; Chait, Holland, and Taylor, 1996; CHEPA, 2005). On the big issues, boards are under enormous pressure to deviate from the standard decision-making processes. This pressure influences how effective boards can be on these issues. Most trustees are not used to the controversy surrounding big issues and are uncomfortable with public hearings where tempers flare and picket lines have to be crossed. They find it difficult to respond to hunger strikes and to deal with negative press and criticism from friends and public figures. The challenge for board trustees is reaching a consensus on difficult issues that affect the educational mission while responding to the needs of diverse constituents and institutional stakeholders. The university is an inherent site of political struggles, and governing boards are usually the final authority for resolving big issues.

Boards operate best when there is a consensus about issues brought to them. When they are asked to make controversial choices, the politics of influence become more important. The fluidity of participation will result in greater volatility than usual. Contradictory views and information will be introduced. As we saw in the school closure case at Glenhaven, this conflict often results in questions by trustees about whether they have the "right" information or whether the data are biased. In addition, since most public boards have to operate "in the sunshine" and are prohibited from having private conversations about board matters, the opportunities to examine alternatives and seek consensus within the board are limited. Sunshine laws represent a significant element in the functioning of public universities, a "still-evolving public policy experiment [with a] potentially profound influence" (Hearn and McLendon, 2005, 31). With the school closure case, sunshine laws mandated that the decision-making process be conducted openly in the public arena. While this allowed all institutional stakeholders a voice in the process, it also complicated what was already a difficult, emotional issue for the university.

POLITICS AND THE ART OF GOVERNANCE

Those who study, conduct research on, and practice the art of governance in colleges and universities must account for the prevalence of political values and legitimacy in institutional behavior. To remain mission centered, institutional stakeholders must engage in difficult and demanding decisions. To be market smart requires an awareness of public needs and the institutional capacity to be responsive to those needs. To be politically savvy requires an ability to understand and manage the following realities:

- External forces are changing faster than internal governance values and processes can adapt.
- Academic goals and missions are ambiguous, and conflict over them is normal.
- Decisions are not made; instead, they flow.

- Participation in governance is fluid, particularly on the big issues.
- Interests of the stakeholders (e.g., job security, salaries, professional control) are legitimate concerns in the debate about governance.

In Glenhaven University, making the decision to close a professional school was only the first step in a difficult and contentious process where a consensus was impossible to achieve. The pressures to be sensitive to changes in the external environment conflict with the more process-oriented, value-driven traditions of internal shared governance. There is too much rhetoric in higher education about managing change. The art of governance is only partially about change; the heart of the matter is defining, implementing, and sustaining an agenda. This requires political awareness, compromise, and negotiation.

REFERENCES

American Federation of Teachers and National Education Association. n.d. *The truth about unions and shared governance*. Washington, DC: Author.

Association of Governing Boards of Universities and Colleges. 1998. *Bridging the gap between state government and public higher education* (a summary of the report). Washington, DC: Author.

Baldridge, J. V., D. V. Curtis, G. P. Ecker, and G. L. Riley. 1977. Alternative models of governance in higher education. In *Governing academic organizations*, ed. G. L. Riley and J. V. Baldridge, 2–25. Berkeley, CA: McCutchan.

Breneman, D. W. 2004. *Are the states and public higher education striking a new bargain?* Public Policy Paper Series No. 04–02. Washington, DC: Association of Governing Boards of Universities and Colleges.

Center for Higher Education Policy Analysis (CHEPA). 2003. *Challenges for governance: A national report*. Los Angeles: University of Southern California.

———. 2005. *Assessing public board performance*. Los Angeles: University of Southern California.

Chaffee, E. E. 1985. Three models of strategy. *Academy of Management Review* 10(1): 89–98.

Chait, R. P., T. P. Holland, and B. E. Taylor. 1996. *Improving the performance of governing boards*. Westport, CT: Oryx Press.

Duryea, E. D., and D. Williams. 2000. *The academic corporation: A history of college and university governing boards*. New York: Falmer Press.

Eckel, P. 2000. The role of shared governance in institutional hard decisions: Enabler or antagonist? *The Review of Higher Education* 24(1): 15–39.

Gumport, P., and B. Pusser. 1997. *Restructuring the academic environment.* Stanford, CA: National Center for Postsecondary Improvement.

Hearn, J., and M. McLendon. 2005. Sunshine laws in higher education. *Academe* 91(3): 28–31.

Ingram, R. T. 1997. *Trustee responsibilities: A guide for governing boards of public institutions.* Washington, DC: Association of Governing Boards of Universities and Colleges.

Jones, D. P., P. Ewell, and A. C. McGuinness, Jr. 1998. *The challenges and opportunities facing higher education: An agenda for policy research.* San Jose, CA: The National Center for Policy in Higher Education.

Julius, D. J., J. V. Baldridge, and J. Pfeffer. 1999. A memo from Machiavelli. *The Journal of Higher Education* 70(2): 113–33.

Kaplan, G. E. 2004. How academic ships actually navigate. In *Governing academia,* ed. R. G. Ehrenberg, 165–208. Ithaca, NY: Cornell University Press.

Kellogg Commission on the Future of State and Land-Grant Universities. 1999. *Returning to our roots: The engaged institution.* Washington, DC: National Association of State Universities and Land-Grant Colleges.

Kerr, C. 1999. Past triumphs, future challenges: A conversation with Clark Kerr. *The Presidency* (Winter): 12–19.

Longanecker, D. A. 2004. *Governing for real.* Paper presented at the Governance Roundtable. Santa Fe, NM: Center for Higher Education Policy Analysis.

Maitland, C., and G. Rhoades. 2001. Unions and faculty governance. *National Education Association 2001 Almanac,* 27–33. Washington, DC: National Education Association.

Martin, J., J. E. Samuels, and Associates. 1997. *First among equals: The role of the chief academic officer.* Baltimore, MD: Johns Hopkins University Press.

McGuinness, A. C., Jr. 2003. *State policy leadership in the public interest: Is anyone at home?* Background paper prepared for Macalester Forum on Higher Education. Boulder, CO: National Center for Higher Education Management Systems.

Mortimer, K. P., and T. R. McConnell. 1978. *Sharing authority effectively.* San Francisco: Jossey-Bass.

Newman, F., and L. Couturier. 2001. *The new competitive arena: Market forces invade the academy* (The Futures Project: Policy for Higher Education in a Changing World). Providence, RI: Brown University.

Pfeffer, J. 1992. *Managing with power: Politics and influence in organizations.* Boston: Harvard Business School Press.

Pusser, B., and I. Ordorika. 2001. Bringing political theory to university governance: The University of California and the Universidad Nacional Autonoma de Mexico. In *Higher Education: Handbook of Theory and Research,* vol. 16, ed. J.C. Smart, 147–94. New York: Agathon Press.

Rhoades, G. 1998. *Managed professionals: Unionized faculty and the restructuring of academic labor*. Albany: State University of New York Press.

Slaughter, S., and L. L. Leslie. 1997. *Academic capitalism*. Baltimore, MD. Johns Hopkins University Press.

Smallwood, S. 2004. Union blues in the sunshine state. *Chronicle of Higher Education* (April 2): A10–A12.

Tierney, W. G. 1988. Organizational culture in higher education: Defining the essentials. *Journal of Higher Education* 59(1): 2–21.

Wellman, J. V. 2004. *Rethinking state governance for higher education*. Paper presented at the 2004 CHEPA Governance Roundtable, Santa Fe, NM.

5

The "New" New Challenge of Governance by Governing Boards

David A. Longanecker

In American higher education, a great deal of time is spent thinking and writing about governance (Kerr and Gade, 1989; Richardson, Bracco, Callan, and Finney, 1999). Those of us in the public sector speak proudly of our tradition of lay governance by our boards of trustees. Individuals within academe maintain that academic governance contributes to the unique strength of American higher education (Burgan, 2004). Academic administrators, particularly presidents and chancellors, who live in both worlds, talk of the unique blend of shared governance that makes American higher education distinctive. All of this is true, of course. The concept of legal governance vested in lay boards of trustees helped shape American higher education into arguably the most accessible and publicly responsive system of higher education in the world. The critical role of board, faculty, staff, students, and others in campus-wide shared governance has sustained quality in an increasingly dynamic environment.

This chapter, however, focuses only on one segment of this structure: the role of public governing boards in the governance process. Board governance, whether effective or ineffective, plays a significant role in public higher education (Ingram, 1998). Under the federalist system in the United States, the authority to organize and fund higher education is given to the states, which in turn utilize lay boards of trustees to manage colleges and universities. Governing boards are charged with ensuring that the public trust in the institution is maintained; the board is also held responsible for ensuring that institutions appropriately exercise their responsibilities. The governing board makes fiscal decisions that are congruent to state policy and in the best interest of the institution (McGuinness, 1997) and is given general oversight regarding academic matters. Trustees also are generally held responsible both for supporting the institution and its actions and for assuring that the institution is accountable to its various constituencies. These multiple roles often can come into conflict and may be difficult to reconcile.

Beyond these roles, the nature of a governing board's responsibilities varies, depending upon the board type. Self-perpetuating boards (those that select themselves) govern most independent, private institutions of higher education. Trustees determine the structure and stature of the board and select individuals to fit institutional or system-wide needs. Most public college or university boards, on the other hand, serve explicitly for and at the request of an external public constituent or set of constituents. The state governor or legislature appoints many, if not most, public higher education board members to their position, though some are actually elected within their state or a specific political jurisdiction of the state (ECS, 1997). For the appointed or elected members of these governing boards, the job of governing can be quite complex. Trustees are legally responsible *for* their institutions and can develop a strong affinity for them; yet they also are responsible *to* those who appoint or elect them—whether the governor, the state legislature, or the voters. And if the rhetoric about higher education is correct, then the consequences of a board's actions are very substantial (AGB, 1996). Indeed, the future economic, civic, and social development of our society and the role of public higher education in that development can be influenced by the actions of governing boards. The role of governing boards, therefore, is important.

Equally important, however, is what governing board members bring individually to the job. While representing the public interest in higher education, individual trustees also bring unique cultural and social perspectives to their work. Despite oft-heard commentary that suggests otherwise, I maintain that most trustees come to the job armed with high intelligence, clear and appropriate values, great vision, and many abilities. They also bring a wide array of personalities; some are well adapted to the group interaction necessary for people to work together and effectively govern, while others are less well prepared to work collaboratively.

As Judith Ramaley notes in chapter 8, trustees are increasingly affected by the growing perception of higher education as a private good with individual benefits as opposed to a public good with social benefits. McGuinness (2002) concluded, "States are moving away from their traditional roles as 'owners-operators' of public institutions and [instead] moving to [the] selective subsidy of institutions . . . linked to a narrower definition of how postsecondary education contributes to the public good." These factors collectively contribute to how effective a board is in governing its institution, as trustees are challenged to respond to social, political, and economic demands. Maintaining a balance between individual characteristics, group dynamics, and role expectations contributes to one of the true dilemmas in the governance of American higher education: How can boards govern for the real world rather than for an idealized world?

The rest of this chapter addresses the ways in which the characteristics of American public higher education boards—who becomes a board member, to whom she or he is beholden, and in what domain she or he governs—affect how realistically they contribute to the life of the institution or system they govern. Unfortunately, there is little past research or literature to help inform the discussion that follows. As Kezar and Eckel (2004) documented in their synthesis of the research and literature on governance, virtually all of the existing studies of governance focus on structural theories, suggesting "that the most important aspect in understanding governance is to examine organizational structures such as lines of authority, roles, procedures, and bodies responsible for decision making" (5). Their research shows that very little literature in this area has focused on the sociological or psychological theories of organizational dynamics. In effect, "human relations, cultural and social cognition theories remain underutilized theoretical frameworks in the study of governance" (4). It is precisely these human dynamics that this chapter explores.

WHO GOVERNS?

The goal of public governing boards is to oversee institutional policies, to ensure the "best interests" of the institution, and to serve as mediators between the institution, the state, and the public (Pusser and Ordorika, 2001). Trustees must respond to immediate needs and long-term analyses: "The essence of the trustee function," noted Rauh, "lies in the continuing assessment of *purpose* and in *planned evolution*" (Rauh, 1969, 7, emphasis added). In order to accomplish these goals, public governing boards commonly consist of laypeople who are not academics nor hold employment in colleges or universities. Most trustees are selected (by appointment or self-selection) or elected because they are change agents. Seldom do individuals accept such an important position simply to sustain the status quo. Committed board members want to make a difference, a difference that they and others can see and one that improves the institution or system for which they have accepted responsibility.

Herein lies the difficulty. Governing is not predominantly concerned with change, it is concerned with sustaining effort. At least with most public governing boards, the guidelines are fairly well established; the institutional mission has already been set out by the state, not by the governing board. The board is to govern its institution or system in a fashion that contributes to the state's goals for higher education, which generally include some combination of ensuring broad access to high-quality education and doing so in a manner that contributes to the economic, civic, and social vitality of the state, hence the role of a public governing board to serve in the public interest. The governing board ultimately "ensures the public responsibility and accountability of the university" (Glion Declaration, 1999). Most boards must work within this established set of parameters.

Some scholars contend that the status quo nature of board governance, which I described as normal and to some extent required, is what is wrong with governance in American higher education (CHEPA, 2004, 2005). I disagree. While change is constant and necessary, and the American higher education exists as a dynamic system, most change is incremental, not radical in nature. And that is for good reason; ours is not the first "wise generation." If I am correct, however, and the role of most governing boards is to manage within a modest change environment, then that is clearly not a situation in which most leaders and change agents want to be involved. Trustees want their unique contribution to governance to improve the institutions under their charge. The two most common areas of focus by trustees are mission expansion and institutional growth.

EXPANDING THE MISSION OF HIGHER EDUCATION

Perhaps the most common way this change agenda materializes in American higher education is through efforts to enhance institutions by expanding their mission. Whether attempted overtly or covertly, governing bodies seek to gain status for their respective institutions in the prestige hierarchy of American higher education. The current national demand for educational accountability has resulted in institutional status erroneously interpreted as a measure of quality. In the United States, the increase in institutional status is frequently perceived as the measure of an effective governing board.

In the public sector of higher education, this attempt is readily apparent in the efforts by many community colleges to extend their mission to include baccalaureate-level education, in addition to their traditional diploma, certificate, associate degree, and vocational offerings. Recent events in Arizona depict this tendency. The state of Arizona has experienced rapid population growth in recent decades, with a resultant 50 percent projected enrollment growth in higher education by 2020 (ABOR, 2004). Yet the number of four-year institutions to serve this population has remained unchanged. The state Board of Regents concluded, "The university system is not well prepared to cope with the impending demand because each university presently is required to be all things to all people. . . . But none has the capacity or sufficient public resources to carry out all of these responsibilities equally well" (ibid., 4).

When the state Board of Regents identified the need for additional baccalaureate education in the state and investigated how to create new institutions to serve that need, a number of Arizona community colleges signaled their interest in becoming new baccalaureate institutions. Although this runs contrary to the efficient mission differentiation that has guided Arizona higher education in the past, the reaction is natural within the prestige hierarchy of public higher education in the United States. Typically, a community or regional district locally controls community college boards. Under this type of governance, members of these boards can seek to advance their communities' interests with less regard for the collective interests of the state. A natural tendency of many communities is for their modest college to become a great university.

This avarice for change through mission creep is not unique to community colleges. Again, using Arizona as a case study, the state Board of Regents maintained: "Arizona's universities and community colleges must continue to collaborate and work closely together" to facilitate the desired mission differentiation that was a core objective of the "system redesign" (ABOR, 2004, 6). Even within the three universities governed by the Board of Regents, however, it was difficult fostering this desired differentiation. The baccalaureate-focused institutions, which included the east and west campuses of Arizona State University, the south campus of the University of Arizona, and northern Arizona University, feared that focusing on baccalaureate education would diminish their ability to expand into great research institutions. While the goal to become a preeminent public research university is one unlikely to materialize, such a goal was still in their proverbial field of dreams.

Mission creep is seldom what the state needs or has in mind in terms of higher education institutions. While such actions often do lead to some institutional aggrandizement, they also inevitably lead to more costly, less broadly accessible higher education. As a result, "good" stewardship by a governing board—as it works to expand the scope and prestige of the respective institution—often undercuts a primary need of the state and the interest of the public: the need to provide broad access to quality education as cost-efficiently as possible (Richardson, Bracco, Callan, and Finney, 1999).

Indeed, cost-effectiveness, an assumed state priority, often runs counter to the objectives of board members. While trustees often are quite engaged in determining how the resources that flow *within* the institutions under their charge can be used as cost-effectively as possible, board members seldom show as much restraint when it comes to resources that flow *into* their institutions, particularly those that flow from the public purse. From the governing board's perspective, external funds are particularly significant to fulfill the public good role of higher education. Governing board members, like so many leaders of American higher education, often bemoan the fact that the share of all state resources being devoted to higher education has declined steadily over the past forty years. Yet trustees are less likely to acknowledge that, despite this declining share, the actual funding per student, adjusted for inflation, has increased in most states. In most cases, the focus of trustees influences them to see the glass as half full rather than half empty.

THE GROWTH OF PUBLIC UNIVERSITIES

Another way in which governance works to move the "change agenda" forward is through growth. In this respect, higher education is similar to many other industries. Growth provides the marginal revenue needed to change the way in which things are done. New "contemporary" classrooms, additional academic programs, expanded athletic facilities and teams, and additional administrators can be supported with growth funds. Growth, therefore, becomes an imperative for achieving change.

Governance fosters growth. In many circumstances, this also enhances some of the agendas of external constituencies. As seen in the previous case study of higher education in Arizona, the democratization of higher education can enhance access. In an era of demographic growth, it is essential for higher education to expand—to both ensure and enhance public benefits. In other circumstances, however, growth can negatively impact other public needs. The state or local community most often must share some of the additional costs of growth in public higher education, thus making the overall enterprise more costly to taxpayers.

Furthermore, growth subtly changes the nature of the institution and the education that it provides (Kezar, 2004). Even without an overt change in mission, a growing institution becomes a place quite different from that originally envisioned. Boise State University offers an example of this phenomenon. Its "official" mission today is quite similar to what it has been for the past twenty years. Yet the nature of the institution has changed phenomenally, as it has changed from a modest undergraduate institution into the largest institution in Idaho, with a robust research and graduate education mission and the most successful Division I athletic program in the state. This expansion has contributed substantially to both economic development and expanding educational opportunity in Idaho, but it has happened incrementally, through the approved actions of the state governing board, not through explicit changes in the mission of the institution.

Within the independent sector, institutional growth often takes a somewhat different form. Governance within the private sector more often focuses on securing a comfortable market niche, preferably one higher on the prestige hierarchy than that which the institution currently holds. In this environment, maintaining an institution's size and mission can actually enhance its attractiveness within an overall expanding market for higher education, because the institution can become more selective—thus more prestigious.

CHARACTERISTICS OF PUBLIC GOVERNING BOARDS

If the desire for dramatic change is often a hallmark of public governing boards (one that does not always serve them well), then there are other qualities related to board composition that also have a profound effect on the way it functions. One example is intentional diversity (Van der Walt and Ingley, 2003), which is essential for the democratic nature of governance in American higher education, particularly among public-sector governing boards. But diversity—of political views, constituency obligations, sociocultural backgrounds, or even of overall perspectives—can impede effective governance. Due to the influence of individual characteristics, as I previously noted, boards composed of people with distinctly different perspectives often have difficulty coalescing so that they can effectively govern in a collaborative fashion. This dilemma of democracy has led some scholars, such as Dill and Helm (1988), to argue for professional competence over democratic representation in the composition of governing bodies. The limits of democracy in governance can be seen perhaps most significantly on politically charged boards, particularly elected boards, in which the interests of public higher education and the institutions involved are muddled with partisan politics.

Recent activities by the Nevada Board of Regents reflect the unique difficulties that elected board members face, and thus the difficulties that such boards have in coming to a consensus regarding significant issues. I maintain that no state faces a greater challenge in preserving access to higher education in the new millennium than does Nevada, which will see an increase in demand for higher education of more than 100 percent over the next few years (UCCSN, 2003). Planning for this growth, however, has proven extremely difficult for the Regents of the Community College and University System of Nevada, in part due to the elected nature of the board. While praising the current governor, the system chancellor noted, "I trust the public more than I trust governors. . . . I do not see shortcomings in the present board that all human beings do not have" (Rogers, 2004). Yet political problems have arisen—some regents place the state's needs above the parochial interests of their specific communities and institutions, while others do not. As a result, historic battles between Las Vegas and Reno have impeded rational planning, regarding both research capacity and expansion of undergraduate education at the state's two major universities. For example, plans to create a new baccalaureate college unraveled when some regents feared impeding the progress of their respective institutions. Even when the regents have worked together to move forward a positive agenda for the future, they have found it difficult to work with other critical stakeholders, such as the governor and legislature, because sharing power and decision making often feels like an abdication of their constitutional responsibility (UCCSN, 2003).

Many governing board members also possess extensive personal managerial experience. Trustees have built careers as successful managers in the business or nonprofit sector, and they pride themselves on their managerial acumen. Oftentimes these individuals will say that their most important responsibility is to select a good chief executive officer (CEO) for the institutions they govern (Michael, Schwartz, and Cravcenco, 2000); their second most important role is to then step back and let the CEO manage the operation. If only they practiced what they preach—too often, governing boards composed of people with substantial management experience succumb to the temptation to micromanage rather than to govern.

Finally, I maintain that most board members, whether they admit it or not, have an interest in being recognized for the good deeds they do. This all-too-human element of governance has both positive and negative consequences. On the positive side, the belief that governance will promote the public good is so strong in American higher education that virtually all who serve on boards recognize that their reputation for service will depend on how well they attend to this expectation. Thus the natural need for positive recognition drives them in the right direction. In this respect, governance in higher education closely parallels governance in the other nonprofit and religiously oriented service institutions but stands in stark contrast to the workings of governing boards in venues such as corporate America.

But the desire for positive recognition also can have negative consequences. Probably the most obvious one is the strong tendency to shirk responsibility when something goes wrong. I see this weakness reflected frequently—for example, when boards blame the CEO for problems for which they themselves are in part responsible, or when boards are involved in covering up a public relations problem. I witness this on Saturday afternoons each fall, as governing board members around the country enjoy the glories associated with college football. Most of these governing board members fully realize that these athletic enterprises, particularly in the most profitable levels of intercollegiate athletics, contribute little, if anything, to the true academic purpose of the institutions they govern. Collegiate athletics can, in fact, often pervert the educational purposes of the institution (see, e.g., the Knight Commission's 2001 report, "A Call to Action"). Yet seldom do boards intervene, unless a crisis arises.

When a crisis does arise, boards often compound the problem rather than redress the concerns. "It is in these stressful and highly politicized situations that the dual nature of the trustee—as a steward of the institution and as a representative of the public—becomes most troublesome," concluded Rauh (1969, 122). The University of Colorado's Board of Regents is one example. The manner in which it dealt with the institution's recent crisis of confidence (see, e.g., Jacobson, 2004), relating to the apparent lack of discipline and civilized behavior within the athletic department, reflects the difficulty that an elected board faces when it must deal with an issue that might tarnish an institution's reputation. The regents clearly felt that they had to seriously address the charges against the university. Their actions also suggested, however, that they wanted to do so in a way that did not erode their individual political futures. The trustees clearly did not see themselves as "responsible" for what allegedly occurred. The inability to reconcile their desire to do the right thing with their reluctance to become personally tainted in the process ultimately led to a muddled response that left the university, but not the regents, at risk. Elected board members cannot escape the fact that they are politicians and thus are affected by the same forces that affect all politicians who desire to remain in office.

In sum, I argue that governing boards are composed of exceptional people with exceptional talent. But certain aspects—who those people are, why they accept such a responsibility, and what they want and need from the position—can result in a dysfunctional governing board operation. Too often board members ignore the responsibilities for which they were selected in an attempt to create new roles for public universities not appropriate for their intended purpose.

To Whom Is the Board Beholden—and How Does That Influence Real Governance?

Recent decades have witnessed a change in the role of the state and federal governments in social life. McGuinness (2002) noted that these changes have affected assumptions regarding the state's role in postsecondary education. In particular, the state now often focuses on the student as a client and consumer of the institution, as opposed to a focus on the provider (the institution). In addition, quality is frequently defined in terms of outcomes, such as graduation rates and assessment of student learning. The work of governing boards is no longer solely "coordination of institutions and regulatory oversight." Instead, boards must work from the perspective of "policy leadership in the public interest" (McGuinness, 2002).

As mentioned in the introduction, higher education governing boards come in three versions: self-perpetuating boards, externally appointed boards, and elected boards (MacTaggart, 1998). Within each of these categories, however, there is often another factor that distinguishes board members. Some members are selected simply because of who they are personally: influential businesspeople, philanthropists, community, religious, or civic leaders, or simply friends of the appointing authority. Others are selected because of their association with a specific constituency: students, faculty, alumni, congressional districts, churches, and so on. Both of these conditions—who selects the members of the governing board and who they represent—affect how they govern.

The boards of independent institutions generally have the easiest time finding an avenue to *real* governance. Because most self-perpetuating boards select their own membership, they are more likely than other boards to compile a board whose members are congenial and dedicated to the same general perspective of the institutional goals. Simply put, I maintain that members of self-perpetuating boards are less beholden to others than they are to the governing board of which they are a part. This difference is significant. Furthermore, members of self-perpetuating boards often are selected because of their already established commitment to the existing institution, which makes them less likely to dream of governing an institution that does not and cannot exist, rather than governing the *real* institution for which they are responsible.

Of course, not every independent institution faces the utopian governance environment just described. Some do not have the luxury of self-selecting their governing boards, operating instead under externally appointed boards, as is the case with public higher education. This is particularly true of many religiously affiliated institutions, as witnessed in recent years with a number of the colleges and universities associated with the Southern Baptist Church. In response to an increasingly conservative focus by the Southern Baptist Convention, some affiliated institutions have altered their charter (Baylor University, Carson-Newman College), created a self-perpetuating board (Samford University, Wake Forest University), or completely severed ties with the convention (Grand Canyon University, Stetson University) (McMurtrie, 2003). The relationship between the convention, trustees, and the institution can lead to substantial conflict with the actual activities and directions of the institution. The trustees, while maintaining legal authority for institutional functions, also are influenced by the religious doctrines of the church.

Self-perpetuating boards also face unique difficulties when the institutions they govern encounter extremely difficult times, either financially or academically. The usual response of these governing boards is then to find new professional leadership—hiring a new president. Yet there are some circumstances so severe that new leadership cannot be expected to fix them. Leadership can legitimately address fiscal mismanagement but cannot solve fiscal insolvency. It can legitimately address academic discord but cannot resolve a fundamental disconnect between an institution's real and achievable niche in the higher education marketplace and the place where its governing board wants it to be.

In contrast, an external authority typically appoints individuals to most governing boards—the governor (which is the norm), the legislature, or some combination of the two (MacTaggart, 1998). One case study (Pusser and

Ordorika, 2001) found that gubernatorial appointees are typically individuals who are major political contributors. Many of these individuals also are appointed because of their affiliation with a specific constituency. In many states, for example, board members are selected to assure geographic representation from the whole state. Certain boards must be politically balanced, requiring that members reveal their political affiliation. In other states, boards are recognized as being politically affiliated solely with the appointing authority. Obviously, in these cases, political affiliation also is a nontrivial feature of the board's membership.

Ensuring equal geographic representation requires congressional district boundaries or urban/rural designations. Within systems that include multiple types of public institutions, members often are selected because of their affiliation with a specific type of institution. In some respects the members of these boards have the most difficult governance tasks of any of the three generic types of boards—in part because they serve multiple masters. While they certainly recognize allegiance to the authority that appointed them, their legal responsibility is to the institution or system in which they serve. As servants of the public good, these governing boards find that other "publics" also expect them to serve their desires and needs. These can be difficult expectations.

Perhaps the most difficult blending of these roles, however, occurs in those cases where boards are beholden to the governor as the appointing authority but legally and ethically beholden to their institution or system. This is a complex role, for two reasons. First, many governors are *uncomfortable* with their relationship with their state's public higher education system. With most other state services, governors have direct control: they appoint the head of the state agency, they control the budget, and they direct public policy within the laws established by the state legislature. But higher education is unique. Seldom does the governor appoint an institutional or a system president or chancellor; the governing board holds that role. Usually, the governor and the state control only a modicum of the budget, with substantial resources coming from tuition (often outside of the governor's official purview), industry-supported customized training funds, externally funded research that may or may not coincide with the state's interests, foundation gifts, fees for auxiliary services, and so on. Much of policy is vested in the governing board. As a result, many governors feel unable to direct one of the state's most important public services—yet they still feel responsible.

Second, higher education often is not a high priority for governors. This is in part because of the lack of control but also because other services simply garner more political support. Governors often focus their efforts on other areas of state activity. Elementary and secondary education is much more important to voters, so it receives more attention. Highways affect the average individual citizen more directly than does higher education, so they garner more attention. When public safety is on everyone's mind, it too upstages higher education. Health care and its costs cannot be ignored, so once again, higher education goes to the back burner. This works, however, because the governor could not greatly affect higher education even if she or he tried. Furthermore, higher education seems to thrive without much intervention. After all, it is overseen by the governor's hand-picked representatives, who tell the governor that the state's institutions are doing a fine job, establishing broad access to high-quality higher education for all the citizens of the state, and so on.

So why does this situation make good governance difficult for boards? Some would say the situation sounds ideal—an appointing authority that often does not care much about what one is doing and generally trusts one to do the job well. The problem is that governing with only tacit support from the representative authority can be troubling, from a number of perspectives. First, the governor expects no problems. When something goes awry, the governor holds the board responsible for tarnishing her or his reputation as a state leader and often usurps the role she or he had originally delegated to the board. An example is the University of Colorado's recent high-profile problem within its athletic department, which prompted Governor Bill Owens to call for a special investigation by the state attorney general (Hoover, 2004). The governor simply could not allow such an issue to surface and fester without demonstrating his serious concern and willingness to act. The University of Colorado's regents, who are elected rather than appointed by the governor, have no allegiance to him—and thus appreciate no allegiance from him.

Perhaps more important, though, is the difficulty boards generally have in getting the attention or capturing the imagination of the governor so they can pursue the issues they feel are essential to the state. In recent years, for example, public governing boards in many states have experienced difficulty in enlisting the governor's help in curbing large budget cuts for higher education—from a gubernatorial perspective, higher education was not a priority. Appointed board members often look to the appointing authority for signals about what is expected. If the appointing authority is essentially disengaged from the board, then there will not be many signals to follow—unless, of course, the board governs in a fashion unacceptable to the governor. Therein exists the dilemma. Publicly appointed governing boards serve multiple masters, but the expectations of those different masters are not always clear.

Perhaps even more importantly, those expectations, even when they are understood, are often not in sync. Governors live in a real world. They want good higher education, but they generally understand the limits and possibilities of what they have. As discussed earlier in this chapter, boards often want change—trustees want to make a big difference, improving upon the situation that lies before them. Many, if not most, institutions want to boost their reputations and stature. For example, many public research universities boast strategic plans that call for them to find their place among the "top 10" or "top 50" public research universities. Yet the likelihood that they will ever achieve this goal is remote, both because the current top 10 or top 50 institutions are not going to idly sit back and be replaced and because, in many cases, the aspiring institutions have no financial commitment from the state to pursue this goal. Additionally, many governing boards also have an overinflated impression of the institution or system as it exists today. Garrison Keillor once quipped on his radio show *Prairie Home Companion* that his home state of Minnesota's medical school was one of the "100 top 10" medical schools in the country. Likewise, board members often become true believers in those organizations with which they are most closely associated and thus have difficulty judging what the institution can realistically become—because, in fact, they do not fully accept what the institution really *is*.

The temporal nature of publicly appointed boards further exacerbates this dilemma. Most appointed board members serve for a relatively short period of time—terms of four to six years, with limited reappointment possibilities. Because effective governance requires knowledge about the institution or system being governed, governing board members are relatively less effective during the first couple of years of their tenure than they are in later years (Chait, Holland, and Taylor, 1996). This means that appointed board members have only a few years in which they can effectively govern. This short-time horizon can foster difficulty in developing a consensus around ideas—because developing a consensus requires time. It also leads to a "reinvention of the wheel," because historical understanding disappears regularly. That is one reason public higher education policy is revisited so frequently. Exceptionally good thinking may have gone into the last generation of policy on tuition, financial, institutional budget allocations, and so on, but those were decisions made by previous board members. The new board was not a part of building a consensus around those policies. Furthermore, as change agents, they are probably quite convinced that they have better ideas than previous members.

Elected boards bring a very different set of dynamics to governance; specifically, of all boards, they exhibit the ultimate constituency orientation. The benefit of elected boards is that they clearly have a reflection of the public good as defined by the public, not by public do-gooders. Yet publicly elected boards also can have extreme difficulty dealing with *real* circumstances, as opposed to *desired* circumstances. If they have the responsibility for setting tuition, which most elected boards do, then they often envision tuition more as a tax than as a revenue source. As publicly elected officials, they often are very reluctant to "raise taxes." Tuition and tuition policy consequently become political tools rather than a critical source of revenue (McGuinness, 2002).

It also is more difficult for elected boards than it is for any other boards to "take the fall" for bad decisions. While I have argued earlier that this is difficult for any board, it is more difficult for politicians than for appointed boards. Yes, whether they admit it or not, elected board members are politicians; as a result, they act as politicians. Such trustees represent their constituents' needs and desires, not the elusive greater public good. And because they are legally responsible for governing, beholden to no one other than their direct constituency, they are less likely as a group to develop consensus on setting their agenda. Such individuals do not have a responsibility to "share governance" with the governor, legislature, business community, or academic stakeholders. Indeed, they often believe that sharing such a responsibility would be abdicating their own responsibility. This is particularly true in states where the elected nature of the governing board also is tied to the constitutional autonomy of the institution or system being governed. It is less true in the community college sector, much of which is governed by elected boards, because these local boards generally are closely tied to the community, all of which is to suggest that the constituency to whom a board is beholden significantly affects the way in which that board governs.

WHAT IS GOVERNED?

In American higher education, we have boards that govern single institutions; we have multi-campus boards that govern institutions with similar missions; we have "superboards" that govern all institutions within a specified jurisdiction (usually a state); we have coordinating boards that represent unique state interests by herding all of the above; and we have boards that combine some or all of the above responsibilities (ECS, 1997). The nature of these responsibilities greatly affects the way in which a board governs.

Single Institutional Board

A governance structure with purview over only one institution has a relatively straightforward task—to maintain the integrity of the academic and financial affairs of the institution and to advance the mission of the institution through appropriate innovation and support. The way in which governing boards undertake this task varies, depending in great part on how the trustees are selected and the kinds of individuals who comprise the board. But their task does not differ much from one institution to another. Boards will often say that their most important task is to select and retain an exceptional president. But what *is* an exceptional president? Not a defender of the status quo, certainly—that would be far too pedantic. No, a great president, like a great board member, is a change agent, someone committed to making the institution better than it is today. Better, however, means different—and not all colleges and universities in America need to be different than they are today.

This drive to be better and/or different is not a difficult challenge for governance of the independent sector of higher education. By definition, these institutions are independent, so they can rightfully choose whatever course they want. For public institutions, however, this quest for difference can create significant problems. The missions of individual public colleges and universities have generally been crafted to guarantee that the missions of various institutions within a state or system fit together. The desire is for balance throughout the system—an effort to make the sum of the parts equal the desired whole. When one institution decides to move outside the parameters of this differentiation of missions, it can upset the balance, creating unnecessary duplication of missions between institutions or gaps in coverage of student access and diminishing institutional fulfillment of the public good.

Multiple Institution/System Board

Governing a system of institutions is more complex. In theory, this complexity should be moderated if the system governs similar institutions with similar missions. But the experiences of the California State University (CSU) System, for example, would suggest that similar missions do not, in and of themselves, create similar institutions. Nor do individual institutions within a system have less ambition than self-governed institutions to become something better (read: different) than they are today. The administration of the Cal State System lists as its priorities: "access, quality, teacher and workforce preparation, partnerships with K–12 education, and accountability" (CSU, 2005). Yet California State University, Fresno, is bent on becoming an athletic powerhouse; Cal State, Los Angeles, is an urban university; San Francisco State is a multi-ethnic international university; and Sonoma State legitimately claims to be a public liberal arts college of distinction. All are within the CSU System.

One substantial difference between individual and system governance is that the board is less likely to have an aggrandized affinity for any single institution. This can have both positive and negative consequences. On the positive side, because the board oversees many institutions, the focus tends to be on what is needed to accomplish the mission—and how to accomplish it—rather than on who is doing what and how. The focus on *the place*, which dominates single-institution governing boards, is supplanted by a focus on *policies*, *practice,* and *performance.* Yet the span of responsibility is often so large in a system that individual institutional integrity and ownership can become sacrificed. Clark Kerr, the great leader of the University of California and architect of the California master plan (which created the three distinct public systems in California), mused late in life about his work. He feared that the University of California had lost something through its megasystem. The geographic communities in which the University of California campuses were located and the cultural communities they served did not share an affinity for these institutions, as happened elsewhere in the country, with institutions that were "owned" more directly by their communities (Kerr, 2001).

Governing Boards of Multi-Campus Systems

Perhaps the most difficult governing task, however, falls to the superboards of multi-campus systems that include institutions with quite differing roles and missions. More superboards exist in the United States than people recognize. When speaking of superboards, most individuals think of the University of Wisconsin System or the two New York systems (State University of New York [SUNY] and City University of New York [CUNY]). Yet in the Western United States alone, Alaska, Hawaii, Oregon, Utah, Nevada, Idaho, Montana, North Dakota, and South Dakota all essentially have superboard governance structures (ECS, 1997). Idaho is particularly unusual, because it not only governs higher education throughout the state (except for a handful of locally controlled community colleges), but it also has statewide responsibility for all elementary and secondary education.

Superboards face unique challenges. Perhaps the most insidious one is that all institutions within their systems are not created equal. Inevitably, the flagship campus or campuses will command a greater share of attention and affinity. Such institutions have the biggest budgets, the most exciting programs, and the infatuation of big-time college athletics. Thus they command the most attention, which leaves other institutions disappointed because their accomplishments are not always recognized. This dichotomy also leaves these less-attended-to institutions greatly desirous of improving their status in the hierarchy of institutions. I should not, however, overplay this. Many institution leaders within megasystems appreciate the relative anonymity they experience with such boards. In the long run, however, these less-attended-to institutions begin to feel neglected.

These megasystems share all of the advantages of other multi-campus systems and have some of their own. The diminution of specific institutional affinity (with the exception of the flagship institution) allows them to approach policy issues more dispassionately. Size provides economies of scale in purchasing services and administering programs that could not be achieved by smaller institutions acting separately. Furthermore, because of the inevitable budget constraints that these governing boards face, their finance policies tend to reflect more attention to cost-effective strategies than do those of less diverse governing structures. Unlike multi-campus systems that lack the breadth of institutional missions reflected in the superboard governance structures, these boards also must balance institutional missions to create a mosaic in which the sum of the parts will equal the desired whole for the entire state.

From a state's perspective, however, all institutional governing boards face two problems that are difficult to overcome, both deriving from the governance responsibility for ensuring the vitality and growth of the institutions. First, the focus on one or a specific set of institutions makes it extremely difficult to govern with an eye to the overall picture of institutional providers available to serve the state. Even a superboard faces this dilemma; such members have difficulty in intentionally incorporating the health and vitality of the private for-profit and nonprofit sectors into their vision of service. Why would they accept responsibility for the fate of institutions not officially under their banner of responsibility? In fact, they often view other institutions or sectors negatively—as "the competition." Yet the failure to consider and nurture the health of nonpublic higher education hurts the state as a whole; a strong, nonpublic sector contributes to the effective and efficient overall delivery of higher education in the state. Recognizing this, however, is difficult for a governing board that is primarily responsible for public institutions.

Second, a focus on one or a specific set of institutions tends to accentuate a focus on the *providers* rather than the *customers*. At least in the public sector, the reason for providing public financial support for higher education is to serve citizens' needs, not to support institutional needs. Colleges and universities are a means to an end, not an end into themselves. Yet as owners and operators of these public institutions, governing boards naturally and rightfully focus on institutional interests, not on the state's students. Without doubt, they focus on their customers, but they focus less on the broad issues of access than on serving well the niche of students they most desire to assist. This market-oriented approach results in exactly what other markets have historically experienced: market failure. The most attractive students are in high demand, and less desirable students get left behind in one way or another. This may well be in the institution's best interest, but it is far from being in the state's best interest. This conflict further defines the difficulty in board members not only reaching consensus of the public good as an operating principle but agreeing on its definition.

Statewide Coordinating Boards

This inherent conflict between institutional and broader public interests has led to the creation of statewide coordinating boards in many states. Coordinating boards were a result of the need for states to manage the growth in public higher education as well as "the need to make the most efficient use of resources and to meet the public demand for access to quality programs of study" (Marcus, 1997, 400). Technically, these boards do not govern, so they should not be considered governing boards. They do not have legal responsibility for the outcomes of higher education in the same fashion as legally established governing boards. Yet they often do have policy authority that allows them to *nearly* govern. Many control, in some way, tuition, financial aid, and the allocation of institutional subsidies. Many have the authority to approve or disapprove academic programs. And many have a significant responsibility to advise state government on levels of financial support and regulatory policy.

All of these policy authorities significantly affect both the academic and fiscal integrity of individual institutions and thus mirror the real governance vested in legally established governing boards. Oftentimes, these coordinating boards see their work as keeping the dreamers from the governing boards in the real world. These coordinating bodies perceive their role as bringing it all together, and doing so as cost-effectively as possible. Not surprisingly, the containment role of coordinating boards often conflicts with the change agenda of governing boards. Coordinating boards focus on what *is* and realistically *can* and *should* be, and they do so taking the perspective of the whole state. Governing boards focus on what they would like their institutions to become, not on how to sustain what they are today, and they do so from a narrower perspective. Both are essential to sustaining the vitality and breadth of American higher education.

CONCLUSION

The role of governing boards in the governance of higher education involves exceptional commitment, complexity, contradictions and, often, as a result, conflict. Yet this combination can account for the dynamic nature that has made American higher education the envy of the world. Questions now exist, however, about whether this American model—which tends to weigh institutional interests more heavily than public interest, and which tends to be driven more by market forces than by public needs—can continue to serve the public good as well in the future as it has in the past. The continuous growth of American higher education over the past decade (in terms of the students served, the research conducted, and the public resources available to accomplish both) fostered existing governance structures. In a more resource-constrained environment, however, and with an essentially developed economy and a mature system of higher education, it is likely that governance structures must evolve to fit the modern era.

REFERENCES

Arizona Board of Regents (ABDR). 2004. *Executive summary: Redesigning Arizona's university system.* Retrieved July 3, 2005, from http://www.abor.asu.edu/special_editions/redesign/SPBDmtg%20603exec%20sum%20reorg.pdf.

Association of Governing Boards (AGB). 1996. *Stronger leadership for tougher times: Report of the Commission on the Presidency.* Washington, DC: Author.

Burgan, M. 2004. Why governance? Why now? In *Competing conceptions of academic governance: Negotiating the perfect storm,* ed. W. G. Tierney, vii–xiv. Baltimore, MD: Johns Hopkins University Press.

California State University (CSU). 2005. *CSU Issues and Ideas: Priorities.* Retrieved July 3, 2005, from http://www.calstate.edu/issues_ideas.

Center for Higher Education Policy Analysis (CHEPA). 2004. *Selection and appointment of trustees to public college and university boards.* Los Angeles: Center for Higher Education Policy Analysis.

———. 2005. *Assessing board performance.* Los Angeles: Center for Higher Education Policy Analysis.

Chait, R., T. Holland, and B. Taylor. 1996. *Improving the performance of governing boards.* American Council on Education Oryx Press Series on Higher Education. Phoenix, AZ: American Council on Education and Oryx Press.

Dill, D. D., and K. P. Helm. 1988. Faculty participation in policy making. In *Higher education: Handbook of theory and research, vol. IV,* ed. J. C. Smart, 319–55. New York: Agathon Press.

Education Commission of the States (ECS). 1997. *State postsecondary structures sourcebook: State coordinating and governing boards.* Denver, CO: Education Commission of the States.

Glion Declaration. 1999. *The university at the millennium.* Statement from the 1998 Glion Colloquium: The Future of the Research University, Switzerland. Retrieved January 3, 2006, from http://www.glion.org/?a=6202andp=1512.

Hoover, E. 2004. Colorado's governor demands accountability over sex-party allegations. *Chronicle of Higher Education* (February 13): A35.

Ingram, R. 1998. *Transforming public trusteeship.* Public Policy Paper Series. Washington, DC: Association of Governing Boards.

Jacobson, J. 2004. Grand jury is said to criticize Regents over supervision of Colorado football. *Chronicle of Higher Education* (September 10): A37.

Kerr, C. 2001. *The gold and the blue: A personal memoir of the University of California, 1949–1967.* Berkeley: University of California Press.

Kerr, C., and M. Gade. 1989. *The guardians: Boards of trustees of American colleges and universities, what they do, and how well they do it.* Washington, DC: The Association of Governing Boards of Colleges and Universities.

Kezar, A. 2004. Obtaining integrity? Reviewing and examining the charter between higher education and society. *The Review of Higher Education* 27(4): 429–59.

Kezar, A., and P. Eckel. 2004. Meeting today's governance challenges: A synthesis of the literature and examination of a future agenda for scholarship. *The Journal of Higher Education* 75(4): 371–99.

Knight Commission. 2001. A call to action: Reconnecting college sports and higher education. Report issued by the Knight Foundation Commission on Intercollegiae Athletics. Miami: Knight Foundation.

MacTaggart, T., ed. 1998. *Seeking excellence through independence: Liberating colleges and universities from excessive regulation.* San Francisco: Jossey-Bass.

Marcus, R. 1997. Restructuring state higher education governance patterns. *Review of Higher Education* 20(4): 399–418.

McGuinness, A. 1997. The function and evolution of state coordination and governance in postsecondary education. In *Education Commission of the States. State Postsecondary Structures Sourcebook: State Coordinating and Governing Boards.* Denver, CO: Education Commission of the States.

———. 2002. Reflections on postsecondary governance changes. *ECS Policy Brief.* Education Commission of the States. Retrieved January 3, 2006 from http://www.ecs.org/clearinghouse/37/76/3776.htm.

McMurtrie, B. 2003. Religion and politics. *The Chronicle of Higher Education* (July 4): A20.

Michael, S. O., M. Schwartz, and L. Cravcenco. 2000. Evaluating higher education leadership: Indicators of trustees' effectiveness. *The International Journal of Educational Management* 14(3): 107–19.

Pusser, B., and I. Ordorika. 2001. Bringing political theory to university governance: The University of California and the Universidad Nacional Autonoma de Mexico. In *Higher education: Handbook of theory and research, vol. 16,* ed. J.C. Smart, 147–94. New York: Agathon Press.

Rauh, M. 1969. *The trusteeship of colleges and universities.* New York: McGraw-Hill.

Richardson, R., K. Bracco, P. Callan, and J. Finney. 1999. *Designing state higher education systems for a new century.* Phoenix: American Council on Education-Onyx Press.

Rogers, J. E. 2004. *The state of the system*. University and Community College System of Nevada. Retrieved September 3, 2005 from http://www.system.nevada. edu/News/Front-Page/The-State-of-the-System.pdf.

University and Community College System of Nevada (UCCSN). 2003. *2003 Annual Report*. Retrieved November 15, 2004, from http://www.system.nevada.edu/ News/Publicatio/2003–Repor/index.htm.

Van der Walt, N., and C. Ingley. 2003. Board dynamics and the influence of professional background, gender, and ethnic diversity of directors. *Corporate Governance* 11(3): 218–34.

6

Renewing the Place of Academic Expertise and Authority in the Reform of University Governance

Craig McInnis

Professor Rory Hume resigned from his position as vice chancellor and president of the University of New South Wales (UNSW) in April 2004 after serving less than two years of a five-year contract. Faculty at UNSW protested vigorously in support of Vice Chancellor Hume, yet the cause of the breakdown in his relationships with the governing council of one of Australia's leading research universities is not entirely clear. Ironically, a "Wyatt R. Hume Award for Distinguished Leadership Advancing the Principle of Shared Governance" was proposed when Hume departed from his previous position as executive vice chancellor of the University of California, Los Angeles (UCLA). The award proposal noted that Rory Hume "exemplified the best of what can be achieved when the academic senate and the administration are able to work co-operatively to achieve the shared interest of advancing the quality and integrity of the university" (Australian Higher Education Supplement, 2004, 30).

Around the same time, faculty at the University of Adelaide in South Australia claimed that proposals from the governing council were "downgrading the status and role of the academic board." The possibility existed for the vice chancellor to take the role of presiding chair and the board's agenda to be restricted "to matters of academic policy referred to it by management and others." The vice chancellor argued that this was a "sensible safeguard against the rise of all-powerful committees" (Healy, 2004, 3). Currently the academic board determines policy and practice in education, research, and research training. Membership of similar boards in Australian universities has typically included all professors and, increasingly, a considerable number of senior administrative staff.

The events at UNSW and Adelaide are not unrelated. They come in the wake of a major program of national reform in Australian higher education that commenced in 2002 and is now in an ambitious implementation stage. A significant part of that reform concerns the structure, roles, and accountability of governing bodies. It is too early to draw conclusions from the UNSW or Adelaide cases that might inform the analysis of university governance and its future. What is clear, however, is that they highlight most emphatically the ambiguities and complexities facing faculty as they struggle to find a voice in the process of governance. These examples also suggest that it is time to move beyond the focus of higher education analysis on leadership styles and organizational structures if faculty are to establish a role for themselves as natural partners in university governance.

The issues are, of course, international. Amaral, Jones, and Karseth (2002) summarized European and Canadian developments as:

> a general trend toward the centralization of authority in institution-level governing structures and administrators and a decline in the "academic voice" in institutional decision-making. Traditional forms of academic governance, with a strong reliance on collegiality, became the target of fierce criticism, being diversely, or simultaneously, branded as inefficient, corporative, non-responsive to society's needs, and unable to avoid declining quality standards of teaching and research. (289)

This account is fairly typical of what prevails in the literature and the public arena. The responses of many policy analysts are disturbingly parochial. The blame for the loss of faculty voice is often directed at local leadership and administration, as though they could, Canute-like, stem the tide of international trends. So far, analysis of governance has been resoundingly unsuccessful at guiding any change in Australian universities. This is partly, I suspect, the outcome of intense frustration at the lack of viable options and the difficulty faculty (and others) have in imagining alternative arrangements that might improve faculty participation in governance. It is perhaps also the outcome of theoretical perspectives locked into contexts that are no longer relevant.

The notion of shared governance is not commonly discussed or understood in Australia. Collegiality—and the myths and fantasies that go with it—is the cornerstone mantra of those who express concern at the loss of faculty voice and participation. Collegiality is an expression of faith in the past from those who see managerialism as the cause (as though it were an end in itself) of all that troubles higher education. Faculty who studied, taught, and researched in a small elite system funded almost entirely by the public purse are, not surprisingly, the most likely to look backward. The higher education press is swamped with sad and bitter swan songs denouncing the evils of commercialism and the rise of managerialism. The critics were working in a vastly different system to that which challenges many of the fundamental assumptions in Australian higher education today. The parting remarks of one recently retired Australian vice chancellor are a salutary reminder of the dangers of backwards-looking analyses:

> "God professors" as they were known made and broke careers with essentially zero formal downward accountability to their academic staff. . . . The most powerful of the university's internal committees, the professorial board, ancestor of today's academic board or academic senate, was typically, but not universally, chaired by the vice-chancellor; however, its agenda was controlled and managed by the person who was unquestionably the greatest wielder of de facto power in the vast majority of Australian universities until comparatively recently, namely the registrar. Those contemporary academics nostalgic for a golden age would do well to contemplate whether this "community of scholars" would be more to their liking. (Chipman, quoted in DEST, 2001, 344)

Against this background of complex times in Australian higher education, the ways in which academics might shape a new role in advancing the quality and integrity of their universities is a challenge. In order to be forward looking and think marginally outside of the square, I have quite deliberately avoided using expressions such as "regaining" or "renewing" in terms of faculty roles in governance. There are some symbolic initiatives that might be considered as well as a few more practical suggestions that might shift the nature of the contribution of faculty to institutional governance. How can colleges and universities take account of, and indeed affirm, the role of academic expertise and authority in the face of demands for responsive governance? A useful starting point is to take a perspective of governance as the structuring of relationships. What that means is an active process of considering the best ways of arranging governance to promote the integrity of the institution and its members, as distinct from an organizational chart that finds a place for key stakeholders.

GOVERNANCE IN THE AUSTRALIAN UNIFIED NATIONAL SYSTEM

It is probably helpful at this point to identify distinctive features of the Australian higher education system that partially explain the specific nature and focus of debates about university governance. It is a national system. Almost all universities are public. The descriptor "Unified National System" should not be read as a government-run uniform system. Indeed, Australian universities have an exceptionally high level of autonomy. They decide what they will teach, who they will employ, and what they will research. While most receive a significant proportion of their income from the federal government by way of block grants, this has declined dramatically since the 1980s, when even resource-rich, research-intensive universities relied on approximately 70 percent of their income from government. Today, such universities require only 30 percent or so directly from government and generate the difference from a diverse range of sources. With this change, the somewhat paradoxical relationship between declining government funding and increasing government regulatory requirements is a cause for concern across the universities.

The governing bodies of Australian universities have the capacity to make investment and commercial decisions without interference from the government. What makes for some interesting tensions with respect to governance is that, although the Commonwealth government is the primary source of funding and regulation, and also the major force for policy, for historical reasons the states actually have legislative responsibility for the universities and, in particular, for the composition of their governing councils.

University councils or senates are considered the principal governing bodies of Australian universities. The number of members of these bodies will vary, from as few as thirteen to as high as thirty-five and are the product of diverse historical and political factors. They are headed by an elected chancellor. The vice chancellor and some other senior academics serve as *ex officio* members. On average, about 34 percent of council members are elected, about 20 percent are *ex officio*, and around half are appointed by state governments or by the councils themselves (DEST, 2001, 328). The composition and backgrounds of the latter category are frequently the subject of debate. An analysis of the backgrounds of council members in 2001 showed that "the external representation on university councils is made up of members of business and the professions (31 percent), community representatives (10 percent), alumni (6 percent), public servants (6 percent), and politicians (4 percent)" (ibid.).

Until a series of major national reforms in 1988, the councils were larger bodies representing a wide range of stakeholders, including faculty, students, state and federal politicians, and special ministerial appointees from community organizations. The 1988 reforms represented the first major effort to reduce the size of councils and to change their role and composition. Then, as now, councils were considered too large and hindered in their decision-making capacity by their tendency to fall into advocacy roles for competing stakeholders. In some cases, political alliances in these mini-parliaments made it almost impossible for some university presidents and senior executives to manage effectively. The 1988 reforms encouraged councils to move toward a corporate board of directors' style with the vice chancellor or president taking the role of chief executive officer.

THE NATIONAL REFORMS 2002–2004

Current proposals for the reform of university governance generally start with the observation that traditional structures are unwieldy and poorly positioned to respond to a rapidly changing higher education environment. A key assumption is that streamlined smaller bodies, with more external expertise and less internal faculty involvement, can best provide focused whole-of-institution leadership. The future of university governance in Australia has been a key plank in the reform process initiated by the Commonwealth in 2002. A national discussion paper, developed by Minister Brendan Nelson and the Department of Education Science and Training (Nelson, 2002a), generated a broad-ranging discussion in the higher education sector. The section on governance reform starts with a view from the United States of the current realities of complexity and accountability:

> We can no longer pretend that the detached, amateurish academic leadership model is sufficient. Nor is it any longer sufficient to rely upon politically selected lay boards for their governance. Like other major institutions in our society, we must demand new levels of accountability of the university for the integrity of its financial operations, the quality of its services, and the stewardship of its resources. (Duderstadt, 2000, 16)

A separate-issues paper for the public discussion of the reforms—*Meeting the Challenges: The Governance and Management of Universities* (Nelson, 2002b)—asked first and foremost if governance structures in Australian universities were "appropriate to meet the changing nature of university activities in the 21st century" (3). An earlier national review of university management considered that several factors were working against the effectiveness of the operation of the governing bodies. In particular, a lack of clarity about the primary roles of the governing bodies was perceived; they were generally too large and lacking a diverse base of appropriate skills, and they did not appear to "take ultimate responsibility for strategic direction and the universities' external and internal accountability" (Higher Education Management Review, 1995).

In its submission to the recent reform review, the University of Adelaide reiterated the government themes, arguing that "there is currently a high level of dysfunction in the governance and management arrangements at some Australian universities." They identified, among other things, "debilitating divisions within governing bodies, often linked to special interest groups; difficult relationships between governing bodies and executive managers; and an inability of governing bodies to respond quickly and decisively to change" (Nelson,

2002b, 17). This imperative, repeated in almost every advanced economy where the performance of universities is now integral to national advancement, is essentially about responsiveness to commercial realities. Closely linked is the concern for accountability and risk management. From the government perspective in Australia, as elsewhere, a simple if not simplistic answer is to create "streamlined governing boards . . . to provide leadership that can deliver the educational mission of universities while supporting the commercial activities necessary to the financial management of a large organization" (xi).

From this and the catalogue of deficiencies in university governance raised in the debates, it appears that the primary obstacles to faculty participation focus on the lack of role definition, not just for faculty but for most participants. The vice chancellor's role seems to be more easily defined as chief executive officer, but the role of faculty is barely considered. As Marginson and Considine (2000) so emphatically argued, "Executive dominance, explicitly corporate in form and substance, has become part and parcel of every university. The new system of executive governance is focused almost exclusively on the office of vice chancellor" (62).

Nevertheless, a number of spectacular departures of Australian vice chancellors under pressure of their chancellors and council in recent years suggest that the power of the chief executive is far from unfettered. Increasing numbers of executive leaders are coming from backgrounds that are not firmly rooted in traditional academic roles and values. The "God professors" referred to earlier drew their authority from their positional status, whether their expertise was matched to the task of governing or not. Government is not convinced that the authority or expertise of faculty is adequate in the current environment: "The promotion of leading academics to senior management positions also needs more considered attention. Management responsibilities should be professionally exercised" (Nelson, 2002a, 29).

The shift of governance bodies from assemblies of sectional interests to custodians of institutional futures is quite problematic in Australia. A common theme of government inquiries, state and federal, is that the "effectiveness of university governing bodies is reduced by confusion about the role of some members" (Nelson, 2002b, x). A review of governance in one state noted that the acts explicitly define the duty of council members to perform solely in the interests of the university taken as a whole with regard to its objects (Victorian Department of Education and Training, 2002, 26). This is a major sticking point. Underlining rather pointedly the vagueness and ambiguities in governance, the national reform discussion paper drew attention to the fact that the University of Western Australia "has no stated objects and neither the University nor its governing body have any stated functions" (Nelson, 48). As the national reforms gathered momentum in the implementation phase, it became apparent that the governance proposals would be stalled by a fundamental flaw in arrangements. The Commonwealth requirement that universities reform governing councils (by, for example, reducing the size of councils) if they were to qualify for additional funds faltered, because the states had the responsibility to detail how governing councils should operate.

The implementation of the governance reforms included the establishment of National Governance Protocols for Higher Education (DEST, 2004). These reforms define the government agenda with an incentive of an ultimate 7.5 percent increase in core government funds contingent on compliance with the protocols. To be clear, the universities cannot be compelled to comply—the government can generally only persuade them with financial incentives or penalties. The emphasis of the protocols reflects many of the issues and tensions raised throughout this paper. This is not the place to detail these requirements; a few examples will suffice to illustrate the intent of the government.

Protocol 1 requires that a university should have its objectives or functions specified in its legislation. The inference is that some universities currently do not. Of the various "prime responsibilities" of a governing body, listed in *Protocol 2*, some of the more noteworthy include: approving the mission and strategic direction as well as the annual budget and business plan; overseeing and reviewing management and performance; approving and monitoring systems of control and accountability; overseeing and monitoring the academic activities; and approving significant commercial activities. In an obvious effort to break down the potential divides and sectional interests created by stakeholder delegates, *Protocol 3* specifies the duties of the members of governing bodies to include acting in the best interests of the institution as custodians as a whole and "in priority to any duty a member may owe to those electing or appointing him or her." Further efforts to shift the weight of power and influence of the sectional, and indeed, the faculty interests, are evidenced by the requirement that "there must be a majority of external independent members who are neither enrolled as a student nor employed (by the university)" (DEST, 2004, 3).

THE REALITIES OF FACULTY LIFE AND ASPIRATIONS

Far too much analysis of faculty participation seems to be divorced from current realities. Indeed, it is as if nothing had changed over the last decade or so other than the imposition of managerialism and market competition. Enders quite rightly calls attention to "another blind spot of national and cross-national governance studies in higher education: the micro-level of academic work and life" (2004, 376).

Basically two things conspire to distance academics from governance that have little to do with the ogres of managerialism and corporatism. First, aspirations to engage in shared governance are tempered if not worn away by the everyday realities of dramatically increasing workloads and significant shifts in the configurations and priorities of academic work (McInnis, 2000). In Australia, as elsewhere, this has hit hardest at those academics who take primary responsibility for the everyday functioning of the university at the level of the school and department—that is, the mid-career experienced and tenured faculty. The proportion of faculty satisfied with their job dropped from 67 percent in 1993 to just 51 percent in 1999 (ibid.). It was this group that typically had the energy and motivation to take a close interest in the workings of the university. The sheer demands on their time have put them out of the governance loop more by default than design.

Without rolling out the litany of complaints about the increasing and fragmented demands on academic work, it is important to be reminded by an academic at this level, when asked to comment on his role in governance, that

> the input one can make as an individual [is] partly a workload issue; there seems to be less time available, more students, and that sort of thing. We don't have morning tea breaks or afternoon tea breaks in the common room, which used to be a very important discussion point. The professors did tend to pull rank and that sort of thing, whereas they wouldn't in a formal meeting necessarily, but [they] did set a more interactive committee process, and people were involved. Nowadays it's all looking to leadership from the top. It's a top-down process, and I think the top managers set the strategies and so on, without any other consultation, and then implement them. (Evans, quoted in Cain and Hewitt, 2004, 74)

More pertinent is the inherent contradictions within the faculty reward system. Just half of faculty surveyed nationally in 1999 saw their contribution to the committee life of the university rewarded for promotion. Interestingly, fewer than half believed it ought to be rewarded (McInnis, 2000).

Alongside, and directly related, is the increase in the number of casual and part-time teaching staff. The everyday reality is that these people have the least interest in spending unpaid time on matters of governance. The declining involvement of the reduced core of tenured faculty in governance is compounded by the lack of faculty with whom to share additional administrative loads. They see their role in governance undermined by the rapid increase in administrative tasks largely focused on meeting the demands of accountability and compliance processes.

The second development reducing the weight of influence of the faculty is the dramatic increase in their dependence on the specialist skills of professional and technical staff. It is becoming exceedingly difficult, if not impossible, for faculty to continue to claim moral authority over colleagues on whom they depend so much for the quality of their academic work and on whom institutions now rely for their success in the competitive markets of higher education (McInnis, 2002). The reconceptualizing of academic work and identity is being driven primarily by the rapid increase in the number of these professional and technical staff with their own expertise and authority, and with quite reasonable expectations that their voices will be heard in the governance process. When surveyed almost a decade ago, the senior professional administrators were inclined to look to faculty acknowledgment of their contribution as a source of satisfaction (McInnis, 1998). It is quite likely that they are now less interested in what the professors think of them. Henkel pointed out that while the "manifest function" of these higher education specialists was to provide support and advice, they are now more widely regarded as change agents "in what had hitherto been regarded as uncontested academic territory" (2000, 62). The squeezing out of academic expertise and authority in these circumstances is unsurprising.

The impact of changing academic work roles on the capacity of faculty to engage in governance also needs to acknowledge that the next generation has less concern for these issues. Indeed, early career academics are, on the whole, quite positive about the future and less bothered by what occurred before (McInnis, 2000). Likewise, Henkel (2000) concluded that younger academics are starting from a notably different set of assumptions from their older colleagues; they are more inclined to accept the new demands being made on them and are essentially adaptive in their approach. Little is known about their specific views on faculty roles in governance from the Australian and British research. It may be, then, that too much attention to the voices of the old guard hinders thinking about what is possible for faculty participation in governance in the future.

FACULTY IDENTITY AND EXPERTISE

For many years, faculty identity has turned most clearly on the autonomy they have to pursue their own academic interests. Given security of employment, and sources of funds to support their activities, academics were prepared to tolerate substantial declines in salary and work conditions (McInnis, 2000). Most of the time, these academics were not involved directly in governance at the higher levels, but they did spend an inordinate amount of time on committee work and administrative tasks that fed into the governance processes at school and department levels. Of all the activities in which faculty engage, administrative and committee work has the least to do with their sense of identity. Henkel's (2000) analysis of academic identity also showed that academic identity focuses on autonomy but is also shaped by the disciplines and institutions in which they work. However, Henkel noted that the "succession of new demands upon institutions has increased the scope for ambiguity and fluidity" in work roles (236). The contrasting view when it comes to governance is that there are distinct choices to be made. As one prominent dean commented in a recent critique of governance, "You were really saying to academics that if they wanted to be involved in serious decision making, they couldn't be academics any more. And we've driven that down three levels of management, and I feel very antagonistic to that" (MacIntyre, in Cain and Hewitt, 2004, 59).

What is often overlooked and untapped is the essentially entrepreneurial nature of faculty when it comes to rewards and performance (McInnis, 2001). Understanding this has considerable significance for changing the potential engagement of faculty in governance. Expecting faculty to adopt and advance institutional goals in the same way as professional administrators might has always been somewhat perilous. It is not unreasonable for governing bodies to see faculty as an obstacle to change, and almost certainly as a handicap to institutional capacity to respond rapidly to external demands. However, faculty expertise and authority are more closely aligned to the goals of the contemporary, market-oriented aspects of university operation than might be realized. Clark identified the potential of collective entrepreneurial action as a driver of transformation in universities to "fashion new structures, processes, and orientations whereby a university can become biased towards adaptive change" (1998, 4).

In contrast to the view that the capacity of governing bodies to respond to rapidly changing contexts is hindered by faculty, there is the possibility that particular kinds of faculty can in fact play a key role in responsive governance. An analysis of forms of motivation fostering entrepreneurial activity in a range of work environments concludes that innovation in corporate organizations comes from much the same sources as those that drive academics (Amabile, 1997). If rewards systems support creativity with such characteristics as autonomy in work, a high level of personal challenge and excitement in the work itself, and extrinsic motivators and rewards that confirm competence without connoting control, then faculty support for entrepreneurial behaviors of the institution seems more likely.

Disconnecting these elements of faculty *personae* from the governance process seems fatally flawed. Henkel's (2000) conclusion that faculty have (and comfortably sustain) multiple identities with respect to their work and membership of the organization is also relevant. The everyday realities of the academic workplace cited earlier are clearly pushing the governance role to one side, or forcing faculty to choose between institutional administration and their core academic heartland activities. Rethinking governance arrangements to account for, and indeed to take advantage of, the natural predisposition of faculty to be creatively entrepreneurial is a potentially useful start.

CREATING A PLACE FOR FACULTY EXPERTISE AND AUTHORITY

Returning to the key question how might faculty participation in governance be improved, the issue is not about the functions of the decision-making bodies; it is about the nature of the relationships within and across the various bodies, and the extent to which faculty in the current context are able to make a contribution. Gallagher (2001) distinguished governance from management along these lines: "Governance is the structure of relationships that bring out organizational coherence, authorize policies, plans, and decisions, and account for their probity, responsiveness, and cost-effectiveness" (2). The structuring of those relationships to embrace faculty—on the basis of their expertise and authority—requires a mix of symbolic and pragmatic steps to ensure that they are embedded in governance processes. Articulating the roles of the members of the governing board and getting a clear sense of consensus among them as to the reasons they are there would be an unusual exercise in many universities.

On the symbolic side, institutions need to develop a new accord confirming and commending the significance of faculty participation in policy making on academic matters. Until recently there seemed little need to articulate the nature and extent of these contributions. The rapid changes in the positioning of institutions have left little or no space for these relationships to be formally redefined. To reinforce the significance of such an accord, the reward system of universities has to be reconfigured to acknowledge the part faculty play in governance. While this has apparent weaknesses in terms of shifting motives away from the intrinsic rewards and formalizing their involvement in terms of workloads, it has perhaps more merit than wishful thinking about recreating assemblies of the past. Nevertheless, the reality in many institutions remains that

> governance . . . by peers and collegial governance through academic boards and committees most frequently functions to preserve the status quo and to reproduce existing structures. This tradition poses a formidable challenge to the manager with plans and strategies to change the institution. (Anderson, Johnson, and Milligan, 1999, 9)

A circuit-breaking accord would provide a new platform from which to restructure relationships. The Hoare Report, as previously noted, argued that governing bodies of universities should have three primary roles: ultimate responsibility for external accountability, strategic planning oversight for the university, and responsibility for the overall review and performance monitoring of university operations, relying on the advice of the academic board or senate for monitoring academic standards and performance. The report also made specific mention of some other responsibilities it believed governing bodies should attend to, including "ensuring that there is an independent and vigorous academic board" (Higher Education Management Review, 1995, 42). The nature of an independent and a vigorous academic board providing advice to the governing council varies considerably across Australian universities. The recent case at Adelaide illustrates the almost endemic tensions involved.

At Adelaide, one option proposed was for the vice chancellor to chair the academic board with a deputy chair (and convenor) elected from among the academic members of the board. It was argued that this arrangement would "bridge the academic and management structures of the university," and that it would "underscore the importance of the academic board." However, it was acknowledged that

> this proposal may not sit comfortably with some members of the university community who may fear it represents a barrier to collegialism. However, it is a structure used traditionally in many universities and would allow us to draw together the need for collegiality and effective management, which need to operate cooperatively. (University of Adelaide Council, 2004, agenda item 4.1.4)

This does not really advance the long-term likelihood that faculty participation in governance at the academic board level will increase or be any more attractive to faculty than other arrangements from other institutions. The structure of the relationships in this instance is most likely to depend on personalities rather than roles, a typically tenuous arrangement.

> Now that the Board has been defined as part of the governance structure rather than an ill-defined part of the management structure, care must be taken to ensure that it is able to provide the Council with the advice and oversight envisaged by the Act, while being consistent with the obligations placed on the Vice-Chancellor. (University of Adelaide Council, 2004, agenda item 4.1.4).

Applying principles for good practice for governing bodies as described by McKinnon for organizational benchmarking purposes to academic boards and senates more generally is essential (McKinnon, Walker, and Davis, 2000). To increase and improve faculty involvement in governance requires, among other things, distinguishing between the governance role and the responsibilities of management in such a way as to overcome the debilitating ambiguities and role tensions discussed earlier. Likewise, formal processes to induct new members of the academic boards and senates into their duties and to systematically review and report publicly on their own efficiency and effectiveness are essential.

The emergence of ad hoc or short cycle working groups operating outside of the formal decision-making structures is a significant opportunity for institutions and faculty to utilize academic expertise and authority. These have something of the "flying gang" or "emergency crew" characteristics that sort out institutional derailments and policy bottlenecks. They usually come together on the basis of an executive decision that a problem has to be resolved quickly and effectively. The ad hoc groups tend to ignore established hierarchy and to focus on getting together the best available minds to assess issues and provide solutions. A clear understanding exists that once the job is done, they stand aside and allow the formal system and processes to resume business as usual. Ironically, ad hoc working groups in Australian universities are frequently formed to reform governance from within.

This is not a matter of preference or a proposal for action. The growth of ad hoc policy groups is a reality that has been largely overlooked in the analysis of university governance and management. How they should work, and under what conditions and the extent to which they can be the vehicle for drawing on faculty expertise, is not yet clear. These adjuncts to governance processes are a potentially significant opportunity to draw more widely from the rich resource of the faculty knowledge base. However, finding a place for academic expertise and authority in these increasingly fluid relationships will depend in part on faculty letting go of conventional notions of shared governance—that is, the formal assembly. This leaves open the ways in which faculty can be engaged and rewarded for their participation in decision making. It is unlikely to be advanced by the kind of redesign of academic boards and senates that appears to be the first response to the difficulties of institutional responsiveness.

CONCLUSION

With some prescience in relation to the resignation of Rory Hume from UNSW, Chipman observed, "Ironically, there are signs today that we are entering a period of greater, not lesser, intervention by governing bodies and their chancellors in operational issues within universities, often at the behest of academic staff representatives" (in DEST, 2001, 344). In Chipman's case, the faculty made life difficult for him as vice chancellor of a regional university by going directly to the chancellor and members of council to get what they wanted when he as vice chancellor stood in their way. In Hume's case at UNSW faculty protested against council on his behalf. The crucial postscript here is that an independent inquiry conducted in 2005 unambiguously vindicated Hume's actions and strongly criticized the council. It is not easy to be creative in the face of the enormous pressures facing universities, especially for vice chancellors. To take up a point well made by Marginson and Considine (2000), it is disappointing, however, that universities in Australia and elsewhere have not pioneered creative organizational structures, including arrangements for governance, that do not simply mimic those of the corporate world. Had they done so, the participation of faculty in governance may have been less problematic than the current scenario. Taking account general faculty predispositions toward creative entrepreneurialism in their work, and recognizing their primary work motives, seems a good start to rethinking their role in governance.

REFERENCES

Amabile, T. 1997. Entrepreneurial creativity through motivational synergy. *Journal of Creative Behavior* 31(2): 18–26.

Amaral, A., G. A. Jones, and B. Karseth. 2002. Governing higher education: Comparing national perspectives. In *Governing higher education: National perspectives on institutional governance*, ed. A. Amaral, G. A. Jones, and B. Karseth, 279–98. Dordrecht: Kluwer Academic.

Anderson, D., R. Johnson, and B. Milligan. 1999. *Quality assurance and accreditation in Australian higher education: An appraisal of Australian and international practice. Evaluations and Investigations Programme No. 00/1*. Canberra: Higher Education Division, DETYA.

Australian Higher Education Supplement. 2004. *Man of values and integrity* (April 14): 30.

Cain, J., and J. Hewitt. 2004. *Off course: From public place to marketplace at Melbourne University*. Melbourne: Scribe.

Clark, B. 1998. *Creating entrepreneurial universities: Organizational pathways of transformation*. Surrey, England: Pergamon.

Department of Education, Science and Training (DEST). 2001. *The national report on higher education in Australia*. Canberra: Department of Education, Science and Training, Commonwealth of Australia. Retrieved September 4, 2005 from http://www.detya.gov.au/highered/otherpub/national_report/default.htm.

———. 2004. *National governance protocols*. Retrieved on September 18, 2004, from http://www.dest.gov.au/highered/governance/nat_gov_prot.htm.

Duderstadt, J. 2000. Financing the public university in the new millennium. Paper presented at the University of Washington, Seattle. Retrieved January 10, 2006 from http://milproj.ummu.umich.edu/publications/u_washington_talk2/.

Enders, J. 2004. Higher education, internationalization, and the nation-state: Recent developments and challenges to governance theory. *Higher Education* 47: 361–82.

Gallagher, M. 2001. *Modern university governance—A national perspective*. Paper presented by the First Assistant Secretary, Higher Education Division, Department of Education, Training, and Youth Affairs at "The idea of a university: Enterprise or academy?" conference organized by the Australia Institute and Manning Clark House, the Australian National University, July.

Healy, G. 2004. Adelaide Uni rethinks academic leadership. *Campus Review* (February 25): 3.

Henkel, M. 2000. *Academic identities and policy change in higher education*. London: Jessica Kingsley.

Higher Education Management Review. 1995. *Report of the Committee of Inquiry*. Canberra: AGPS.

Marginson, S., and M. Considine. 2000. *The enterprise university: Power, governance, and reinvention in Australia*. Melbourne: Cambridge University Press.

McInnis, C. 1998. Dissolving boundaries and new tensions: Academics and administrators in Australian universities. *Journal of Higher Education Policy and Management* 20(2): 161–73.

———. 2000. Changing perspectives and work practices of academics in Australian universities. In *International perspectives on higher education research. Vol 1. Academic work and life: What it is to be an academic and how this is changing*, ed. M. Tight, 117–45. New York: JAI Elsevier.

———. 2001. Promoting academic expertise and authority in an entrepreneurial culture. *Higher Education Management* 13(2): 45–55.

———. 2002. The impact of technology on faculty performance and its evaluation. In *Evaluating faculty performance, New Directions for Institutional Research, No. 114*, ed. C. Colbeck, 53–62. San Francisco: Jossey-Bass.

McKinnon, K., S. Walker, and D. Davis. 2000. *Benchmarking: A manual for Australian universities*. Canberra: Department of Education, Training, and Youth Affairs, Commonwealth of Australia.

Nelson, B. 2002a. *Higher education at the crossroads: An overview paper*. Canberra: Department of Education, Science, and Training, Commonwealth of Australia.

Nelson, B. 2002b. *Meeting the challenges: The governance and management of universities*. Canberra: Department of Education, Science, and Training, Commonwealth of Australia.

University of Adelaide Council. 2004. *Agenda*, meeting 1/2004. Retrieved February 23, 2004 from http://www.adelaide.edu.au/governance/council/meetings/2004/meeting1_04.pdf.

Victorian Department of Education and Training. 2002. *Review of university governance*. Melbourne: Victorian Department of Education and Training, Victoria.

7

Institutional Autonomy and State-Level Accountability

Loosely Coupled Governance and the Public Good

Jay Dee

The dual demands of public accountability and institutional autonomy represent a critical challenge for public higher education governance. Observers generally agree that institutions need some degree of autonomy from the external environment in order to preserve academic freedom and promote unfettered exploration of new domains of knowledge (MacTaggart, 1998; Newman, 1987). External interests in accountability, however, have grown in recent years, as state governments have become increasingly concerned about holding the line on college costs. State leaders also have come to associate higher education with economic competitiveness and hope to obtain a competitive advantage when their higher education systems are able to produce a highly trained workforce. As a result, higher education policy making is now viewed as too important to be left solely to institutions (Alexander, 2000; Salter and Tapper, 1994). State governments are now much more involved in determining the priorities for public higher education and have introduced new accountability measures to monitor public college and university performance on a range of indicators.

The campus-state relationship can be characterized, at least in part, as a tug-of-war between campus interests in institutional autonomy and state policy makers' concerns about accountability. In order to address this tension, Hearn and Holdsworth (2002) suggested that "each state needs to establish a point between the two extremes" (10) of complete autonomy and absolute accountability. Higher education scholars have speculated as to where appropriate boundaries should be drawn between states and campuses. They have addressed questions such as: When does an accountability request become an unreasonable intrusion? (Newman, 1987); and When does institutional insistence on autonomy reflect disengagement from the public good? (Braskamp and Wergin, 1998). As McLendon (2003a) noted, "Because neither absolute autonomy of the campus from the state nor complete accountability of the campus to the state is likely to be feasible, the vexing question confronting policymakers is where, precisely, the line should be drawn between campus and state" (57).

The idea of drawing a line between the campus and the state reinforces the notion that higher education institutions and external actors have separate interests rather than a common interest in the public good. Moreover, delineating a midpoint between accountability and autonomy suggests that these concepts are opposing points on a single continuum. Any increment in additional accountability comes at the expense of institutional autonomy, and efforts to protect institutional autonomy are viewed as attempts to circumvent public accountability.

This chapter offers a different way to conceptualize campus-state relationships that have traditionally focused on separate interests and distinct boundaries. I will explore how the dual demands of public accountability and institutional autonomy can be addressed through a governance system that builds connections between campuses and state governments. I will call upon a frequently utilized organizational term, *loose coupling*, but employ it in a new way to understand how campus leaders and state policy makers can work together to develop shared commitments and build trust-based relationships that maintain high levels of both public accountability and institutional autonomy to advance the public good.

Governance systems advance the public good when institutions are engaged in a system of mutual obligation with the communities in which they are embedded. The interests of the campus and those of the community become so entwined that nearly every major institutional action also advances a public purpose. Acting in the interest of the campus becomes synonymous with acting in the interest of the community. State policy makers can promote this form of governance when they extend their view of accountability beyond merely ensuring that campuses meet performance benchmarks and begin to work with campuses to develop shared commitments toward the public good. These shared commitments transcend the narrow focus of outcome measures and instead connect state and campus leaders on issues of civic engagement and social responsibility. The focus shifts from compliance and measurement to mutual obligations toward revitalizing neighborhoods, tackling health care disparities, improving K–12 schools, and promoting the use of sustainable resources, to name but a few examples.

Unfortunately, the predominant relationship between campuses and the state is one of compliance-based accountability and insular autonomy (Alexander, 2000; Braskamp and Wergin, 1998). The state ensures that funds are spent appropriately and that performance benchmarks are met, and campuses seek to protect themselves from outside interference. An emphasis on promoting the public good through accountability and autonomy does not permeate the relationship between most states and campuses. In order to develop and support governance systems that promote the public good, state and campus leaders need new frames of reference for understanding and enacting accountability and autonomy.

PUBLIC ACCOUNTABILITY

Accountability refers to the responsibilities that institutions have to be answerable to external entities. Historically, higher education institutions were able to address external accountability concerns by demonstrating their commitment to self-regulation (McLendon, 2003a). Accreditation self-studies and voluntary coordination among institutions were viewed as sufficient mechanisms to ensure high-quality, efficient education (Chambers, 1961). Strong norms of professionalism and academic freedom provided a buffer from direct external oversight into higher education. However, the creation of statewide coordinating boards, the development of performance measurements systems, and the enactment of accountability regulations suggest that the era of self-regulation has ended (Alexander, 2000).

Statewide coordinating boards collect data on institutional retention rates, graduation rates, time to degree completion, faculty teaching loads, and job placement rates (Hearn and Holdsworth, 2002). Public institutions also are required to report data that demonstrate financial accountability and fiscal health, including acquisition of grant funding, levels of private giving, and return on endowment investments. State boards use these data to make aggregate assessments of institutional performance, which may be linked to resource allocation decisions (i.e., performance-based funding).

The shift to performance-based accountability can be attributed to state policy makers' concerns about institutional efficiency and effectiveness. "The extraordinary interest in performance-based accountability in the United States has emanated from a taxpayer backlash against increases in public college spending and widespread public concern for improving institutional productivity" (Alexander, 2000, 421). Governors and state legislators have responded to these concerns and have compelled public institutions to demonstrate their effectiveness.

States have enacted policies and regulations that hold public institutions accountable. State policies that ensure financial accountability include the use of detailed line-item budgets and pre-audits for institutional expenditures (McLendon, 2003a). Accountability for personnel decisions may be enforced through standardization of personnel policies and mandated use of state classification systems. State governments retain the authority to set tuition rates at public institutions in order to ensure access and affordability (Hearn and Holdsworth, 2002), and state coordinating boards retain the authority to approve new academic degree programs in order to ensure efficient use of resources.

The effects of state accountability policies permeate the entire institution and extend to specific academic programs and individual faculty members. Academic programs are subject to quality assurance mechanisms such as state-mandated program reviews, and individual faculty members are increasingly being held accountable for their productivity, especially for their interactions with undergraduate students (Colbeck, 2002). Trends toward centralized coordination, performance measurement, and increasing regulatory authority of the state have raised concerns that extensive accountability expectations threaten the autonomy of public higher education institutions.

INSTITUTIONAL AUTONOMY

Autonomy refers to the ability of an institution to determine its own behaviors and to be free of bureaucratic regulations and restrictions. Berdahl (1971) distinguished between "substantive" and "procedural" autonomy. Substantive autonomy refers to setting the programmatic mission and strategy of an institution. Procedural autonomy, in contrast, relates to control over the general management of the institution, including budget decisions, personnel issues, contracts for goods and services, and capital construction projects.

Historically, the rationale for institutional autonomy was framed in terms of benefits to the institution. Institutional autonomy was viewed as necessary to protect academic freedom from political intrusion (Newman, 1987). More recently, higher education leaders have linked institutional autonomy to state interests in economic competitiveness and human capital development (McLendon, 2003b). Institutional leaders assert that they need management flexibility in order to respond to a rapidly changing environment. They seek deregulation in the administrative domain and greater flexibility to initiate new academic programs (i.e., the ability to bypass statewide coordinating board approval). Arguments linking institutional autonomy and economic development suggest that the state has a compelling interest in providing autonomy to higher education institutions, and that autonomy can actually help public institutions become more accountable to state policy goals.

This realization has led to a counter-trend toward deregulation and devolution of authority from the state to the campus. Current governance trends in public higher education reflect state preferences for both centralization and decentralization (Hearn and Holdsworth, 2002). In some domains, states are enacting more extensive accountability requirements, especially in the areas of performance measurement, student learning outcomes, and faculty productivity. These accountability mechanisms centralize authority in the state coordinating boards and state agencies that collect and monitor these data. Other signs, however, point to increasing levels of institutional autonomy, especially for procedural matters and for academic program creation. In these cases, authority is decentralized to the campus level.

Simultaneous trends toward centralization and decentralization suggest that state higher education systems operate in a paradoxical context where campuses encounter policy environments that are both constraining and liberating. This paradox, however, offers higher education leaders and state policy makers an opportunity to construct new campus-state relationships that strengthen both public accountability and institutional autonomy. Virginia's Higher Education Restructuring Act (2005), for example, enables public universities to apply for one of three levels of autonomy, each with increasing levels of campus responsibility for capital building projects, procurement, personnel, and tuition and fees. In exchange, campuses agree to commit themselves to achieving state goals for access, affordability, and student retention; the institution is obligated to develop stronger articulation agreements with community colleges, stimulate economic development, attract externally funded research, and meet financial and administrative management standards. This legislation was based on a proposal developed by three of the state's leading research universities, and the final bill attracted large majorities in both houses of the legislature.

Legislation in Virginia and elsewhere shows that states and campuses can seek new governance relationships that strengthen both accountability and autonomy. These innovative relationships require new ways of thinking about state policy making and institutional decision making. Accountability and autonomy can no longer be conceptualized as competing values; instead, state and campus leaders must negotiate the paradox of maintaining high levels of both public accountability and institutional autonomy.

THE PARADOX OF ACCOUNTABILITY AND AUTONOMY

A conceptual understanding of paradox can yield new insights for policy making in a changed governance environment. Paradox refers to a seemingly contradictory opposition within a social system (Hatch, 1997). Oppositions relevant to organizations as social systems include accountability and autonomy, centralization and decentralization, stability and change, and structure and process, among others. The idea of paradox is central to several theoretical traditions. Marxist social scientists, for example, explain organizational activity in terms of contradictions that are typically resolved in favor of managerial interests (Braverman, 1974; Burawoy, 1982). Paradox also is addressed through structural-functionalist approaches to management that attempt to resolve conflict and forge consensus (Galbraith, 1977). So-called "win-win" approaches to negotiation, for example, attempt to resolve contradictory views and eliminate paradox through the formation of consensus (Fisher and Ury, 1981).

Dialectical perspectives, however, offer a different view that acknowledges and seeks to preserve the interdependent relationship between oppositions (Baxter and Montgomery, 1996; Benson, 1977; Czarniawska-Joerges, 1988). A dialectical conceptualization suggests that organizations can maintain apparent contradictions; for example, higher education institutions can be both highly autonomous and highly accountable. This stands in stark contrast to structural-functionalist approaches that seek to clarify or resolve contradictions in favor of one opposition or the other. Instead, dialectical perspectives suggest the desirability of preserving tensions between contrasts. (Table 7.1 compares functionalist and dialectical perspectives.)

Dialectical conceptualizations of accountability and autonomy require leaders to think in terms of "both-and" rather than "either-or" (Spender and Kessler, 1995). "Either-or" thinking is associated with the functionalist desire to resolve paradox. Campus leaders who think in terms of "either-or" view any external accountability movement as an intrusive constraint on autonomy. And state policy makers take an "either-or" perspective when they issue policy mandates for accountability without consulting the institutions being held accountable. These actors conceptualize accountability and autonomy as opposing points on a single continuum. Some locations along the continuum endorse autonomy, others support greater accountability, but no point successfully integrates high levels of both. High levels of accountability are thought to diminish autonomy and are perceived as a limitation on accountability. Midpoints between absolute accountability and complete autonomy are seen as opportunities for each "side" in the debate to push the position on the continuum closer to their side, some pushing for more accountability and others striving for more autonomy (see Figure 7.1).

Instead, state and campus leaders can think in terms of "both-and." Campus leaders can seek to remain responsive to external accountability expectations *and* preserve high levels of autonomy for institutions and the professionals who work in them. Similarly, state policy makers can ensure that public institutions remain accountable to policy priorities but also give the institutions discretion to demonstrate accountability in ways that are consistent with their unique campus missions. "Both-and" thinking necessitates a shift from bipolar contradictions to two-variable matrices (Bobko, 1985). Figure 7.2 represents a dialectical conceptualization where accountability and autonomy are viewed as two separate continua.

TABLE 7.1.
Comparing Functionalist and Dialectical Perspectives

	Functionalist Perspective	*Dialectical Perspective*
Conceptualizations of account-ability and autonomy	Accountability and autonomy as oppositions; additional increments of one variable diminish the other	Accountability and autonomy as mutually supportive con-structs; additional increments of one variable may strengthen the other
Campus-state relationships	"Drawing a line" between campus and state; maintain-ing appropriate boundaries	Building connections between campuses and state governments
Policy goal	Finding a "midpoint" between accountability and autonomy	Maintaining high levels of both accountability and autonomy
Social cognitions of policy actors	Social construction of sepa-rate interests; "either-or" thinking	Social construction of shared commitments; "both-and" thinking

FIGURE 7.1
Functionalist Conceptualizations of Accountability and Autonomy

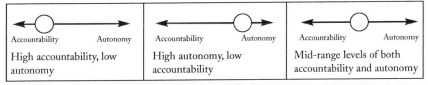

High accountability, low autonomy

High autonomy, low accountability

Mid-range levels of both accountability and autonomy

FIGURE 7.2
Dialectical Conceptualization of Accountability and Autonomy

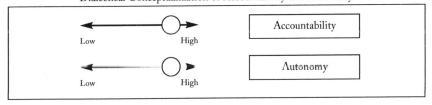

Researcher have begun to study the positive effects of dialectical tensions on organizational decision making and performance (Brown and Eisenhardt, 1997). Organizational theorist Barbara Czarniawska-Joerges (1988) under-lined the need for both autonomy and role-based accountability in organiza-tions. Autonomy "offers organizations flexibility and creativity, which are essential for adaptation to changing environments" (2). But change itself is predicated upon accountability and control structures that provide stability and predictability. "Without control, the organization is invaded by chaos and deadly entropy" (2–3), which eventually forestalls potential change efforts. Organizational change depends upon "both-and" thinking; change requires both flexible, autonomous work arrangements *and* clearly defined accountability relationships among employees. These findings suggest the utility of maintaining a dialectical tension between paradoxical elements in organizations rather than resolving paradoxes in favor of one opposition or the other.

The maintenance of both accountability and autonomy may produce mutually reinforcing effects where high levels of one variable sustain high levels of the other variable. For example, when higher education institutions demonstrate public accountability, they may inoculate themselves against future external intrusions that diminish autonomy. Demonstrations of accountability to state policy priorities may strengthen policy makers' commitment to institutional autonomy. Similarly, states that provide high levels of autonomy to their higher education institutions may reap benefits in terms of innovative academic programs, research agendas, and public service initiatives that address state needs.

Conversely, high levels of institutional autonomy may not be sustainable when institutions neglect external accountability expectations. And states may not be optimizing their higher education systems when institutions are hamstrung by regulations and approval procedures that dampen creativity and discourage innovation. If maintaining an accountability/autonomy paradox is a major objective of educational leadership, then state and campus leaders need a set of understandings and concepts appropriate for addressing this challenge. Karl Weick (1976) was one of the first scholars to explore the accountability/autonomy dialectic in educational organizations. He introduced loose coupling as a metaphor for understanding how organizations, departments, people, and events can be responsive to each other (accountable) yet retain their separateness (autonomy).

LOOSE COUPLING

Loose coupling may be one of the most widely utilized organizational concepts in the higher education vernacular. It has been used most frequently to analyze the internal workings of colleges and universities (Birnbaum, 1988). However, Orton and Weick (1990) explained that the theory has been underutilized in the study of organization-environment interactions, such as those between public campuses and state governments. Higher education scholars have not yet explored the potential of this theory to illuminate issues that pertain to campus-state relationships, but loose coupling is well suited to inform understandings of public accountability and institutional autonomy. Loose coupling theory seeks to explain organizational social structure through an analysis of systematic patterns of interaction among organizational elements (Beekun and Glick, 2001). Coupling is defined "in terms of systematic patterns of relationships among organizational elements located within multiple domains and spanning theoretically relevant dimensions" (Beekun and Ginn, 1993, 1297). *Coupling elements* are any things that may be linked together. Orton and Weick (1990) identified eight coupling elements: "among individuals, among subunits, among organizations, between hierarchical levels, between organizations and environments, among ideas, between activities, and between intentions and actions" (208). The campus-state relationship is one example of coupling between organizations and environments. The *coupling domain* identifies the content area of the relationship between the coupling elements. An organization and its external environment may be coupled in the resource exchange domain (e.g., state appropriations to higher education), the information domain (e.g., sharing retention and graduation rate data), and the policy domain (e.g., state regulations). Finally, *coupling dimensions* refer to the quality of the relationship among coupling elements. Relevant coupling dimensions include responsiveness (i.e., accountability to other coupling elements) and distinctiveness (i.e., autonomy from other coupling elements).

A loosely coupled system is characterized by coupling elements that are both responsive and distinctive. A loosely coupled organization responds to the environment with which it is coupled, but it does so in a way that retains the distinctiveness (autonomy) of the focal organization (Orton and Weick, 1990). Consider, for example, the relationship between a public higher education institution and a statewide coordinating board. In a loosely coupled relationship, the institution demonstrates responsiveness (accountability) to policy priorities determined by the board, but the institution is allowed to chart its own course of action and remain autonomous from the board. The coordinating board provides autonomy to the institution, but it does not yield its position as an independent intermediary between the institution and state government. In other words, the coordinating board does not abdicate its responsibility to hold public institutions accountable, but it gives discretion to institutions for deciding how to be accountable to state expectations. The accountability goals are specified by the board, but the means to achieve them are determined by the individual campuses.

Loose coupling preserves the paradoxical tension between accountability and autonomy. In contrast, tight coupling resolves the paradox in favor of accountability. A tightly coupled system is characterized by responsiveness without distinctiveness. In a tightly coupled relationship, an institution may be subject to prescriptive regulatory demands and have little discretion in determining its own strategy and programmatic goals. Decoupling resolves the paradox in favor of autonomy. Institutions avoid inspection and evaluation by external actors. The role of the state, in this instance, is that of "resource provider" rather than "regulator" (tight coupling) or "coordinator" (loose coupling). The state ensures that public institutions have adequate resources to fulfill their mission, and then it steps back and allows the institutions to govern themselves. Loose coupling makes it possible for colleges and universities to develop flexible responses to a wide variety of accountability expectations. Different elements of the institution can specialize in responding to particular segments of the external environment (Weick, 1976). In contrast, tight coupling between a college and its external environment may cause the institution to "freeze" internally (Birnbaum, 1988). As Pfeffer and Salancik (1978) noted, when "everything is connected to everything else, it is difficult to change anything" (69). Loose coupling, therefore, should not be viewed as an organizational deficiency in need of repair. Instead, it is an adaptive social structure that facilitates accountability to the external environment, and preserves the organization's autonomy from the environment.

LOOSE COUPLING AS A DIALECTICAL PERSPECTIVE

Loose coupling is intended to be conceptualized dialectically. In other words, it embodies the maintenance of a tension between responsiveness and autonomy. Too often, according to Orton and Weick (1990), scholars interpret loose coupling as "the endpoint of a scale that extends from tightly coupled to loosely coupled. Tightly coupled systems are portrayed as having responsive components that do not act independently, whereas loosely coupled systems are portrayed as having independent components that do not act responsively" (205).

These interpretations conflate loose coupling and decoupling. As Orton and Weick (1990) argued, "When loose coupling is portrayed as decoupling, the diminished emphasis on connectedness, responsiveness, and interdependence dissolves the dialectic" (207). Scholars may arrive at inappropriate conclusions when the dialectical conceptualization of loose coupling is dissolved. Lutz (1982), for example, criticized loosely coupled colleges and universities for their lack of accountability and lack of attention to overall mission. He argued in favor of tighter coupling for higher education governance: "If coupling were tighter, control, communication, participation, and prediction would be improved and goals better achieved" (667). Similarly, Balderston (1995) maintained that loose coupling is likely to fail in times of rapid change due to lack of institutional responsiveness to the external environment. These uses of loose coupling, however, stray from Weick's intended conceptualization of a dialectical relationship between accountability and autonomy. The key for organizational leaders is to maintain the dialectic of loose coupling by developing governance systems that are both responsive and autonomous.

Loose Coupling and Public Higher Education Governance

Historical trends in higher education governance can be traced through an analysis of campus-state couplings. Relationships were largely decoupled during the early years of public higher education in the United States. The mid-1800s were characterized by a trend toward granting constitutional autonomy to flagship universities. Gradually, however, institutions ceded their constitutional autonomy in exchange for increased funding from the state. Beginning in the 1910s, loose coupling emerged between higher education institutions and newly formed regional accreditation associations that sought to ensure minimum levels of quality and to facilitate institutional improvement (Bogue and Saunders, 1992). Institutions were accountable to accreditation guidelines established by the regional associations, but the autonomy of institutions was preserved by linking accreditation review to a self-study process whereby institutions are evaluated in terms of self-determined goals and objectives. This system of accreditation is unique to the United States; elsewhere, national ministries of education determine institutional effectiveness criteria and conduct quality evaluations of their higher education institutions. The campus-state relationship is more tightly coupled in these nations. It is important to recognize that the U.S. system of accreditation is loosely coupled to the U.S. Department of Education (DOE), which certifies the regional associations and communicates expectations for institutional quality reviews. For example, based on DOE directives, regional associations are now much more insistent that institutions assess student learning outcomes (Lubinescu, Ratcliff, and Gaffney, 2001). The DOE did not specify how the regional associations were to hold institutions accountable for student learning outcomes; instead, it allowed the associations to determine their own accountability mechanisms.

Higher education observers have noted the potential of accreditation to facilitate institutional improvement and establish or renew commitments to the institution's mission (Martin, Manning, and Ramaley, 2001). From the perspective of state governments, however, the system of accreditation is decoupled from the state. Regional associations accredit institutions across several states and are not particularly sensitive to policy priorities of individual states. Therefore, states have developed other mechanisms to ensure accountability to their interests.

The 1950s through the 1970s were characterized as a period of "widespread growth in state intervention and a concomitant decrease in the autonomy of colleges and universities" (McLendon, 2003a, 67). The growing size and complexity of public higher education invited greater oversight from state authorities. Massification of enrollments reflected state interests in building human capital and enhancing economic competitiveness. Two additional trends contributed to tighter couplings between states and public campuses: (1) the expanding capacity of state executive and legislative branches to oversee and regulate public-sector institutions, and (2) the proliferation and strengthening of statewide coordinating boards.

Tight coupling remains a prominent trend in higher education governance. Performance-based funding, for example, seeks to link state appropriations to institutional performance on indicators determined by the state. But as the decentralization and deregulation efforts of the 1980s and 1990s indicate, the prevailing policy trend is toward both centralization and decentralization (Hearn and Holdsworth, 2002). Therefore, states and campuses need to develop relationships that ensure both institutional flexibility and responsiveness to public needs.

Dill (2001) was one of the first to underline an agenda for public higher education governance that strengthens both institutional autonomy and public accountability. Consistent with Berdahl (1971) and others (Francis and Hampton, 1999; Richardson, Bracco, Callan, and Finney, 1999), Dill advanced ideas for deregulation and procedural autonomy. He encouraged states to provide lump-sum (rather than line-item) appropriations and to give institutions autonomy to control purchasing and contracts, set and retain tuition, develop personnel policies, and initiate facility construction projects. But Dill also recognized that new accountability mechanisms are necessary: "The early lessons on deregulation in higher education reflect the experience in commercial markets such as the aviation industry. That is, government deregulation along one dimension may require a need to regulate more stringently along another dimension" (Dill, 2001, 29). Dill offered a series of performance-based mechanisms that states can use to ensure that institutions address the public good. The combination of deregulation, devolution of authority, and performance-based assessment contributes to a loosely coupled governance system where public institutions retain autonomy, yet states ensure that policy priorities are addressed. The next section of this chapter extends Dill's analysis and offers additional recommendations for maintaining high levels of both public accountability and institutional autonomy.

RECOMMENDATIONS FOR LOOSELY COUPLED GOVERNANCE

Dill's (2001) analysis was not explicitly framed in the context of loose coupling theory, yet it is evident that his recommendations call for both expanding the domain of institutional autonomy and making sure that institutions are subject to a range of new accountability mechanisms. The aggregate result of these recommendations is a loosely coupled relationship between the campus and the state. Dill focused on procedural autonomy and performance measurement. The following recommendations build upon and extend this framework to include loosely coupled relationships with statewide coordinating boards and state legislatures.

Policy Inducements Rather Than Policy Mandates

Mandates are policies handed down by state governments and statewide coordinating boards that prescribe certain behaviors that the focal organization must enact. "Typically, mandates are designed and implemented without input from higher education leaders" (Hearn and Holdsworth, 2002, 12). Policy mandates produce tight coupling between organizational behaviors and state priorities. Policy inducements, on the other hand, provide incentives for institutions to craft their own unique responses to state expectations. Inducements "shift much of the burden of proving satisfactory performance from the state to the institutions" (Colbeck, 2002, 5).

Policy inducements reflect a loosely coupled relationship between higher education institutions and the state. In order to receive incentive rewards, institutions need to be responsive to state priorities, but the institutions retain significant latitude regarding how they choose to respond. Incentive-based policies enable institutions to craft flexible responses that are more likely to address both state priorities and unique campus needs. Hearn and Holdsworth (2002) argued that inducements are likely to be more effective than mandates in terms of improving student learning outcomes. "Mandated and generalized program review policies across a state's higher education enterprise may not positively influence student learning as much as incentive-based policy instruments that allow for institutional flexibility in implementation" (30). Incentive-based policies may strengthen institutional autonomy and enable colleges and universities to become more accountable to the needs of their students.

Customized Performance Measurement
Rather Than One Size Fits All

One of the major areas of contention regarding statewide performance measurement systems is that the indicators do not reflect the unique missions and cultures of the diverse public institutions within a particular state (Barak and

Kniker, 2002). Accountability policies are more likely to improve institutional performance when they are sensitive to local contexts and allow for the creation of indicators that will uniquely fit the institution's mission (Jones and Ewell, 1993).

Loosely coupled performance measurement systems enable colleges and universities to customize the set of indicators that will be used to evaluate institutional performance. In order to maintain responsiveness to the state, however, these indicators need to be aligned with state priorities. Martinez (2002) described how the state of South Dakota developed a performance-based funding system that was guided by five state priorities (access, economic development, academic improvement, collaboration, and enhancing non state revenues) but allowed each institution to establish its own targets for each of the five areas. This system ensured both accountability to state priorities and institutional autonomy in determining operational goals and indicators of success.

Capacity-Building Audits Rather Than Competitive Rankings

Statewide coordinating boards were established to minimize competition among public institutions and across sectors of higher education. However, when performance measurement systems are used to compare or rank institutions across a public higher education system, institutions are pitted against each other (Alexander, 2000). The stakes may be especially high where performance measures are linked to state appropriations. Marginal institutions may be at a competitive disadvantage in securing needed resources. The net effect of such policies may be one "of punishing students at universities with ineffective administrations" (Dill, 2001, 30).

As an alternative, Dill (2001) recommended the use of capacity-building audits that focus on institutional improvement and the sharing of best practices. The role of the statewide board, in this scenario, is to facilitate the development and training of a network of "academic auditors" within each institution. Faculty members and administrators are given opportunities to learn best practices for assessment and quality assurance and then are charged with the task of enacting and monitoring an agenda for organizational improvement. Institutions that attain high levels of quality assurance capacity (i.e., have an extensive network of trained academic auditors) are able to sustain high levels of accountability without extensive oversight from external authorities. The result is higher-level performance at less expense to both external authorities and the organization being overseen. Capacity-building audits ensure a loosely coupled relationship between campuses and state governments. Campus leaders are empowered to define institutional problems and craft solutions that uniquely fit their institutional context. State policy makers also gain assurances that the audit process will yield institutional accountability to state interests in institutional improvement.

Campus-Based Assessment Rather Than Mandated Measures

Institutions have developed extensive systems of student outcomes assessment that measure cognitive and noncognitive gains achieved in college. These systems were developed in response to policy makers' concerns about the quality and cost of undergraduate education. Regional accreditation associations and statewide coordinating boards now expect public institutions to engage in the ongoing assessment of student outcomes. These associations and boards, for the most part, allow institutions to select their own measures of learning outcomes. Increasingly, however, there are pressures for standardization across public higher education systems, especially for placement testing, which may require uniformity for purposes of facilitating transfer across sectors and among institutions (Jones and Ewell, 1993).

Where uniformity is important, states may choose to mandate the type of assessment tests used by all public institutions (Mills, 1998), however, these institutions may resist such efforts and retain locally developed assessments that duplicate the functions of the mandated tests. This is neither efficient nor effective in terms of the state interest in uniformity across higher education sectors. Instead, states can allow the public institutions themselves to decide collectively which assessments need to be uniform and where locally developed tests can be retained. These decisions can be charged to a statewide assessment council or systemwide governance body composed of campus representatives. For example, the Faculty Senate of the State University of New York, a sixty-four–campus system, developed a campus-based assessment system that provided flexibility in the selection of assessment measures. Senate representatives decided that only three of the twelve general education learning areas (mathematics, basic communication, and critical thinking) would be assessed using externally referenced, standardized measures. But each campus was able to retain its existing assessment plan, and institutions had the authority to select or develop their own measures of student learning for the remaining nine learning areas (State University of New York, 2004). Campus-based assessment preserves loose coupling by delegating measurement decisions to the institutional level. Institutions retain the authority to create their own assessment plans, as long as the plans remain accountable to state interests in the efficient and effective delivery of undergraduate education.

Autonomy for Academic Program Creation Rather Than Centralized Approval Processes

In the interest of financial accountability to taxpayers, state governments have attempted to limit program duplication within public higher education systems. Proposals for new academic programs and degrees are often subject to review by state coordinating boards. Dill (2001), however, argued that "program review procedures in the United States and other countries are becoming overwhelmed, and universities are complaining about their inability to respond quickly to public needs for innovative programs" (24). In this instance, accountability mechanisms may actually make institutions less responsive to public needs. (See Table 7.2.)

Loosely coupled program approval processes are needed to ensure both financial accountability and institutional autonomy to develop new degree programs. States legislatures can delegate to public institutions the power to create new degree programs in areas designated "high need" or "state priority." States may identify significant labor market needs in areas such as allied health, high technology, or K–12 science and math education. Institutions would have the autonomy to create new degree programs in these priority areas but would still be subject to state-level reviews for new programs in non-

TABLE 7.2.
Recommendations for Loosely Coupled Governance Systems

Structures and Policies	Autonomy	Accountability
Policy inducements	Not prescriptive; allows institutional flexibility for implementation	Incentives contingent on responsiveness to state priorities
Customized performance measurement	Institutions select indicators and measures of effectiveness	Indicators must be aligned with state priorities
Capacity-building audits	Campus leaders are empowered to enact and monitor an agenda for improvement	Accountability becomes an explicit role for campus leaders; no need for costly oversight from external authorities
Campus-based assessment	Measurement decisions delegated to the campus level	Assessment plans must be responsive to state interests in improving undergraduate education
Autonomy for academic program creation	Institutions have the flexibility to quickly create new academic programs	Flexibility is provided in areas designated "high need" by state government

priority areas. In this way, institutions are unburdened from state-level oversight but remain accountable to state policy priorities.

Summary of Governance Recommendations

Loosely coupled governance systems employ structures and policies that foster high levels of both public accountability and institutional autonomy. This section of the chapter identified five structures and policies that reflect a loosely coupled relationship between state governments and public campuses (summarized in Table 7.2). Formal structures and policies are important because they affirm and legitimize the loosely coupled relationship between states and campuses. But they do not explain how loosely coupled governance systems are created and sustained. The next section of this chapter explains how loosely coupled systems originate, and how campus leaders and state policy makers can maintain these systems once they have been established.

CREATING AND SUSTAINING A LOOSELY COUPLED GOVERNANCE SYSTEM

Couplings are produced and reproduced through social cognitions and thought patterns that reflect collectively shaped images of the relationship between coupling elements (Spender and Grinyer, 1995; Weick, 1988). Over time, coupling elements converge on a particular image for the relationship. Tight couplings are produced by images that depict separate interests; in this instance, thought patterns reinforce notions of dominance by one party and compliance for the other. Loose couplings are constructed through images that depict shared commitments.

Shared Commitments

Shared commitments are conscious, intentional, public statements that reveal mutually agreed upon motivations and justifications for action (Staw, 1980). Public statements of shared commitment enable organizational members and external constituents to transcend mere shared perceptions and values and enter into a community of practice that sustains purposive action. Shared commitments are oriented toward action and have a self-sustaining capacity once they have been initiated. In other words, once a shared commitment has been articulated publicly, it becomes much more difficult to dissolve, because both parties have a stake in its continuation (Weick, 1988).

Spender and Grinyer (1995) claimed that shared values alone are insufficient to initiate and sustain loose coupling. Instead, shared commitments toward institutional improvement are needed to alleviate tendencies to revert to tighter coupling (i.e., enforce accountability through compliance) or drift toward decoupling (i.e., autonomy without concern for accountability). In higher education governance systems, shared commitments provide a common framework for addressing expectations for public accountability and institutional autonomy. Shared commitments ensure that the autonomous behaviors of institutions are reconciled with systemic interdependences and collective goals rather than idiosyncratic preferences. Institutions engage in autonomous behaviors, but their behaviors are guided by commitments shared between the state and the campuses. Formalized mechanisms for tight coupling between the campus and state are unnecessary when institutional activities originate from an a priori framework of collective understanding.

Shared commitments are critical prerequisites for loosely coupled governance. Policy reforms that seek loose coupling may be ineffective if states and campuses do not share commitments toward institutional improvement. Policy incentives, customized performance measurement systems, and capacity-building audits are unlikely to effect changes in institutional behavior if states and campuses have not articulated a common vision for the future. Campus-based assessment systems and degree approval processes are unlikely to address state needs when institutions and state actors have differing conceptualizations of policy priorities. Shared commitments provide the foundation for a loosely coupled relationship built on publicly expressed visions for future courses of action. Once shared commitments are in place, the level and quality of trust among system actors may determine whether shared commitments and loose coupling can be sustained.

Trust

The conceptual literature on trust is extensive, and this chapter examines trust only as it relates to loose coupling. (For a more comprehensive treatment, see Hardin [2002] and Seligman [1997]. William Tierney expands on the notion of trust in chapter 9.) Trust is a vital form of social capital in social systems (Coleman, 1990; Putnam, 1993) and can be defined as "a psychological state comprising the intention to accept vulnerability based upon positive expectations of the intentions or behavior of another" (Rousseau, Sitkin, Burt, and Camerer, 1998, 395).

Loose coupling depends on positive expectations that both parties will uphold their shared commitments. Loose coupling also requires trust-based assurances that institutions will be granted behavioral latitude, and that direct oversight will be minimal. In a loosely coupled system, state governments trust that institutions will act in accordance with the public good, and institutions trust that their autonomy will not be infringed upon by external intrusion. Under conditions of trust, norms of secrecy are displaced by public self-disclosure, and preferences for direct oversight and compliance are replaced with trust-based relationships that preserve institutional autonomy. Trust-based relationships obviate the need for extensive oversight and ease concerns regarding the potential for intrusions into internal institutional affairs.

It is important to acknowledge, however, that the parties in these trust-based relationships are differentiated by asymmetric information (Barber, 1983). Administrators and faculty leaders know more about the higher education enterprise than do external actors. The wider external community relies on assurances that colleges will perform as expected and provide needed services. External perceptions of consistency in the words and actions of successive institutional administrations may strengthen such assurances over the long term (Henkin, Singleton, Holman, and Dee, 2003). State policy makers gain confidence in institutional leadership and trust that institutions are capable of advancing the public good. On the other hand, institutions lose public trust when "members of the public and stakeholder groups believe the organization neither intends to take their interests into account, nor would it have the competence/capability to act effectively even if it tried to do so" (La Porte and Metlay, 1996, 342). Violations of trust jeopardize loose coupling and may portend state-level responses that constrain institutional autonomy.

CONCLUSION

As Alexander (2000) noted, "Controversies over institutional autonomy and government control are as ancient as universities themselves" (413–14). In recent years, dual demands for accountability and autonomy have produced simultaneous trends toward centralization and decentralization in the campus-state relationship. Campus leaders and state policy makers are challenged by seemingly paradoxical demands for compliance to the state and flexibility from the state.

This chapter explored how the paradoxical demands of accountability and autonomy can be addressed through a governance system that strengthens connections between campuses and state governments. I employed a frequently utilized organizational concept, loose coupling, in a different way to delineate a framework for campus-state governance relationships. In a loosely coupled governance system, campus leaders and state policy makers engage in "both-and" thinking, where accountability and autonomy are viewed as mutually reinforcing constructs that advance the interests of both institutions and the publics they serve. I recommended five structures and policies that support loose coupling between state governments and public colleges and universities. These structures and policies ensure that campuses remain accountable to state priorities but also provide significant discretion to institutions for designing the means to achieve these goals and for selecting measures of success that pertain to unique campus missions.

Structures and policies are necessary but not sufficient conditions for establishing and maintaining loosely coupled governance systems. Loosely coupled campus-state relationships are created and sustained through trust and a shared commitment to the public good. These shared commitments transcend the traditional focus on measuring institutional outcomes and instead unite campus and state leaders on an agenda for civic engagement. When notions of the public good permeate the campus-state relationship, accountability is not simply an aggregate of benchmarks; the public good also entails a focus on social responsibility. And institutional autonomy is not viewed simply in terms of a need to ensure academic freedom—it also involves operating as a partner with the community within which the institution is embedded and with which it has mutual obligations toward the betterment of society.

Loosely coupled governance systems serve the public good by producing benefits that extend beyond the institutions and state governments that participate in them. Society at large benefits when institutions use their autonomy to respond to state policy priorities, and the public good is advanced when state governments ensure accountability through flexible mechanisms that preserve local autonomy. Loose coupling enhances the likelihood that campus leaders and state policy makers will work together to fulfill their mutual obligations to the external constituencies that support and depend upon them.

REFERENCES

Alexander, F. K. 2000. The changing face of accountability: Monitoring and assessing national performance in higher education. *The Journal of Higher Education* 71(4): 411–31.

Balderston, F. 1995. *Managing today's university: Strategies for viability, change, and excellence* 2nd ed. San Francisco: Jossey-Bass.

Barak, R., and C. Kniker. 2002. Benchmarking by state higher education boards. In *Using benchmarking to inform practice in higher education. New Directions for Higher Education, no. 118*, ed. B. Bender and J. Schuh, 93–102. San Francisco: Jossey-Bass.

Barber, B. 1983. *The logic and limits of trust*. New Brunswick, NJ: Rutgers University Press.

Baxter, L., and B. Montgomery. 1996. *Relating: Dialogues and dialectics*. New York: Guilford Press.

Beekun, R., and G. Ginn. 1993. Business strategy and interorganizational linkages within the acute care hospital industry: An expansion of the Miles and Snow typology. *Human Relations* 46(11): 1291–1318.

Beekun, R., and W. Glick. 2001. Organization structure from a loose coupling perspective: A multidimensional approach. *Decision Sciences* 32(2): 227–50.

Benson, J. K. 1977. Organizations: A dialectical view. *Administrative Science Quarterly* 22: 1–21.

Berdahl, R. 1971. *Statewide coordination of higher education*. Washington, DC: American Council on Education.

Birnbaum, R. 1988. *How colleges work: The cybernetics of academic organization and leadership*. San Francisco: Jossey-Bass.

Bobko, P. 1985. Removing assumptions of bipolarity: Towards variation and circularity. *Academy of Management Review* 10. 99–108.

Bogue, E. G., and R. Saunders. 1992. *The evidence for quality: Strengthening the tests of academic and administrative effectiveness*. San Francisco: Jossey-Bass.

Braskamp, L., and J. Wergin. 1998. Forming new social partnerships. In *The responsive university: Restructuring for high performance*, ed. W. G. Tierney, 62–91. Baltimore, MD: Johns Hopkins University Press.

Braverman, H. 1974. *Labor and monopoly capital: The degradation of work in the twentieth century*. New York: Monthly Review Press.

Brown, S., and K. Eisenhardt. 1997. The art of continuous change: Linking complexity theory and time-paced evolution in relentlessly shifting organizations. *Administrative Science Quarterly* 42: 1–34.

Burawoy, M. 1982. Introduction: The resurgence of Marxism in American sociology. In *Marxist inquiries: Studies of labor, class, and states*, ed. M. Burawoy and T. Skocpol, S1–S30. Supplement to the *American Journal of Sociology* 88.

Chambers, M. 1961. *Voluntary statewide coordination*. Ann Arbor: University of Michigan Press.

Colbeck, C. 2002. State policies to improve undergraduate teaching. *Journal of Higher Education* 73: 4–25.

Coleman, J. 1990. *Foundations of social theory*. Cambridge, MA: Belknap Press of Harvard University Press.

Czarniawska-Joerges, B. 1988. *Ideological control in nonideological organizations*. New York: Praeger.

Dill, D. 2001. The regulation of public research universities: Changes in academic competition and implications for university autonomy and accountability. *Higher Education Policy* 14(1): 21–35.

Fisher, R., and W. Ury. 1981. *Getting to yes.* Boston: Houghton Mifflin.

Francis, J., and M. Hampton. 1999. Resourceful responses: The adaptive research university and the drive to market. *Journal of Higher Education* 70(6): 625–41.

Galbraith, J. 1977. *Organization design.* Reading, MA: Addison-Wesley.

Hardin, R. 2002. *Trust and trustworthiness.* New York: Russell Sage Foundation.

Hatch, M. 1997. *Organization theory: Modern, symbolic, and postmodern perspectives.* New York: Oxford University Press.

Hearn, J., and J. Holdsworth. 2002. Influences of state-level policies and practices on college students' learning. *Peabody Journal of Education* 77(3): 6–39.

Henkin, A., C. Singleton, F. Holman, and J. Dee. 2003. Trust in schools: Extending the perspective to institutions. *Journal of Research in Education* 13(1): 22–30.

Jones, D., and P. Ewell. 1993. *The effect of state policy on undergraduate education: State policy and college learning.* Denver, CO: Education Commission of the States.

La Porte, T., and D. Metlay. 1996. Hazards and institutional trustworthiness: Facing a deficit of trust. *Public Administration Review* 56(4): 341–48.

Lubinescu, E., J. Ratcliff, and M. Gaffney. 2001. Two continuums collide: Accreditation and assessment. In *How accreditation influences assessment. New directions for higher education, no. 113*, ed. J. Ratcliff, E. Lubinescu, and M. Gaffney, 5–21. San Francisco: Jossey-Bass.

Lutz, F. 1982. Tightening up loose coupling in organizations of higher education. *Administrative Science Quarterly* 27: 653–69.

MacTaggart, T., ed. 1998. *Seeking excellence through independence: Liberating colleges and universities from excessive regulation.* San Francisco: Jossey-Bass.

Martin, R., K. Manning, and J. Ramaley. 2001. The self-study as a chariot for strategic change. In *How accreditation influences assessment. New directions for higher education, no. 113*, ed. J. Ratcliff, E. Lubinescu, and M. Gaffney, 95–115. San Francisco: Jossey-Bass.

Martinez, M. 2002. Understanding state higher education systems: Applying a new framework. *Journal of Higher Education* 73(3): 349–74.

McLendon, M. 2003a. State governance reform of higher education: Patterns, trends, and theories of the public policy process. In *Higher education: Handbook of theory and research, vol. 18,* ed. J. Smart, 57–143. Dordrecht, Netherlands: Kluwer Publishers.

———. 2003b. Setting the governmental agenda for state decentralization of higher education. *Journal of Higher Education* 74(5): 479–515.

Mills, M. 1998. From coordinating board to campus: Implementation of a policy mandate on remedial education. *Journal of Higher Education* 69(6): 672–97.

Newman, F. 1987. *Choosing quality: Reducing conflict between the state and the university.* Denver, CO: Education Commission of the State.

Orton, J., and K. Weick. 1990. Loosely coupled systems: A reconceptualization. *Academy of Management Review* 15(2): 203–23.

Pfeffer, J., and G. Salancik. 1978. *The external control of organizations: A resource dependence perspective.* New York: Harper and Row.

Putnam, R. 1993. *Making democracy work.* Princeton, NJ: Princeton University Press.

Richardson, R., K. Bracco, P. Callan, and J. Finney. 1999. *Designing state higher education systems for a new century.* Phoenix, AZ: Oryx Press.

Rousseau, D., S. Sitkin, R. Burt, and L. Camerer. 1998. Not so different after all: A cross-discipline view of trust. *Academy of Management Review* 23(3): 393–404.

Salter, B., and T. Tapper. 1994. *The state and higher education.* Essex, England: Woburn Press.

Seligman, A. 1997. *The problem of trust.* Princeton, NJ: Princeton University Press.

Spender, J.C., and P. Grinyer. 1995. Organizational renewal: Top management's role in a loosely coupled system. *Human Relations* 48(8): 909–26.

Spender, J.C., and E. Kessler. 1995. Managing the uncertainties of innovation: Extending Thompson (1967). *Human Relations* 48(1): 35–56.

State University of New York. 2004. *Faculty senate bulletin: Strengthened campus-based assessment.* Albany: State University of New York Press.

Staw, B. 1980. Rationality and justification in organizational life. In *Research in organizational behavior, vol. 2,* ed. L. Cummings and B. Staw, 45–80. Greenwich, CT: JAI Press.

Virginia Higher Education Restructuring Act. 2005. HB 2866, Chapter 933, State of Virginia. Retrieved September 3, 2005 from http://www.lcg1.state.va.us/cgi-bin/legp504.exe?051+ful+CHAP0933

Weick, K. 1976. Educational organizations as loosely coupled systems. *Administrative Science Quarterly* 21: 1–19.

Weick, K. 1988. Enacted sensemaking in crisis situations. *Journal of Management Studies* 25(4): 305–17.

8

Governance in a Time of Transition

Judith A. Ramaley

It is interesting to trace the conversation about the challenges facing higher education across the decades. Over ten years ago, Paul Ylvisaker made the case that "each decade of [the twentieth century] has seen the pace of change speeding up" (Ingram and Associates, 1993, 226). Ylvisaker explains:

> The most problematic aspects of this change are the causes and con-
> sequences of increasing diversity, the onrush of pluralism in every
> aspect of life and quadrant of the globe. Spirits and voices so long
> held quiescent by traditional constraints have shaken loose and been
> given expression and power by today's electronic and photonic mag-
> nifications of the printing press. . . . One can therefore expect leader-
> ship and decision making to become ever more precarious and
> diffuse. (226)

Ylvisaker continued: "Communications technology and global migration have made all sorts of boundaries permeable and in many ways obsolescent. The boundaries of the campus are no exception. No longer a walled city, the academy is more liquid than fixed" (Ingram and Associates, 1993, 227). Is it any wonder that public and private interests are also becoming blurred?

CHALLENGES FACING HIGHER EDUCATION

The list of things that disrupt the old models of governance—institutional purposes, societal roles, and the very nature and intentions of the classic functions of research, teaching, and service—is remarkably similar from one document to another. It usually includes "economic, political, technological, and demographic changes of enormous magnitude" (Bracco, Richardson, Callan, and Finney, 1999, 23). Often the expectations and pressures are contradictory. Institutions and their boards find themselves caught between competing demands. Down one path reside the ambitions and interests of institutions and their faculty, and down the other is "the financial, strategic and public-policy demands of their state" (Association of Governing Boards [AGB], 1998, 16).

Societal demands have broadened the role of academic institutions to include a multitude of requirements. These demands have confused and blurred our expectations about what we want from higher education: (1) a means to the preparation of leaders for society; (2) a vehicle for the advancement of opportunity in a democratic society; (3) a focus for the conduct of research and advancement of knowledge; (4) a way to contribute to economic development and job creation; and (5) a partner in community development.

Confounding this complexity are larger societal patterns that are reshaping both the nature and the operating context of higher education. To cite Bracco and others (1999, 23):

> Demand for access to higher education from an increasingly diverse student clientele continues to increase as changes in the economy demand greater skills. Technological developments have created entirely new mechanisms for the delivery of education and have introduced new providers into the market. Global competition threatens historical patterns of economic activity.

As campuses are expected to "serve business and industry, provide inventions that will fuel the economy, improve their communities, and promote democratic values for a diverse society" (Kezar, 2001), they must deal with growing enrollments, a declining base of public support, a growing regulatory overburden, and erosion in public confidence. What is to be done?

GOVERNANCE TODAY

"Can state higher education systems designed to manage enrollment growth under conditions of expanding prosperity meet these and other challenges of a new century?" (Bracco et al., 1999, 23). Recent articles on higher education have considered this question, especially in the face of growing public demands for accountability and criticisms that higher education is failing to respond to changing environments and societal expectations (Eckel, 2000). In many instances, the pressures on governance are severe, splitting the debate into an argument between two different cultures—a corporate and political model represented by the governing board that embraces competition, strategy, and a focus on measurable outcomes, and an academic culture, represented by the campus community, that believes in "independence, reflection, and process" (Ferren, Kennan, and Lerch, 2001, 9).

The resulting struggle for a sense of shared purpose and community is made more difficult by the lack of time, a shortage of experience in building effective working relationships, and a tenuous connection between the campus community and the governing board. A sense of shared purpose would offer a first step toward a new conception of shared governance as well as new ways to respond to changing societal expectations during a period of growing complexity and limited financial support (Ferren et al., 2001). As several observers have put it, the members of the campus community are increasingly fragmented and isolated from each other as well as distanced from their own administrators (Martin, Manning, and Ramaley, 2001)—not to mention the members of their governing board. This fragmentation has a decided impact on the quality of decision making, the timeliness of evaluations, and the health of the consultative and participatory processes that ensure effective governance.

If we turn to the theoretical literature on governance, we find little to guide us as we seek to identify ways to infuse energy, purpose, and capacity into our governance structures and processes. As Kezar and Eckel (2004) pointed out: "Previous scholarship focused almost exclusively on structural theories and to a lesser extent on political theories and provided little explanation of, or few ideas for, improving governance" (373).

When solutions to the challenges of governance are, in fact, put forward, they sound easy in principle. In practice, they are very hard to implement. As Mary Burgan, former general secretary of the American Association of University Professors, once noted, "Shared governance is better honored in words than in deeds" ("A question," 1999). To make her point, Burgan quoted G. K. Chesterton on the subject of Christianity: "It has not been tried and found wanting; it has been found difficult and not tried." Her prescription for shared governance and the blending of reflection and action required in a rapidly moving society was to "work harder to mend—not end—our commitment to information, consultation, and deliberation. This means that all parties must be open to surprising conclusions, to good faith deliberations, and risk-taking during crisis times" (28). This simple, yet profound, solution places very real obligations on all participants to provide accurate, timely information. We also must take seriously an obligation to remain up-to-date and ready to explore options quickly when needed, to take one another seriously, to consult before it is too late and before options have been closed down, and to listen for the value in one another's perspectives.

As patterns of trust and consultation continue to break down, the roles of governing boards, especially boards that oversee multi-campus institutions or state systems, continue to expand. The result is the creation of ever-widening gaps between the preoccupations of governing boards and the interests of the campus community they serve. Based on work by Bruce Johnstone, Fretwell (2001) described an impressive and a frightening catalog of major decision-making areas for which governing boards now are held accountable. The list is daunting and includes the following:

- To determine, reaffirm, and occasionally alter the missions of the system and its constituent campuses.
- To appoint, nurture, evaluate, and, if necessary, remove the chief executive officer from the system and from the constituent campuses or institutions.
- To advocate to the legislature, governor, and other key opinion leaders and patrons the needs of the system.
- To advocate to the constituent campuses the needs of the state.
- To allocate missions and operating and capital resources to the respective constituent institutions.
- To provide a liaison between the executive and legislative officers of state government and the member campuses.
- To mediate disputes over programs and missions among constituent institutions.
- To foster cooperation among campuses, which can cut both costs and enlarge options for students.
- To audit and otherwise assess the stewardship of resources, including the assessment of academic programs.

A more collegial form of governance calls for us to be a true community of learners, where governance becomes a model for public problem solving rather than primarily political negotiation (Rich and Prewitt, 2001). Such a model requires new patterns of interaction and a new discipline of discourse. All disciplines have a set of defining principles. This set of principles defines a culture of evidence and inquiry, but each field or discipline interprets these in specific ways. A discipline is bound by several factors, including the questions asked, the way research is designed, the way scholarly work is carried out, the interpretation and generalization of results, and the language used to discuss the work.

The discipline of good decision making bears a close resemblance to the expectations of any academic discipline. Governance crosses all disciplines and is thus inherently interdisciplinary. The participants tend not to respect or understand the perspectives of other disciplines, especially when expertise develops from work outside of the academy (e.g., corporate or political experience) or from experience in academic management or leadership. Good governance resembles good interdisciplinary scholarship that is directed at pressing and practical problems, while drawing its strength and inspiration from the values of the academy. It is, in short, as I shall soon define, work in Pasteur's Quadrant.

Effective shared governance that involves governing boards, senior administration, faculty, staff, students, alumni, and community leaders is rooted in practical outcomes, both in its inspiration and application. The pattern is clear. Participants in shared governance (1) seek to coordinate progress in basic knowledge with multiple forms of empirical inquiry, interventions, and the wisdom of experience (2) conducted by a multidisciplinary professional community of people who have experience and expertise in different parts of the enterprise (3) in order to develop an approach that would coordinate the resources of research, development, and experience (4) to build up a systematic base of knowledge generated by a research infrastructure that has the capacity to do this kind of engaged work that (5) leads to better and more informed choices on behalf of a campus community and its constituents (Ball, 2003).

It is not surprising that governing boards and shared governance fall short of these expectations. As Lovett (2003, 21) pointed out in her observations about what happens during meetings of system governing boards: "Except for the obligatory references to 'our underfunded system of higher education,' the state's fiscal crisis, and the low graduation rates on some campuses, reality did not intrude into this tableau of cheerfulness, civility, and complacency." No wonder boards tend to seek civility when the top public policy issues are so formidable (AGB, 2003), for example, homeland security, affirmative action, the deteriorating economic and fiscal environment, surging numbers of diverse students, rapid tuition increases, the federal policy environment (reauthorization of the Higher Education Act), federal tax policy, assessment and accountability, scientific research policy and controversies, such as protection of human subjects and stem cell research, and intercollegiate athletics. None of these topics lend themselves to easy solutions. All would benefit from new approaches to consultative decision making and problem solving between the governing board and campus and community members.

RETHINKING THE UNIVERSITY

The answer to the dilemma of shared governance, while complex and, as yet, unclear, must include a change in how institutions interpret their missions. We must seek to reconcile competing interests on campus, across institutions within systems, and within the broader community. We must, in fact, become engaged with society in new ways—through the design and goals of the curriculum, through institutional relationships with the community, and, where appropriate, through the scholarly interests and pursuits of faculty and students.

There are a number of reasons to invent new approaches to our institutional models and to rethink how we approach the classic functions of research, teaching, and service (Ramaley, 2001.) By doing so, we can integrate a number of related, but often distinctive, aspirations and goals espoused by higher education or advanced on behalf of higher education by its many constituencies. It is not necessary for our systems of governance to carry the whole burden for adapting to changing economic and social conditions, but the impetus must be articulated there. Full support and encouragement must be offered to those who pursue new forms of research and teaching. We can respond to societal demands in an effective and affordable manner by rethinking how aspects of scholarship can be brought together in such a way as to link the institution more meaningfully to the larger community.

In doing so, we can address a number of otherwise conflicting demands in an integrated manner (Ramaley, 2001), including preparing students to be good citizens by providing them ways to help the institution itself be a good citizen; fostering and renewing bonds of trust in the community, that is, "social capital"; using the neutrality of the campus to provide a common ground where differences of opinion and advocacy for particular points of view can be addressed in an open and a constructive way and where people with similar goals can come together and create ways to work together; enhancing the employability of graduates by providing opportunities to build a strong resume and to explore career goals; promoting learning both for students and for community members; creating capacity in the community to work on complex societal problems; designing a more effective way for the campus to contribute to economic and community development; building support for public investment in higher education, both to provide access and opportunity for students of all backgrounds to pursue an education and to generate knowledge that will address critical societal needs; and accomplishing a campus mission of service.

Is there a way to bring together these many goals? Many have tried over the years to understand and then reinterpret the conception of a university to shape campuses to both public and private ends and to broaden the working definition of what constitutes scholarship so that both advancement of theoretical knowledge and investigations that address practical problems will be supported and encouraged. The concept of the "engaged university" captures this integration in very concrete terms. Within an engaged institution, as we shall see, the classic traditions of research, teaching, and service will be changed, with significant implications for faculty scholarship, the design and intentions of the curriculum, and the mechanisms by which knowledge is generated, interpreted, and used. To get to that idea, we need first to explore some of the earlier ideas about what a university should be.

CONCEPTIONS OF THE UNIVERSITY AND ITS PURPOSES: DISENGAGED OR ENGAGED?

In his *The Uses of the University*, Clark Kerr (2001) traces the more recent debates about the purpose of the university and concludes with his interpretation of the contemporary American university, which he dubs the "multiversity." After dwelling a bit on the medieval origins of our current academy, he explored "the academic cloister of Cardinal Newman" and the "research organism" of Abraham Flexner (1), which together represent the two ideal, Platonic types from which our contemporary interpretations of the university derive. What are these forebears of our modern institution?

Cardinal Newman derived his vision from the Platonic ideal. He insisted on "the cultivation of the intellect, as an end which may reasonably be pursued for its own sake. Truth of whatever kind is the proper object of the intellect" (1960, 114). As he explained, "A university may be considered with reference either to its Students or its Studies" (74). If the purpose of education is to cultivate the intellect, what is the purpose of Studies, or as we might say today, the disciplines? For Cardinal Newman, all branches of knowledge are connected together and "complete, correct, balance each other" (75). He argued that the university was the "high protecting power of all knowledge and science, of fact and principle, of inquiry and discovery, of experimentation and speculation; it maps out the terrain of the intellect" (quoted in Kerr, 2001, 2). As far as he was concerned, useful knowledge was trash and had no place in the academy. The special purview of the university was to raise the intellectual tone of society, cultivate the public mind, and give "enlargement and sobriety to the ideas of the age" (Kerr, 2001, 3).

Knowledge for its own sake and the concept of education as a means to enrich and improve the public mind were soon eclipsed by the concept of the research university where, as Kerr noted, "Science was beginning to take the place of moral philosophy, research the place of teaching" (2001, 3). The modern university, as envisioned by Abraham Flexner in 1930, was an entity "not outside, but inside the general social fabric of a given era. . . . It is not something apart, something historic, something that yields as little as possible to forces and influences that are more or less new. It is on the contrary...an expression of the age, as well as an influence operating upon both present and future" (quoted in Kerr, 2001, 3).

Yet, even as Flexner wrote, the "modern university" he described was being replaced by a uniquely American form that Kerr called *the multiversity*. As Kerr wrote about the multiversity, other institutional types were appearing and growing to maturity (e.g., the community college, the regional comprehensive university). The hegemony of research as the ideal form and function of a university would soon be solidified as the federal government called upon university researchers to conduct studies that would contribute to the war effort during World War II. Soon after the war, Vannevar Bush (1980) presented to President Truman a prospectus for a continued investment in scientific research that was already widely believed to be "absolutely essential to national security" (17). As he explained, "The bitter and dangerous battle against the U-boat was a battle of scientific techniques—and our margin of success was dangerously small" (17). Beyond the demands of national security, there also was the connection between science and labor; work created by the technology arises from scientific discovery.

For Bush, "Basic research is performed without thought of practical ends ... it results in general knowledge and an understanding of nature and its laws" (18). Basic science was to be conducted in universities and research institutes where "scientists may work in an atmosphere which is relatively free from the adverse pressure of convention, prejudice or commercial necessity" (19). Government laboratories and private industry would translate this work into something practical. Bush saw the conversion of basic research into practical use as a linear process. In his model, research was kept relatively separate from teaching. The university was still viewed as an ivory tower whose function was to look out upon society and elevate its taste and values through the generation of basic research.

SCHOLARSHIP: DISENGAGED OR ENGAGED?

The concept of engagement entered the higher education vocabulary in the mid-1990s. The engaged institution takes many forms—ranging from state and land-grant universities to regional comprehensive institutions, urban universities, community colleges, and liberal arts colleges. Institutions that embrace engagement are committed to direct interaction with external constituencies and communities through the mutually beneficial exchange of ideas and the exploration of common interests. The collaborative application of knowledge, expertise, resources, and information addresses community problems in ways that enrich the experience of students while opening an avenue for scholarly inquiry by both faculty and students. These interactions expand the learning and discovery functions of the academic institution while also enhancing community capacity. The work of the engaged institution is responsive to (and respectful of) community-identified needs, opportunities, and goals in ways that are appropriate to the mission and academic strengths of the campus (Holland, 2001). It is a means to contribute to the public good.

It is possible that a concern for the public good will become the pathway to a fresh interpretation of the role of higher education in the twenty-first century. It also may serve as a starting point for thinking differently about the meaning of faculty work. Most important for this context, a concern for the public good and the practice of engagement may find expression in the composition and membership of governing boards, their committee structure, their policy agenda, and their interactions with the campus community and citizenry at large.

Engagement encourages a rethinking of the core of the academy—namely, the nature of scholarship itself and our expectations for the undergraduate experience. The goal of engaged scholarship is not to define and serve the public good directly *on behalf of* society but to create conditions for the public good to be interpreted and pursued in a collaborative mode *with* the community. In contemporary society, the exercise of citizenship requires constant learning and the thoughtful and ethical application of knowledge. By including its students in engaged scholarship, an institution introduces basic concepts and, at the same time, offers a chance to explore the application and consequences of ideas in the company of mature scholars and practitioners who live and work in the community.

Ernest Boyer's (1990) early formulation of scholarship attempted to match the faculty reward system more closely with the full range of academic functions and to broaden the concept of scholarly work, encompassing innovative approaches to teaching and service. The element of scholarship that he called *the scholarship of application* explores the idea that basic research, called *the scholarship of discovery* in Boyer's model, is not the most legitimate, or even the only legitimate, form of scholarly contributions. Boyer poses three questions that can guide one's thinking today.

1. How can knowledge be responsibly applied to consequential problems?
2. How can knowledge be helpful to individuals as well as institutions?
3. Can social problems themselves define an agenda for scholarly investigation?

Deborah Witte's *Higher Education Exchange* (2004) examined ten years' worth of articles on public scholarship. In her preface, she pointed out that in each article, authors described their experiments with "a different way of relating to the community—both the university community and the community of citizens beyond the campus" (Witte, 2004, 1). Originated before the terms "engaged campus" or "scholarship of engagement" entered our vocabulary, the

Higher Education Exchange helped advance these ideas and served as a forum for examining the definitions of engagement and public scholarship.

We are still arguing about public scholarship and engagement and have yet to agree on whether these are legitimate scholarly activities. David Brown (2004), editor of the *Higher Education Exchange*, spoke to Robert Kingston, editor of the *Kettering Review*, and Peter Levine, a research scholar at the University of Maryland's Institute for Philosophy and Public Life. The interview touched on all three of Boyer's questions about the scholarship of application. Kingston argues that researchers become public scholars "on the occasions and to the degree that [they] use their professional way of thinking and body of knowledge in a manner that is directly helpful to fellow citizens who are confronting (with the scholar) a societal problem that affects them all, although not all in the same way" (Brown, 2004, 17). This is Boyer's first question, the responsible application of knowledge. Kingston excludes the design of a specific, functional solution to a problem (Boyer's third question).

Levine, in contrast, thinks about public scholarship and the role of the public intellectual in three ways, touching on all of Boyer's questions. He discusses community-based research that "involves a genuine collaboration between professional scholars and a concrete collection of other people" (Brown, 2004, 18). He also includes direct involvement in social movements and public advocacy and "research about social issues, communities, or institutions" (ibid., 18–19). In all of these instances, what makes the work public is "the presence of a real dialog between the scholar and those studied" (ibid., 19) and, in many cases, a real collaboration with members of the community.

So what does this have to do with governance? In his Afterword to the commemorative edition of the *Higher Education Exchange*, David Mathews (2004) reflected upon the institutional engagement model and its implications for faculty work and the student experience. In passing, he pauses to comment upon the role of trustees and governance in promoting engagement and the public good. In the past ten years, only one article in the *Higher Education Exchange* examined the civic responsibilities of governing boards or campus governance. In an interview with David Brown in 2001, William C. Hubbard talked about drawing his fellow trustees into a conversation about the relationship of the campus to a democratic public. Such discussions are rare, usually sidelined by more urgent matters of finance, fund-raising, and management challenges.

After reflecting on the sparse literature regarding the duties of trustees to engage the public and to direct attention to issues of the public good and the importance of social responsibility, Mathews (2004) made the case that trustees "are in a position to create more opportunities for their institutions to engage the citizenry at large—those citizens who aren't part of the professional constituencies, alumni organizations, and groups of financial supporters that colleges and universities see every day" (86). He goes on to say that he thinks it would be helpful to begin discussing new governance structures that could link the academy and the public more closely. What grand idea could guide us in thinking about this linkage? One answer is to explore the intellectual space where theory and practice, basic research and use-inspired research, and campus and community can come together—Pasteur's Quadrant (Stokes, 1997).

A New Intellectual Space: Pasteur's Quadrant

Roger Geiger (1993) has pointed out that we academics tend to picture ourselves as "communities of scholars, free and ordered spaces, dedicated to the unfettered pursuit of teaching and learning." In these intellectual spheres, we produce increasingly specialized knowledge, not "wisdom, sagacity, or liberal learning" (335). We do not forge a meaningful link between learning and life. Yet some of our forebearers had a very different concept of knowledge and the role of learning in forming and preserving our way of life. For many early educators, theory and utility could be combined to create an appropriate education for our young people. The Reverend Daniel Clark Sanders, the first president of the University of Vermont, wrote about the purposes of a collegiate education (quoted in Daniels, 1991, 94): "It teaches the young where are the sources of knowledge, the means by which it is attained, where truth may be found without error, and where wisdom has chosen her place of residence. To become a real scholar is to be a student for life."

How might scholarship change in order to link theory and utility? It has been customary to distinguish basic from applied research and research from education. By keeping these vital functions apart, we limit the productive relationship between basic research and technological innovation. Donald Stokes articulated the concept that brings these elements together in his book *Pasteur's Quadrant* (1997). Stokes sought a "more realistic view of the relationship between basic research and technology policies" (2) and hence between private interests (those of the researcher) and the public good (the advancement of technology and its effects on society and the economy).

According to Stokes, we must connect the goals of science (to develop theory and advance understanding) and technology (to solve practical problems and develop new useful products). To pave the way toward this kind of integration, Stokes developed the concept of intellectual spaces that he calls "quadrants," defined by the balance of theory and practical use pursued. No one wants to be in the quadrant framed by low theoretical or practical interest; we trust that few projects reside there. Thomas Alva Edison's work would nicely describe the space framed by high interest in use and low interest in advancing understanding. He was "the applied investigator wholly uninterested in the deeper scientific implication of his discoveries." As Stokes explains, "Edison gave five years to creating his utility empire, but no time at all to the basic physical phenomena underlying his emerging technology" (24).

Niels Bohr represents the classic researcher engaged in a search for pure understanding as he explored the structure of the atom. Occupying the fourth quadrant is Louis Pasteur, who had a strong commitment to understanding the underlying microbiological processes that he had discovered and, simultaneously, a motivation to use that knowledge to understand and control food spoilage and microbial-based disease. He occupies his own intellectual space where basic research is inspired by considerations of its potential use and where research advances both theoretical (basic) knowledge and applied (practical) knowledge. Here we have Pasteur's Quadrant. It has been my goal over the years to encourage more work in this quadrant, while never losing sight of the value and importance of basic research and knowledge for its own sake.

The concept of engagement is guided by the growing integration of research and education, the development of research models that bring together theory and practice, new forms of curricular design and expectations about the goals and outcomes of an undergraduate education and advanced study, and the movement from the classic concepts of research, teaching, and service to a new approach best defined as discovery and learning in an engaged mode. These factors will change the "terms of engagement" and slowly merge public good, private gain, and the self-interests of higher education institutions.

The convergence of these elements can be examined by studying the implications of Pasteur's Quadrant. In Pasteur's Quadrant, the goals of discovery come together with technology. In this quadrant, private gain and public good coexist. While Stokes developed his quadrant model to map a new path from basic research to innovation, the ideas apply equally well to curriculum, governance, and institutions as a whole. It is time to examine how governing boards can seek first to understand the evolving nature of the public university in its various forms (state and land-grant university, comprehensive regional institution, urban/metropolitan university, community college) and then undertake their responsibility to interpret the institution, or system of institutions, its mission, and its societal value to a broader audience while encouraging the institutions for which they bear responsibility to interpret research and teaching in engaged modes.

One theme here, drawn from the concept of Pasteur's Quadrant, is that the relationship between classic research and its applications in both the curriculum and in the development of new technologies is not always linear or derivative. In fact, it may rarely be sequential or linear as Vannevar Bush

(1980) purported. It is both possible and often desirable to advance knowledge while advancing educational and societal goals.

The Stokes model is a conceptual one and is not based on any close study of the actual nature of scientific experimentation. Closer observation of the actual practices of scientists would be required to confirm whether the theoretical categories that Stokes developed actually capture the major forms of scholarship. As a framework for reconciling the apparent tensions between public good and private gain, the model is helpful. My basic premise is that we can contribute to the public good as a natural consequence of work valued by both faculty and students. But research and education must be conducted within institutions that have embraced the habits of engagement. It also is necessary that faculty, governing boards, and administrators care about the educational and societal implications of their work and involve students in work that explores all facets of genuine scholarship. In the course of their undergraduate experience, all students should pursue discovery, integration, interpretation, and application of knowledge to real-world problems. If possible, some of this work should take place in modes common to Pasteur's Quadrant, so they can acquire habits of lifelong learning now essential for the exercise of good citizenship as well as advancement in the workplace.

THE ROLE OF THE GOVERNING BOARD IN CIVIC ENGAGEMENT: THE EXAMPLE OF PROJECT PERICLES

Concurrent to public disinvestment in higher education, higher education institutions have been introducing models of both education and research that increasingly comingle public and private benefits. Many institutions are quietly seeking to earn public support in new ways. In the past several years, the importance of incorporating civic responsibility into both institutional missions and the curriculum acquired much higher visibility. It is difficult to keep up with the articles and books being written about civic responsibility, public scholarship, service learning, and community-based learning. Many colleges and universities are now experimenting with a variety of approaches to learning communities, service learning, community-university partnerships, collaborative research models, outreach, and engagement that bring together students, faculty, and community participants so that they may work on issues that will affect the quality of life in communities and create opportunities for others. These interactions create the capacity to recognize and contribute to the public good. As students engage in service-learning activities, for example, they also are addressing issues of concern to the broader community. Students may frequently produce products such as studies, reports, and advice that help a community manage its most pressing problems. Who benefits in such a model? Clearly everyone does. It is becoming increasingly difficult to untangle the public good from private benefit.

Project Pericles, conceived by Eugene Lang, the founder of the I Have a Dream project, offers one model of how governing boards can incorporate a concern for the public good into their structure and agenda. Although the current membership is drawn from a small segment of the higher education community, Project Pericles offers one way for a governing board to play a meaningful role in linking campus and community. The board's goal is to give attention to public engagement and scholarship while simultaneously reflecting this priority in its structure and priorities. Colleges and universities that sign on to the Pericles project commit themselves to a promotion of civic learning experiences as a regular part of their mission. They seek to instill in their students "an abiding and active sense of social responsibility and civic concern, and the conviction that the processes and institutions of our society offer a person an opportunity to contribute meaningfully to a better world" (Lang, personal communication, February 9, 2004). To become a "Periclean," an institution must meet the following criteria:

- Each Periclean, by a formal resolution of its board of trustees, must make a commitment to the objectives associated with Project Pericles.
- The trustees must establish and provide for maintaining a discrete, standing, multi-constituency committee of the board to oversee the implementation of the Periclean commitment.
- Each Periclean creates, develops, administers, and evaluates a comprehensive and an ongoing program for planning, guiding, and implementing its Periclean commitments as a recognized part of its educational mission.
- The program provides opportunities for involving all of its constituencies—trustees, president, administrators, faculty, staff, students, and alumni—as well as the community.

In other words, Project Pericles is one answer to the question posed by David Mathews (2004) when he wrote about the importance of looking for "new governance structures that could link the public and the academy more closely" (86). Macalester College, a Periclean institution, offers an interesting institutional interpretation of the goals of the project through its Web site, where one can find a paper by Andrew A. Latham, associate professor of political science, associate director of the center for scholarship and teaching, and co-director of Project Pericles. In his paper (2003), Professor Latham provides an introduction to the concepts of civic engagement and describes some of the work at Macalester College that supports "civically engaged scholarly work" (2). The Macalester model offers an interesting window into the ways that governing boards and the broader campus community can promote engagement and the work of Pasteur's Quadrant. In Macalester's conception, as articulated by Latham, engaged/public scholarship has several defining features, all of which are compatible with the notion of the integration of theoretical and use-inspired inquiry:

- Public scholarship addresses issues of pressing or persistent concern to the local and global communities in which we live.
- It provides citizens and civic leaders with the dependable knowledge necessary for reaching responsible public judgments and decisions.
- It enriches public discourse on controversial issues.
- Such scholarship is directly responsive to important public concerns, and/or it enlivens democratic debate and deliberation.

LIFELONG LEARNING: BEING A GOOD CITIZEN MEANS BECOMING A STUDENT FOR LIFE

As the information age continues to develop, the role of higher education extends further into adult life. This often is not reflected on the docket of the governing board or in its committee structure. It also does not usually appear in the form of interactions and consultations that the governing board has with its many constituencies. Until recently, lifelong learning was thought of as "continuing education" and was the purview of continuing education divisions and professional societies. In a survey conducted for the Kellogg Commission (1999), 91 percent of respondents agreed that "lifelong learning" is defined as "the process of intellectual and professional renewal that leads to both personal enrichment and occupational growth" (10). This definition has some significant limitations, because it fails to draw the educational needs of adults into the heart of the academic programs of an institution or onto the agenda of the governing board.

First, the term *renewal* fails to take into account the growing need for the continuous creation, acquisition and application of knowledge, and the patterns of learning associated with "reflective practitioners." In addition, the term *personal enrichment* overlooks the importance of lifelong learning for fostering both effective citizenship and community development. Third, the definition focuses exclusively on individuals and fails to take into account the building of intellectual and problem-solving capacities of groups of people in neighbor-hoods, communities, and organizations. Perhaps most important, the defini-tion fails to address the importance of applying skills and knowledge to solve new kinds of problems that often are disputed and poorly defined.

Continuing education divisions still offer valuable programming for pro-fessionals, and, no doubt, will continue to do so, but it is now becoming clear that lifelong learning is an essential condition for sustaining our democratic way of life as well as for solving practical problems while contributing to our fund of knowledge and theory at the same time—the defining qualities of Pasteur's Quadrant. We need to capture the importance of an enlightened and a capable citizenry to the democratic way of life and the maintenance of our sense of community through the generation of greater social and human capital.

The entire university community must accept the challenges of this kind of learning. The changing societal conditions that will reshape our approach to lifelong learning and the role that universities will play in the generation of community capacity as well as the promotion of personal and occupational enrichment are complex. We must consider a number of issues that are only now beginning to enter our thinking or even our sense of responsibilities as scholars and educators. A learning organization has many features that require a new approach to both shared and individual lifelong learning. According to David Garvin (2000), "a learning organization is an organization skilled at cre-ating, acquiring, interpreting, retaining, and transferring knowledge; and at pur-posefully modifying its behavior based on new knowledge and insights" (11).

Among the societal functions that now require the formation of commu-nities of learning or learning organizations are: (1) the changing role of learn-ing within larger organizations as a mechanism for better product quality and customer service; (2) the movement toward community-based decision making in school systems, health care delivery, social service delivery, and eco-nomic and community development, and the need to provide support for the continuous learning that community decision-making groups must undertake if they are to make wise choices; (3) the expansion of integrative models that blend both pre-service and in-service training (i.e., professional development) as well as community-based research in settings such as school systems, social service agencies, and health care environments; and (4) new options for under-taking college-level work in alternative settings, such as high schools, and new forms of educational articulation that provide better access and opportunity for additional education involving more complex pathways and more effective educational and career planning.

All of these models represent examples of collaborative learning within groups and organizations. Most begin to blur the edges of our traditional cat-egories of teaching, research, and service and represent variations of "engagement" in which knowledge is generated, applied, and interpreted in a collaborative mode. *Learning* is becoming a more complex concept that includes all aspects of scholarly work (discovery, integration, interpretation, and application) conducted by different groups of people in a variety of settings. It is no longer simply the effective absorption of knowledge transmitted by an expert. Many of these approaches depend upon inter-institutional alliances as well as institutional support structures that must be designed and used effectively to blend discovery, learning, and innovation in new and productive ways.

In this conception, lifelong learning must be both an avenue for sustaining individual skills and competence as well as the shared competencies of groups and organizations. In addition, lifelong learning will increasingly include a component of discovery and application rather than the absorption of knowledge recently generated by others. It will mean an integration of research and continuing professional development that advances theoretical knowledge while addressing practical problems and advancing the skill and knowledge of all of the participants.

DEFINING CHARACTERISTICS OF A TWENTY-FIRST CENTURY UNIVERSITY: SCHOLARSHIP DIRECTED TOWARD THE PUBLIC GOOD

What kind of college or university can provide a supportive environment for engaged scholarship and the formation of learning communities? What might be the features of such an entity? In outline, here is one model to consider. The assumption underlying this description is that any engaged institution will be closely linked to other educational and societal institutions in order to create the context and capacity for engaged research and education.

• The primary purposes of twenty-first century engaged higher education institutions are to conduct research on important problems, ideas, and questions; to promote the application of current knowledge to societal problems; and to prepare students to address these issues through a curriculum that emphasizes scholarly work in both the liberal arts and in the professions, where learning is advanced in a mode that encourages civic commitments and social responsibility.

• Scholarly work consists of discovery, integration of new knowledge into an existing discipline or body of knowledge, interpretation to a variety of audiences, and application of knowledge to a variety of contemporary questions. In an engaged institution, all faculty, staff, and students can and should engage in scholarly work, either to address societal concerns, to strengthen the educational environment, or to promote effective use of campus resources.

- Faculty, staff, and students will participate in diverse forms of scholarly work at different times in their careers. No single profile can properly accommodate disciplinary differences and individual interests effectively.
- The classic tripartite mission of research, instruction, and service must support a full range of inquiry and application both within the curriculum and research environments created by the institution and in field, community, and other applied settings. Campuses cannot and must not be insular. Scholarly work that involves instruction and research combined with service must be valued, rigorously reviewed, and effectively rewarded.
- Although many institutions are oriented to address directly the social and economic problems of our society, the engaged institution is distinguished by the comprehensiveness of its academic mission, its range of graduate and undergraduate programs, the effective integration of scholarship and service within both the curriculum and the research mission, and the integral involvement of students in the generation and application of knowledge.
- Success in the college or university of the future will be defined by the rigor of scholarly work; the quality of the educational experience of undergraduate, graduate, and professional students; the effectiveness of the partnerships that link the university with the community; and the impact of the institution on the quality of life of citizens of the state, the nation, and the world.

Conclusion

The challenge of engagement is really to bring together life and work—in the lives of our students and faculty, in the collective work of our institutions, and in our working relationships with the broader community. All of our discussions about the conditions required for engagement and the role of governing boards in creating these conditions have at their heart the problem of achieving coherence and integrity to allow personal meaning and intellectual work to come together: for us, for our disciplines, for our departments, and for our institutions. True engagement offers the opportunity to experience learning in the company of others in a situation where learning has consequences and where individuals are respected and given voice. It is in this process of mutual inquiry where contributions can be made to the public good while at the same time advancing the personal and private interests of the participants. It is this blending of the personal and the public that will help us resolve the tensions that now exist between the expectations of society and its elected representatives, on the one hand, and the higher education community, on the other, about the appropriate roles and responsibilities of higher education in contemporary society.

In an engaged institution, an ideal education lies between the two poles of experience and purpose, thought and action, and self-realization and social responsibility. An education is meaningful when it liberates the spirit and feeds the soul *and* at the same time prepares us to make good decisions, contribute to public life, and live as responsible citizens of our democracy. To foster a society in which learning has consequences, our colleges and universities must direct themselves to bringing together public purposes and private benefits. The public good and private benefit cannot and must not remain competing alternatives. The basic premise of this chapter is that individual aspirations and personal goals can be most productively advanced when research and education are inspired by *both* a thirst for knowledge and a desire for practical outcomes. It is the responsibility of the governing board to reflect upon the convergence of public and private interests and to represent these interests in its membership, its committee structure, and its policy agenda. The governing board must pay attention to the issue of public scholarship and help the institution(s) for which it exercises the duty of stewardship and care to explore the implications and challenges of life in Pasteur's Quadrant.

REFERENCES

Association of Governing Boards (AGB). 1998. *Bridging the gap between state government and public higher education.* Washington, DC: Author.

———. 2003. *Ten public policy issues for higher education in 2003 and 2004.* Public Policy Paper Series 03–02. Washington, DC: Author.

Ball, D. L. 2003. *Mathematical proficiency for all students: Toward a strategic research and development program in mathematics education.* Santa Monica, CA: RAND Corporation, Mathematics Study Panel.

Boyer, E. L. 1990. *Scholarship reconsidered: Priorities of the professoriate.* Princeton, NJ: The Carnegie Foundation for the Advancement of Teaching.

Bracco, K. R., R. C. Richardson, Jr., P. M. Callan, and J. E. Finney. 1999. Policy environments and system design: Understanding state governance structures. *The Review of Higher Education* 23(1): 23–44.

Brown, D. 2001. On the role of trustees: An interview with William C. Hubbard. *Higher Education Exchange* 10: 38–42.

———. 2004. What is "public" about what academics do? An exchange with Robert Kingston and Peter Levine. *Higher Education Exchange* 10: 17–29.

Bush, V. 1980. *Science, the endless frontier: A report to the president on a program for post-war scientific research.* Washington, DC: National Science Foundation. (Original work published 1945)

Daniels, R. V. 1991. *The University of Vermont: The first two hundred years.* Hanover, NH: University Press of New England.

Eckel, P. E. 2000. The role of shared governance in institutional hard decisions: Enabler or antagonist? *The Review of Higher Education* 24(1): 15–39.

Ferren, A. S., W. R. Kennan, and S. H. Lerch. 2001. Reconciling corporate and academic cultures. *Peer Review* 3(3): 9–11.

Fretwell, E. K., Jr. 2001. *More than management: Guidelines for state higher education system governing boards and their chief executive.* Denver, CO: State Higher Education Executive Officers.

Garvin, D. A. 2000. *Learning in action: A guide to putting the learning organization to work.* Cambridge, MA: Harvard Business School Press.

Geiger, R. L. 1993. *Research and relevant knowledge: American research universities since World War II.* New York: Oxford University Press.

Holland, B. 2001. Toward a definition and characterization of the engaged campus: Six cases. *Metropolitan Universities* 12(3): 20–29.

Ingram, R. T., and Associates. 1993. *Governing public colleges and universities.* San Francisco: Jossey-Bass.

Kellogg Commission on the Future of State and Land-Grant Universities. 1999. *Returning to our roots: A learning society.* Washington, DC: Author.

Kerr, C. 2001. *The Uses of the University.* 5th ed. Cambridge, MA: Harvard University Press.

Kezar, A. 2001. Seeking a sense of balance: Academic governance in the 21st century. *Peer Review* 3(3): 4–8.

Kezar, A., and P. D. Eckel. 2004. Meeting today's governance challenges. A synthesis of the literature and examination of a future agenda for scholarship. *The Journal of Higher Education* 75(4): 371–99.

Latham, A. A. 2003. *Liberal education for global citizenship: Renewing Macalester's traditions of public scholarship and civic learning.* Retrieved May 1, 2004, from http://www.macalester.edu/pericles/.

Lovett, C. 2003. Keep the main thing the main thing. *Trusteeship* 11(6): 19–23.

Martin, R. R., K. Manning, and J. A. Ramaley. 2001. The self-study as a chariot for strategic change. In *How accreditation influences assessment: New directions for higher education*, 113, ed. J. L. Ratcliff, E. S. Lubinescu, and M. A.Gaffney, 95–115.

Mathews, D. 2004. Afterward: "What Public?" In *Higher Education Exchange* 10, ed. D. W. Brown and D. Witte, 82–88. Washington, DC: The Kettering Foundation.

Newman, J. H. 1960. *The idea of a university.* Notre Dame, IN: University of Notre Dame Press.

A question for . . . governance experts: A look at campus decision making. Four AGB national conference panelists answer the question: How can boards, administrators, and faculty change the way decisions are made on campus? 1999. *Trusteeship* (March/April) 7(2): 25–28.

Ramaley, J. A. 2001. Why do we engage in engagement? *Metropolitan Universities* 12(3): 13–19.

Rich, R. F., and K. Prewitt. 2001. *Social science information and public policy making.* Somerset, NJ: Transaction.

Stokes, D. E. 1997. *Pasteur's quadrant: Basic science and technological innovation.* Washington, DC: Brookings Institution Press.

Witte, D. 2004. Foreword. In *Higher Education Exchange,* 10, ed. D. W. Brown and D. Witte, 1–4. Washington, DC: The Kettering Foundation.

Ylvisaker, P. N. 1993. Responding to political, social and ethical issues. In *Governing Public Colleges and Universities,* ed. R. T. Ingram, 226–39. San Francisco: Jossey-Bass.

9

Trust and Academic Governance

A Conceptual Framework

William G. Tierney

In the last decade, students of organizational behavior have developed a theoretical interest in trust, motivated in part by a desire to understand how to bring about cooperative behavior (Kramer and Tyler, 1996). Lack of trust, or distrust, generates one set of conditions for civic engagement. Trust and trustworthiness generate another. What are the conditions for change when trust exists? How does trust come about? Who is able to engender trust? Scholars have asked such questions in order to consider how to improve organizational effectiveness. Whereas some have pointed out how power, authority, or contractual arrangements might bring about desired goals, others have asked what part trust plays in sustaining cooperation and, in turn, enhancing organizational effectiveness (Gambetta, 1988; Luhmann, 1988; Tyler and Degoey, 1995).

In what follows, I examine the faculty's role in governance at one institution, offering a provisional schema for how to think about trust in academic organizations. I begin with an overview of two contrasting frameworks that may be used to analyze trust. I suggest that a cultural framework offers more useful possibilities for understanding organizational trust than does a rational choice framework. I focus on two key concepts that utilize a cultural framework for examining organizational life. I then offer one portrait of trust based on research that I have done over the last two years. My purpose here is not to provide a replicable conceptual framework for trust, since the idea is far too untested to make such a claim. Rather, I offer the schema as a trial of some ideas in order to expand research into relatively new terrain, and, of consequence, to improve academic organizations.

Trust in Academic Life: Rational Choice and Cultural Frameworks

Although the concept of organizational trust is related in various ways to interpersonal and societal trust, I concentrate here on the conditions for creating trust in an academic organization. In the end, psychological or normative accounts of how an individual creates trust in his or her life differ considerably from an organization's constituents' ability to create the conditions for trust. Similarly, a citizen's trust in government differs from an individual's trust in his or her organization. My focus here is on trust within organizations.

Trust within a rational choice framework: A great deal of research on trust has utilized a rational choice perspective. The unit of analysis is the individual who exists within a social structure. Rational choice theorists assert that trust is an individual's subjective assumption about what is going to happen (Hardin, 1993; Morse, 1999; Dunn, 1988). The trusted have incentives to fulfill the trust, and the trusters have information and knowledge that enable them to trust. Thus by a series of complex rational expectations, individuals come to trust others.

James Coleman, a leading proponent of rational choice theory, has described the commonsensical idea that "social interdependence and systemic functioning arise from the fact that actors have interests in events that are fully or partially under the control of others" (1990, 300). Continuing from this observation, he argued that the actors are necessarily engaged in an exchange relationship that encourages trust to develop because it is in the interest of both parties. While his assessment of the nature of social relations goes well beyond the idea that society consists of a set of individuals acting independently from one another, Coleman and other rational choice theorists (Putnam, 1995) assumed that conditions for trusting relationships can be replicated, irrespective of the context and the individual.

Trust is a two-party relationship in which an individual commits to an exchange before knowing whether the other individual will reciprocate. The focus of the exchange occurs within a structure of relationships where the motives for trust are instrumental. The researcher investigates the incentives involved in getting the trusted to do what is obligated, and the knowledge needed by the truster to trust. Social obligations, expectations, norms, and sanctions are primary arrangements used to build trust. When trust is absent, or does not develop, it is primarily because of the pathologies of the individuals involved in the interactions. When trust exists, it is because the individuals have utilized the structures in a manner that fosters trusting relationships.

The concern with rational choice when one thinks of colleges or universities pertains as much to ideological notions of the world as to an individual's ability to create change in his or her life and work within an organization. That is, rational choice theorists hold an implicit assumption that a structure exists, but an explicit analysis that an overriding ideological view of the world is framed within that structure is absent. One understands how different phenomena function by analyzing the social networks of individuals within these structures. Those who are unsuccessful can change by altering their view of the world and trying to fit within the overarching structure. Structures from this perspective are neutral and not powerful forces that reinforce ideological hegemony. Trust comes about when individuals hold views of the world that are in sync with the structures in which they reside.

Trust within a cultural framework: An alternative view is to conceive of organizations as social structures that individuals construct and reconstruct. A cultural view of the organization forces an analysis not only of structures but also of the social contexts and histories in which these structures are embedded. Trust gets contextualized and understood not only from an individualistic standpoint but also from a vantage point that seeks to interpret how actors define the individual and how that individual acts and reacts within the organization (Seligman, 1997). From this perspective, one seeks to understand the social bonds and shared identities that enable trust to occur. The focus is on the internal dynamics within the organization as well as on the social forces that help shape the organization. Feelings of a shared identity and interpersonal connections need not be shaped to an impersonal and impervious structure but instead have broad leeway for interpretation and reinterpretation, as individuals enter and exit the organization, relating to it differently over time.

In this framework, rather than pawns within a rigid structure, individuals become social decision makers. Whereas a rational choice framework seeks to understand how individuals might align themselves to the structure, a cultural view enables the researcher to see the organization in much more fluid terms. Organizations simply do not bend one way or another but have ideological parameters framed in part by the larger social structure. The challenge for the researcher, then, is not figuring out how to align individuals with predetermined social structures but instead figuring out how relationships that build commonalities across differences might be developed, promoting agency within individuals.

In order to elaborate on how trust operates within a cultural framework I turn now to two key components that help frame how trust becomes understood in an organization. The first component pertains to how an organization's members come to hold *shared experiences.* How a culture's participants make meaning is an important part of whether trust is pervasive, fleeting, or absent. The second component addresses how one *learns* about shared experiences. The socializing experiences of new members as well as the reiterated interactions and experiences that individuals have with one another lead to the

kinds of epiphenomenal interpretations of organizational life that enable trust
to occur.

Trust as shared experience: Trust does not come about without a framework
and language for common understanding. As Russell Hardin noted, "When I
trust you in the sense that your interests encapsulate mine in at least the matter
with respect to which I trust you, we can, naturally, be said to share interests
to some extent" (2002, 144). One way to share interests is by common interpretation. Two parties view events similarly when they have a mutual interest
in attaining the same goal and see the path to that goal in a similar manner.
Trust occurs when both parties share interests such that what is good for one
party is also good for the other. Such a view is context specific; one party trusts
the other on a specific issue, but both parties may not have developed a generalized trust.

Common interpretations, however, can never be assumed. Individuals
arrive to an organization with their own unique histories and ways of viewing
events. For example, if a college president concludes that his or her institution
is in fiscal jeopardy, it does not mean that the faculty will come to the same
conclusion. A rational choice perspective, however, assumes otherwise, arguing
that when two people are faced with a choice and share the same information
and the same values, they must rationally make the same decision.

Proponents of a cultural framework disagree. A cultural view acknowledges that perfect information does not exist, and that many viewpoints exist
about a particular issue (Tierney, 1988). The challenge for the organizational
leader turns less on collecting and disseminating perfect data so that everyone
will view the information in a similar manner and more on how to build an
organizational culture that incorporates multiple viewpoints and calls upon
cultural symbols, rituals, and communicative processes to highlight organizational goals and overriding ideologies. From this perspective, trust develops
through the ability of individuals to communicate cultural meanings rather
than rational facts.

The adult learns to trust as a means of cooperation. Russell Hardin spoke
of "encapsulated trust" (2002). Individuals trust one another because it is in
their mutual interest to take each other's involvement in the same matter seriously. Such a view incorporates parts of a rational view but, ultimately, it is
inherently subjective. That is, encapsulated trust assumes that individuals
make rational choices about trust, and in part, those choices are framed by the
psychological backgrounds of the parties. However, the focus of encapsulated
trust is not only on future expectations of what will occur but also on past
interactions and interpretations. In an organization, encapsulated trust takes
place when an individual enters into a trusting relationship because of his or
her particular view of the organizational world, a view framed in part by the
culture of the organization. The mores of the organization, the symbolic and

communicative processes that exist, and a host of cultural artifacts enter into how cooperation is likely to occur.

Although there are plenty of stories of office rivalries, demagogic managers, and petty intrigue, a significant body of research highlights the importance of cooperation in organizations. This line of research views individuals as decision makers and active agents who are likely to perform better in an environment that exists through reciprocal obligations rather than individualized desires and wants. The research moves, then, from atomistic analyses that center on an individual's rational choices within predetermined structures toward an understanding of how social connections within an organization are developed, maintained, and enhanced. Other than highly contractual arrangements where all parties are clear about how each is to respond to different situations, what kind of relationships might engender trust?

Academic organizations exemplify the kind of cultural entities where trust has the potential to flourish. A great many people stay in the academy for a significant length of time, and they generally interact with one another because they desire to rather than because of a command. Long-term working relationships are most successful when they embody encapsulated trust. The social context of the college or university has relied more on a sense of collegiality than a legalistic contract. In this light, trust is an orientation toward the organization and toward one another that cannot be precisely or neatly summarized as "rational." One has faith that because one works in the organization, and because the participants in the organization have a particular history with one another, the organization will respond in ways that reinforce trust.

Trust as learned experience: One can neither command nor coerce an individual to trust. Although an individual may do what a superior wants because the latter has power over or has coerced the individual, trust will not be part of the interaction (Luhmann, 1980). A professor may demand certain behaviors from students because of the role that each inhabits. Similarly, if individuals in an organization constantly receive messages that command them to act in one way or another, they may do what they are told. But trust has nothing to do with these interactions. For there to be a trusting relationship it is necessary to believe that the relationship one has with the other individual is useful; the truster also must have confidence in the other individual. While an element of risk is always involved, because one can never be certain that the trusted party will do what is expected, the interactions always occur within the ongoing social contexts of the organizational actors. Trust is learned.

At the most elemental level, an infant learns to trust a parent. The infant is helpless and hopefully learns through repeated actions to trust the parent. When an infant cries and the parent picks him or her up, this is not solely a functional act. The infant learns that he or she matters to the parent. The parent is trustworthy. To be sure, there are numerous examples in which an infant does not learn such a lesson, and some will suggest that trust is instead "imprinted" on an infant. But from a cultural perspective, the infant-parent connection is perhaps the clearest example of trust as learned experience.

Trust, then, is enwrapped in cultural contexts. At the organizational level, the assumption that trust is learned behavior suggests that of necessity one investigate the socializing mechanisms and processes that induct the individual into the culture. Academic life is imbued with socializing experiences. Initiates learn a great deal about academe as soon as, if not before, they become recruits; that is, in graduate school. Institutional pecking orders, the importance of research, how one works with one's colleagues, and what is and is not important are all lessons that individuals learn en route to the PhD. Although these lessons are frequently implicit rather than explicit, one should not overlook their symbolic importance. Similarly, when one arrives on campus as a new assistant professor, the diverse experiences that occur make an inevitable imprint about the organizational culture. How an individual achieves tenure, what one has to do to achieve it, and the inevitable aspects surrounding departmental politics will all teach lessons to the initiate.

Because individuals will interpret events differently, my point here is not to suggest that socialization is a lockstep process that moves individuals through academic life as if they are on a production line in a factory. Indeed, one's past experiences and the different ways organizations treat individuals both lead to differential interpretations. A new assistant professor whose parents were faculty will arrive at the institution with a different set of assumptions than someone who is the first in the family to attend college. In an engineering department, the same kind of tenure process may be assumed for everyone, but that process may be experienced differently depending on one's gender. A woman who is the only female in the department may have very different interpretations about what one needs to do to achieve tenure compared to a man, who might not feel at all out of place.

Thus an individual's experiences and an organization's socializing processes have a significant impact on what one learns about trust. The culture of the organization provides a variety of symbolic processes to teach individuals about trust. An individual receives one message when at the start of the school year a college president says that teaching is important, for example, and another message when a colleague is denied tenure because of a lack of research. In contrast, consider a university in which the message from the provost is that individuals should take intellectual risks, and the faculty are frequently rewarded when they take such risks. In the former example, individuals learn not to trust what the president says, and in the latter, they learn to trust what emanates from the provost. Learning is rarely a singular event but is rather ongoing and multidimensional.

METHODOLOGICAL FRAMEWORK

To provide a sense of these admittedly abstract terms, I turn here to a case study that highlights how trust operates at one institution, with particular regard to faculty involvement in governance. The data were collected by a case study in which thirty-one individuals were interviewed during one academic year; these individuals were asked about their perceptions of the role of the faculty in the governance of the university. Follow-up interviews took place via the Internet and the phone. The point here, of course, is not to suggest that trust operates in this manner in all locations but instead to offer an individual case study in order to be able to advance the notion of trust in academic organizations.

I utilized a qualitative research design in order to give voice to different constituencies and actions. As with any qualitative study, numerous methodological possibilities exist. I could have conducted a life history, multiple interviews of one group (e.g., faculty) across numerous campuses, portraiture, cultural biography, and the like. I chose a case study based on the points raised in the previous section. My intent was to understand the cultural dynamics within an organization. The intense focus on one individual or snapshots of numerous individuals irrespective of site would not have been able to generate contextual data that enabled the ability to understand how members learned to trust (or not). Thus I utilized a case study.

A case study approach is a useful method for this investigation, given that significant contextual relevance can be created (Bogdan and Biklen, 1998). To be sure, as Clark has noted, "No one method of social inquiry is ideal. The approach of open-ended field interviewing on which I rely is deficient in its inability to demonstrate representativeness and in its loose control of bias in deciding what will be reported. But it is better to suffer the slings of such selection than the sorrows of superficial responses than inhere when respondents answer mail questionnaires by simply checking boxes or circling numbers opposite prepared answers unable to explain what they individually mean" (Clark, 1987, xxvi).

Accordingly, some may think that the particular has been emphasized at the expense of generalizing the findings. However, as noted at the outset of the chapter, I am not trying to generalize. Scholars in this area first need to come to terms with the parameters of organizational trust and then eventually move on to testing different hypotheses.

I identified interviewees with the initial help of a contact person and according to criteria I had set, such as the informant's role in governance. Once on campus, interviewees also suggested additional persons with whom I should speak. To the extent possible, I sought a diverse sample rather than trying to get everyone with a similar viewpoint. For example, I sought individuals who had been at the institution for many years, those who were newcomers, and faculty from multiple disciplines in order to gain diverse perspectives on governance. To enhance trustworthiness, I also conducted hour-long interviews with campus members who represented a cross-section of perspectives and vantage points on governance (Glesne and Peshkin, 1992). Some individuals were supporters of the governance process, and others interpreted governance from a different perspective. Although individuals were free to decline to be interviewed, everyone agreed to speak to me. Interviewees included the president, provost, leaders of the faculty senate, deans, junior and senior faculty, and faculty from the humanities, social sciences, and professional schools. I also made sure to interview a mix of male and female faculty. In addition to interviews, I collected and reviewed campus documents, including faculty handbooks, presidential speeches, strategic plans, and minutes from meetings in which decision making took place.

Insofar as the framework is trying to understand the perspectives and interpretations of individuals within an organization's culture, I utilized an interpretive perspective; intentions, circumstances, and actions were carefully considered and filled with multiple meanings (Denzin, 1989). I did not assume that the organization's "reality" awaited me to find and discover it. Instead, I worked from a constructionist perspective that sought to understand how the participants made sense of that reality. This perspective is not predictive; it seeks to make sense out of social interaction within a particular context. My purpose in developing a diverse sample was to ensure that I had as complete an interpretation of events and activities as possible rather than only one interpretation. I analyzed and coded the data using a grounded theory method that sought to develop themes inductively through a constant comparison of data (Glaser and Strauss, 1967). Interviews were transcribed by three methods: taping, taking notes, and, on a few occasions, simply listening and writing up a short summary immediately afterwards. Different methods of transcription bring forth different kinds of data, which is an additional way to check one's findings. I triangulated data through interviews, document analysis, focus groups, and secondary follow-up interviews. I utilized a pseudonym to disguise the institution and to provide generic identifiers (e.g., "a senior professor") to mask the identities of the interviewees.

PRAIRIE HOME COMPANION UNIVERSITY

Prairie Home Companion University (PHCU) is a large public institution with a history of successful shared governance. The institution has been in existence for over a century, and faculty have been centrally involved in governance from its inception. The main organ of governance is the faculty senate and an executive council. In addition, a shared congress includes staff and students. Senior administrators serve on the academic senate, and the faculty and administration have a tradition of working together to solve problems. The senate and its executive committee are well funded and staffed with a suite of offices and five full-time employees; more importantly, the culture of the university both expects and rewards faculty involvement in governance.

When asked what advice faculty would give to a new president, a consistent theme emerged. "He has to get to know the faculty; don't go around us," said one. Another added, "We would never hire someone who was uncomfortable with the tradition around here of consultation." A third said, "He had better take governance seriously. Someone from a radically different kind of place would have a pretty steep learning curve." A fourth added, "Embrace the governance structure. It's the way we do things." A final person said, "See the faculty as an ally. I know that's not the way it is at other places, but here we all see the need to get along and work with one another."

Similar kinds of comments occurred when individuals spoke about faculty involvement at PHCU: "We expect leadership from the faculty. You have tenure, so use it." A second person contrasted his experience at PHCU with other institutions: "We have a stronger governance system here than at other places. Faculty expect to be consulted, and by and large, we are." "Don't get the wrong impression," said another. "This is not a democracy without flaws. Faculty have their typical turf battles, and we avoid difficult decisions. Faculty still make the process slower than it should be. But if you're interested in faculty engagement, I'd say for the kind of institution this is we are aware of what's going on." A fourth person concurred: "Faculty are never satisfied. They will always say they want more consultation, but when I look at other places, this place is far better than most, and it functions pretty well." In an interview with two individuals, one said, "Some issues are perennial, and you wonder why we keep repeating ourselves." The other summarized, "But it goes to the heart of involvement. Faculty feel they can speak up on anything, and they do."

Individuals also felt included in decisions at their school and department levels. "I'm not sure if it comes from the top or the bottom, but people's voices are heard here," said one. "Department meetings are, on the whole, collegial, and if a dean ignored us, he'd be in trouble." Another added, "At my previous university, department meetings were a joke. They were never held, and if they were, no one went. Here they're important." A dean noted, "When I came here I learned pretty darn quick to involve the faculty. Part of it is being a public. Also where we're located. People expect discussion and debate."

Communication appeared to play a role in faculty engagement. "This is a big institution with a small college feel to it," said one person. Another remarked, "I suppose, no, I know, people who can ignore governance here and get lost in their labs and research. But the tilt is toward involvement rather than away from it. When you hear what's going on, you're supposed to be an active listener, rather than passive." When asked how he finds out about what's going on at the institution, a third suggested, "I guess I find out in lots of ways. E-mail. Newspapers. Reports. Word of mouth. It's sort of like the sports page. You can ignore it, but usually from osmosis you just know." A leader in the senate explained, "We work at trying to communicate, to let the faculty know what's going on. It's hard with so much competing for faculty attention, but it's imperative."

One example of faculty engagement pertained to a search for a new president. When the current president took a job at another institution, the PHCU Board of Trustees created a search committee that contained relatively few faculty. "They made a mistake," commented one person. "It creates bad faith. There are fewer faculty on this search than the last one." Another person explained, "It was a misstep on their part, but off the record I've heard from the chair and understand why it was done. They'll still take our voice into account." A third person concurred, noting, "There is a growing consensus amongst the faculty about who we want, and we have been quietly writing letters to the search committee. Senior faculty and university professors also have written. I don't know what the outcome will be, but I'm sure we'll be listened to." A fourth person added, "The board knows to avoid conflict, so I'm not sure why they created a committee with so few faculty, but we also have used informal channels, and I'd be surprised if they chose someone out of step with the faculty."

Three interesting points arise in the responses to the presidential search committee. First, although the interviewees viewed the structure of the search committee as important, they also were not overly concerned that the structure did not meet their expectations. Rather, the culture of the organization is what mattered. The means of communication and the shared belief that they would be heard enabled the faculty to focus on whom they should hire as president rather than on the structure utilized to make that decision. Second, not all voices are equal. University professors (campus-wide, endowed chairs with tenure) play an important role in the organization. When they express an opinion, the expectation is not that what they say will be agreed to, but that they, as faculty, will be heard. Third, a presidential search is an unusual case. A college president is ordinarily a key actor in creating and maintaining (or destroying) the conditions for trust. Here, then, we have an example in which the culture has created trust through shared and learned experiences, so that even when the president is not involved, trust thrives.

This example also demonstrates the importance placed on socialization. Indeed, one key concern of the faculty is that individuals new to the organization have different expectations and obligations. One person stated, "I suppose it's common everywhere, but the younger ones seem less involved; they want to focus more on their research or have national ambitions." A second observed, "There's increasing pressure to increase our research standing, and you can't do everything. It takes away from service. It's not a crisis, because there are still many of us involved, but I wonder if that will change." A third continued, "When crises erupt, people come out of the woodwork, but in the meantime everyone goes about their business. I'm not sure, though, if we're in a new ball game. Everyone seems so busy, and governance takes so much time. We should streamline the process." A department chair commented, "If I were to make a prediction I'd say that faculty will still be involved in ten years at the department level, but less so at the university level. It's not that they're uninterested in university politics. It's that there's no time, so you make choices." Another interviewee agreed, saying, "I think there has been an erosion of faculty governance. It's nothing overt, or a power grab, it's just the times."

Although senior faculty felt that early career faculty seemed disengaged, assistant professors and new faculty had a different opinion. "The message is pretty clear here," said one assistant professor. "Sure, it's like all research universities; you've got to do research to survive. But people expect you to interact. My friend at [X University] says he doesn't even know if his place has a senate. I do." Another person added, "I came here because of my department. If it hadn't been a good group of scholars, I never would have come. But I was surprised at what they expect of us. The department has meetings, and you're supposed to show up!" An assistant professor in her third year pointed out, "People tell me what I need to hear: to do research, to go to conferences. But I also know there's a sense that when I get tenure I'll be expected to contribute more toward service, and that's fine with me. I just first need to get tenure."

The nature of socialization at PHCU is primarily implicit and informal. Individuals do not go through training, and there is no manual for what is expected of a faculty member. However, numerous lessons are implied and internalized. As one individual commented, "It's quite natural for faculty to work in administration for a spell. There's a lot of coming and going from one to the other." The individual went on to explain that such interaction was common and that it contributed to trust between faculty and administration. Another individual concurred: "I was in the administration once before, and then I went back to the faculty, and now I'm back again. It gives me a useful perspective." Again, such back-and-forth movement between the administration and faculty not only provides individuals with useful perspectives but also shared experiences that enable trust to develop.

A related example pertains to faculty appointments. The pervasive assumption at PHCU is that virtually all committees on which faculty serve will be vetted by a senate committee. "Shadow committees, or kitchen cabinets that have formal power, won't fly around here very well," explained one person.

"If a president just appointed individuals to important committees without the senate's input, that would be seen as a real problem. It's just not done." Another commented, "We expect leadership from the faculty. For a president to handpick people for an important committee would be a sign that he doesn't understand our culture."

Additional examples pertained to construction projects and athletics. "I guess we feel like this is our place, or that we at least have a say in how things are supposed to be around here," reflected one person. "We expect to have input when something goes up." Another said, "I don't care, frankly, about some building somewhere on campus, but I'm glad we've got a process for review, because I know some people do care. This isn't a monarchy." A third person lamented, "College athletics is a problem, that's for sure. The faculty can never have enough oversight of it. Problems are always going to arise, but I think the administration protects themselves and the university when they bring us in. There can't be much, 'I told you so,' because we're involved." Another person added, "A few years back, we had a problem. Then they brought in the faculty, sort of after the fact . . . I don't think you can lay it on the president's doorstep though. The faculty should have been involved, had oversight, from the get-go. If there's a silver lining, it's that we assume we're supposed to be in the mix."

The point here is not that everyone sees the organizational world similarly, or that PHCU is an academic utopia, where everyone trusts one another. However, the comments reflect common perceptions about the nature of faculty governance. Indeed, when queried about what an indicator of effective governance might be, one respondent said that "the administration [should be] managing in a way that reflects academic values." Another person noted, "The extent to which academic community is strengthened would be an indication [of effective governance]." A third stated, "These are all indirect effects—faculty involvement, the way people are socialized, the way they see their role here—but I think that most of us believe that when faculty are engaged with the goings-on around campus, that the place is just more effective in fulfilling its mission."

"This place is overgoverned," complained one person. A second asked, "On what campus is there too little governance, too few committees?" She continued, "We need to streamline things here, but because we are inefficient does not mean we are ineffective." A third noted, "Governance today is often silly. The issues are so complex, and we don't have the time to attend to them, so we may take a quick pass at something and then defer to the administration, but there's been an erosion of faculty involvement. It's not at the breaking point, I don't know when that is, but we're heading down that road—everybody is." Another person noted, "Governance is ailing here. Discussions aren't as robust as they used to be. I think people were exhausted by the fight we had with the board a few years ago. That left a mark, because it was a time in the history, at least in the time I've been here, where you really felt that they were out to screw you. We won. But it left a bad taste. It violated the culture." Another respondent summarized these issues, saying, "It all comes down to time. Maybe the people who trained me felt like I do now, but I don't think so. I find myself in a race, and governance isn't a good use of my time if I am to accomplish what they want me to do—to get grants, publish, move the university in a position of prominence."

Indeed, how one defined effective governance had more to do with cultural markers pertaining to the nature of faculty-administrative relations than it did with typical "bottom-line" indicators that one might find in a business. "Do the faculty trust the administration, or is the administration arbitrary in their decision making?" asked one individual. Conversely, a senior administrator noted, "I have to be sure I can speak confidentially to the executive committee and its chair. Sunshine and open meetings are fine, but I have to be able to be frank. It's a marker of effectiveness, because it says we can get things done because we trust one another." A third person stated, "The administration needs to be open to conversation and discussion of major policies, and they have to respect faculty governance." Another person added: "I like benchmarking and comparative indicators. How are our graduation rates? How do we measure up? But those are less important than the nature of relations that have been built up between the administration and the faculty." Again, one respondent summarized the situation, saying:

> I know if I just say we [the faculty] have to be perceived as a stakeholder that it's not enough. Simply being invited to the table doesn't mean governance is effective, but think of it as an entry card. You can't be effective where there's no communication and everybody is watching out for their back. I've worked at a place where everyone distrusts one another, and it's not good.

When I asked individuals about the future, I was less interested in whether their predictions would turn out to be true than on what their view of the future suggested about their present perceptions. Although many of the previous comments forecast a troubled future, they also highlighted a culture in which the faculty are engaged citizens of the university. "We will be more managerial in five years," commented one person. "The kind of 'Mr. Chips' world that has existed is probably a thing of the past." Another said, "Collaborative relationships with the administration have to continue, but I don't know if they will." A third added, "The apple cart could be overturned. I'm not sure if that's a bad thing, but I know that what we have now is working." A long-time member of the faculty said, "I hope we streamline things. Every twenty years or so we should abolish committees and think through what we do. But I hope we maintain our core, the academic values, the belief in what we're doing and one another." Explained another, "One thing that all these committees have served to do, is to let us get to know one another. Otherwise we're just isolated within our departments and disciplines. University citizenship helps us see the whole rather than the part. It won't work if we lose that." Another added, "We have resisted the corporate model, even though our committees might seem bureaucratic. I'm not sure if that will remain. I'm not sure if consultation and trusting one another will be what we're about in the future."

"I hope this isn't going to be some 'happy-faculty' story," summarized another person in a focus group. "Our salaries are too low, the state underfunds us, we have real problems to confront. It's not like simply because people are involved that everything works." A colleague added, however, "He's right. We especially don't get enough from the state. In the long run that's going to do us in, but if governance was a bust, then we'd have no chance. We're at least well organized, and everybody seems to be pulling together." A third pointed out, "Who isn't short of money right now? The answer isn't that someone's going to give us a pot of gold. At least I don't think that will happen. The answer is being able to sit down and plot out a direction—together. That's the good news in hard times."

DISCUSSION

My focus here has been on trying to articulate an intellectual framework for examining organizational trust from a cultural perspective. In doing so, the framework differs from that expressed by proponents of rational choice. Although the rational choice model has been helpful in analyzing how the self-interest of individuals leads to decision making, it ignores the larger social and cultural contexts in which interactions occur. Rational choice theorists begin their analysis with an eye toward replicability: What might be learned from PHCU, they will ask, that will be replicable at other institutions? Proponents of a cultural model begin with no such premise. Rational choice theorists would have focused on the structure of individual relationships within PHCU and assumed that trust came about through instrumentalities: one individual trusted another because the individuals were in a reciprocal relationship. If trust failed, it was because of the pathologies of the individual.

The PHCU is a useful portrait, however, because even though individuals bring their own backgrounds and history to the university, it is the culture of the organization that creates trust. To be sure, individuals bring their own interpretations to an organization's culture, but they "read" the organization through shared experiences that they learn over time. Trust, then, is a highly contingent term rather than a static notion based on one-to-one structural relationships. The challenge turns on understanding the conditions for the creation and maintenance of trust such that an organization's actors have bonds of affiliation and mutual obligations to one another and the institution.

For example, while the norm at PHCU that I employed as an exemplar for trust and trustworthiness was to have the faculty shift back and forth between administrative and faculty positions, I am not suggesting that all institutions should have such a standard. Rather, the perception of such shifts is what is of interest. Consider the following quotation from a faculty member at a different institution:

> A few years ago I took a turn as a dean. During the summer I packed up my books in boxes and as I was taking them over to the administration building, a professor who I know rather well bumped into me. I thought he was going to help me with the boxes. Instead he told me, "I just want you to know that as long as you're in that building, you're one of them. I won't be talking to you." I thought he was kidding. You know what? He wasn't! He didn't talk with me until I finished my term and moved back to my faculty office. (Tierney, 1989, 118)

Clearly, at this institution, the perception of faculty movement into administration is quite different than at PHCU. The point is not that faculty need to avoid administrative life at one institution and undertake it at another. Instead, the challenge is to understand how similar actions are interpreted in different cultures, and to consider what one might do to improve the conditions for trust and trustworthiness.

Further, I have purposefully confined this discussion to interactions that take place within organizations. Trust is invariably quite different, depending on the level of analysis. As I have noted, organizational trust may resemble the trust an infant places in his or her parent, or a citizen places in his or her government, but in the end, both examples are different. Trust in organizations involves an analysis of individual and group interactions as well as an understanding of the ties that bind people to one another. From this perspective, trust is not an atomized gesture between one social actor and another, but instead it is embedded in a network of social relations created within the organization's culture.

Trust is particularly important in organizations where risk taking needs to occur and where task requirements are not clearly delineated (Creed and Miles, 1996; Luhmann, 1988; Meyerson, Weick, and Kramer, 1996). An organization that does not need to innovate or succeeds by adherence to the status quo may not depend as much on an environment of trust insofar as expectations and outputs are clear and defined. Legalistic mechanisms or contract-like arrangements also might substitute for trust in organizations where an individual's work requirements are clearly delineated and can be articulated into codified tasks. Ultimately, any organization's goal will be first to define and then to accomplish the goals the participants have set for themselves. A key characteristic of effectiveness, of course, is to secure compliance from the organization's actors to accomplish what has been set. Although compliance may occur in any number of ways—threats, coercion, incentives, or contractual arrangements, to name a few—organizations that operate in dynamic environments where risk is involved and participation is not mandatory are more likely to need to call upon trusting relationships. Voluntary involvement in (and acceptance of) decisions calls upon a different form of engagement than in a hierarchical organization where participants follow orders and undertake routinized tasks.

At postsecondary institutions, trust and trustworthiness are key variables in achieving high performance. Colleges and universities in the twenty-first century are in highly unstable environments that necessitate risk-taking behavior. Academic organizations have tried to institute more managerial and hierarchical mechanisms in response to the turbulent external environment (Rhoades, 1998). However, colleges and universities continue to use decentralized decision-making processes, in which power is diffuse and shared. Although one may argue about the advantages and disadvantages of tenure, one of its key attributes is the concept of shared governance. The result is that the participants in colleges and universities will face change not through a hierarchical chain of command but through a system that necessitates collaboration and cooperation. A level of trust is critical if individuals are going to take risks and participate in shared decision making. A culture of obligation and cooperation is fundamental. Bureaucratic structures that try to outline and constrict individual behaviors are not useful, but trust also does not naturally develop in an organization simply because a leader sees its utility. Instead, it needs to be nurtured over time. The manner in which trust manifests itself will be highly contingent upon the culture of the organization.

The PHCU is an example of an institution in which trust has been built and maintained within the culture. As the comments cited earlier make clear, PHCU is not an academic utopia where everyone sees things the same way. However, countless examples exist at other colleges and universities where faculty feel as if they do not have adequate representation on one or another committee, and decisions are determined by bureaucratic appointments rather than through substantive discussions. Similarly, the advice PHCU faculty provided to a new president or new faculty revolved around issues of trust. Such comments need to be taken as indicators of the shared interpretations of reality that the faculty have rather than as static notions of advice that will be given to all new presidents and all new faculty irrespective of institution or culture. Individuals also worried that because of stronger socializing mechanisms by discipline, new faculty would be less psychically engaged in the university than before. Because of focus and tempo, individuals confessed to a concern that faculty would not spend as much time on university governance. Although these concerns are undoubtedly rooted in real-world dilemmas about what the future may bring, the comments also highlight what the actors currently consider important. Indeed, even their concept of effectiveness was wrapped in the ability of individuals to trust one another.

The example of PHCU offers a glimpse into a culture in which trust is learned and shared by the actors' experiences with one another. The environment also helps structure responses of individuals within the culture, allowing that the response to future challenges may differ from how the organization's participants currently respond. In this light, trust and trustworthiness are conditioned by environmental and individualistic determinants, but the culture that has been built over time through shared interpretations of reality also helps condition those same environmental and individualistic variables.

As noted at the outset, my goal here has not been to provide a tested model of trust and trustworthiness that might now be utilized in a decision-making analysis of the many problems that institutions confront. Instead, I have sketched what the cultural determinants of a trust-based model might involve and then presented PHCUniversity as an example of an institution where trust appears to be incorporated into the fabric of the institution. Trust is a cultural construct that helps individuals interpret reality, and it shapes their visions not only of how to respond but of what type of response they will develop. Again, I am not suggesting that trust is a generic virtue that individuals or organizations hold, as if some institutions are virtuous and others are not. However, I am arguing that a culture where trust is embedded in the organization's fabric is likely to be better prepared for dealing with the myriad problems that exist on the horizon than those institutions that reach for bureaucratic and hierarchical solutions.

Although many areas remain for further research, perhaps one of the most pressing questions is how to best develop high-quality conditions in an environment where trust exists. The argument has been that trust enables risk-taking behavior and foments action in organizations that lack clearly delineated lines of authority. What has not been determined in the context of normative, social institutions is whether risk taking leads to excellence. Obviously, institutional survival ought not be an adequate standard for whether trust is a key organizational component; colleges and universities should focus on excellence, not merely survival. Trust and trustworthiness, then, are necessary but not sufficient criteria for effective academic governance in the twenty-first century.

REFERENCES

Bogdan, R. 1998. *Qualitative research for education: An introduction to theory and methods.* Boston: Allyn and Bacon.

Brennan, G. 1998. Democratic trust: A rational-choice view. In *Trust and governance,* ed. V. Braithwaite and M. Levi, 197–217. New York: Russell Sage Foundation.

Clark, B. 1987. *The academic life.* Princeton, NJ: Carnegie Foundation.

Coleman, J. 1990. *Foundations of social theory.* Cambridge, MA: Belknap Press.

Creed, W. E., and R. E. Miles. 1996. Trust in organizations: A conceptual framework linking organizational forms, managerial philosophies, and the opportunity costs of control. In *Trust in organizations: Frontiers of theory and research,* ed. R. M. Kramer and T. R. Tyler, 16–38. Thousand Oaks, CA: Sage.

Denzin, N. 1989. *The research act.* Englewood Cliffs, NJ: Prentice Hall.

Dunn, J. 1988. Trust and political agency. In *Making and breaking cooperative relations,* ed. D. Gambetta, 73–93. New York: Basil Blackwell.

Gambetta, D. 1988. Can we trust? In *Trust: Making and breaking cooperative relations,* ed. D. Gambetta, 213–37. New York: Basil Blackwell.

Glaser, B., and A. Strauss. 1967. *The discovery of grounded theory: Strategies for qualitative research.* Chicago: Aldine.

Glesne, C., and A. Peshkin. 1992. *Becoming qualitative researchers: An introduction.* White Plains, NY: Longman.

Hardin, R. 1993. The street-level epistemology of trust. *Politics of Society* 21: 505–29.

———. 2002. *Trust and trustworthiness.* New York: Russell Sage Foundation.

Kramer, R. M., and T. R. Tyler, eds. 1996. *Trust and organizations: Frontiers of theory and research.* Thousand Oaks, CA: Sage.

Luhmann, N. 1980. *Trust: A mechanism for the reduction of social complexities in trust and power.* New York: Wiley.

———. 1988. Familiarity, confidence and trust: Problems and alternatives. In *Trust: Making and breaking cooperative relations,* ed. D. Gambetta, 94–108. New York: Basil Blackwell.

Meyerson, D., K. E. Weick, and R. M. Kramer. 1996. Swift trust and temporary groups. In *Trust in organizations: Frontiers of theory and research,* ed. R. M. Kramer and T. R. Tyler, 166–95. Thousand Oaks, CA: Sage.

Morse, J. R. 1999. No flames, no freedom: Human flourishing in a free society. *Social Psychology and Policy* 12: 290–314.

Putnam, R. D. 1995. Bowling alone: America's declining social capital. *Journal of Democracy* 6(1): 65–78.

Rhoades, G. 1998. *Managed professionals: Unionized faculty and restructuring academic labor,* Albany: State University of New York Press.

Seligman, A. B. 1997. *The problem of trust*. Princeton, NJ: Princeton University Press.

Tierney, W. G. 1988. Organizational culture in higher education: Defining the essentials. *Journal of Higher Education* 59(1): 2–21.

———. 1989. *Curricular landscapes, democratic visas: Transformative leadership in higher education*. New York: Praeger.

———, ed. 2004. *Competing conceptions of governance*. Baltimore, MD: Johns Hopkins University Press.

Tyler, T. R., and P. Degoey. 1995. *Collective restraint in a social dilemma situation: The influence of procedural justice and community identification on the empowerment and legitimation of authority*. Unpublished manuscript, University of California at Berkeley.

Williams, B. 1988. Formal structures and social reality. In *Trust: Making and breaking cooperative relations*, ed. D. Gambetta, 3–13. New York: Basil Blackwell.

10

Defining Governance for Public Higher Education in the Twenty-First Century

Karri Holley

The American public university has long been a remarkably adaptive social institution. As the authors in this volume have discussed, the growth and development of public higher education are intertwined with innumerable significant national events over the last century. Public universities assisted millions of returning veterans in receiving a college education due to the GI Bill. Scientists trained at the nation's public universities have contributed to important advances in medicine and health. Such institutions have "grown up with the nation . . . [the public university] has transformed the very society it serves" (Duderstadt and Womack, 2003, 9). Yet the rapid and conflicting demands of the twenty-first century raise questions regarding the ability of colleges and universities to maintain their internal focus on education, research, and knowledge production while responding to external demands for accountability and social engagement. James Duderstadt, former president of the University of Michigan, has noted, "A fundamental issue [is] whether the university, as we know it in the last years of the twentieth century, [is] prepared to educate citizens, to serve the society of an unimaginable future" (2000, 11).

The implications of this unimaginable future encourage us to redefine our understanding of higher education as well as the role of the state, the need for social resources, and the significance of the public good. In particular, the implications also challenge the fundamental components of the modern public university, such as tenure and academic freedom, the liberal arts education, and institutional governance. Indeed, the definition of such terms is not singular or undisputed. Much of the debate over the future of higher education in the new century rests on the competing and often conflicting interpretations of what colleges and universities are—or what they *should* be.

The preceding chapters represent authors with an expertise in the theory and practice of higher education. By assembling their chapters in a single text, the goal was to bridge the often artificial dichotomy between research and practice and to provide multiple perspectives for grappling with the concepts of institutional governance and the public good. The focus has been on public universities, which are related to the public good in a way that other types of institutions are arguably not. If higher education is conceptualized as a public good, then what are the implications for governance in a rapidly changing new century? How can the process of governance enable colleges and universities to be more responsive to the multiple needs of the public? My purpose in this chapter is to provide the reader with a brief summary of the viewpoints presented by the preceding authors and to offer implications for the challenges facing higher education. In doing so, I focus on the contested interpretations of the "university" and the "public good." I also explore the need to clearly define expectations of public colleges and universities in the twenty-first century.

GOVERNANCE, THE PUBLIC GOOD, AND HIGHER EDUCATION

If higher education is a public good, then the changes in recent decades regarding the role of the state and the provision of social resources alter the underlying assumptions in terms of public higher education. The challenges that exist require colleges and universities to (1) respond creatively and decisively to declining social resources, increasing social demands, and conflicting expectations, while (2) simultaneously retaining elements of the core values of higher education. Change and continuity are inherently conflicting modes of behavior for organizations. Institutional change implies a change in institutional processes, such as governance, which the preceding chapters set out to consider.

Contested Interpretations

When we speak of governance in higher education, we refer to a process that takes place on many interrelated levels. The previous chapters explored various aspects of this process—from the analysis by Craig McInnis (chapter 6) of faculty involvement in university governance, framed by the context of rapid social change, to Jane Wellman's (chapter 3) discussion of state governance structures in light of political and economic pressures. Just as the university is inherently a part of its local, regional, and global community, so do its governance processes span the width of these components. Decisions that are made at the institutional level involving faculty, administrators, and trustees will affect the relationship between the institution and the state. The understanding of public higher education "governance" cannot be encapsulated as a single process but rather one that is constructed and shaped by multiple social, economic, and political influences.

The concept of the public good, as Brian Pusser outlined in chapter 1, has long been inherently ambiguous and evolving. The public good is often defined according to an individual perspective, although it ultimately refers to a collective good. In the end, the concept of the public good speaks to a symbiotic relationship between the institution and society. The dualistic nature of this relationship, as Pusser further noted, results in endless debate regarding such topics as access, accountability, institutional autonomy, and funding. One feature of a symbiotic relationship is that each component requires the other in order to ensure survival. The questions raised in this volume only reinforce this interdependency in terms of the debate regarding higher education's role in serving the public good. What social needs does the institution fulfill? Perhaps more significantly, what social needs *should* the institution fulfill, and how do we ensure that it is capable of doing so? Conversely—and just as significantly—what public resources should be made available to the institution in order to meet those social needs?

In the Introduction, William Tierney underscored this complex interdependence by noting that the public good rests on a shared commitment between higher education and society. This relationship is unique; corporations and other businesses do not exist because of a shared commitment with the public. In higher education and society, each component relies on the other to fulfill a social contract. Herein lies the conflict that the authors have explored. Education, specifically at public universities, exists because of the obligation to serve public needs and to provide a place for the growth of knowledge. It is difficult to arrive at a broad, shared consensus regarding the relationship of higher education to the needs of the public, and even more difficult to outline a linear framework of how higher education governance can work to fulfill institutional and public needs.

Add to this dynamic the forces of privatization and politicization. Karen Whitney, in chapter 2, illustrated how privatization has occurred as a gradual process that has altered the pattern of state funding and support for higher education over several decades. Influences such as privatization, noted Burgan, "have intensified issues of governance by inserting nonacademic interests into the heart of education, adding layers of external complexity to institutions, and intensifying the stakes involved in devising new ways of handling them" (Burgan, 2004, vii).

This conflict calls into question the purpose of governance, its relationship to the institutional mission, and the methods by which successful governance can be achieved. As Jane Wellman noted in chapter 3, public university governance within the institution, the system, and the state serves several key functions. First, governance protects the autonomy of the institution by serving as a buffer against external interference in the academic process. In addition, governance enables institutional stability and includes multiple stakeholders—such as the faculty, the administration, and the public—in decision making. Finally, state governance allows for the efficient and fair allocation of public resources to meet social needs; the board of trustees is one mechanism for holding the institution accountable for the use of public resources.

The goal of governance, then, is to ensure the accountability and integrity of the institution. But how these goals should be achieved is a question that elicits multiple responses. Although the purpose of governance may be well defined, the practice of governance is not. Colleges and universities are inseparable from their social context and cultural environment. In chapter 4, Kenneth Mortimer and Colleen O'Brien Sathre illustrated how complex and contested the practice of governance can be when the institution must respond to social, political, and market influences. Even as the institution attempted to come to a decision that furthered its ability to respond to social needs, a consensus could not be reached on the most responsive means to do so.

From multiple perspectives, then, issues such as institutional mission and academic policies can be deeply decisive. Some stakeholders were dissatisfied with decisions made at Glenhaven University, the site of Mortimer's and O'Brien Sathre's case study. Yet this case study also is a reminder of the value of institutional process. "In higher education, process *is* substance," concluded Birnbaum (1988, 223, emphasis added); colleges and universities are well served to retain and encourage the integrity of the governance process.

Defining Expectations

One cannot regard all public colleges and universities as sharing the same goals, finances, relations to the state, or governance structures. Each institution has evolved from a unique history, purpose, and tradition. Jane Wellman provided a comparative outline of state governance structures and the relationships of institutions to the state in chapter 3; her framework illustrates the rich diversity of public higher education in this country and the difficulty in defining expectations for public universities in terms of fulfilling the public good. "With renewed interest in defining and pursuing a public agenda for higher education which transcends institutional advancement," noted MacTaggart (2004), "[we] should focus on what governance structures best support the pursuit of fundamental public needs" (129). Focusing on a single goal—supporting fundamental public needs—is one means of coping with the ambiguous expectations that exist in the relationship between universities and the state.

In chapter 5, David Longanecker detailed the multiple masters that boards of trustees are required to serve, and the ongoing dilemma that has resulted; the expectations of these different masters for the trustees, governing boards, and the university are not always clear and are sometimes conflicting. These competing interests, particularly in an era of constrained resources, are difficult to reconcile. How can boards of trustees fulfill their duty to ensure that the public trust in the institution is maintained, and that the university adequately fulfills its responsibilities, when expectations are unclear and inconsistent? Judith Ramaley continued this discussion in chapter 8 as she outlined the need for the university to redefine its mission and its relationship to the public in light of increasing demands on higher education. Ultimately, Ramaley noted, colleges and universities must change their position from an institution that serves the public good *on behalf* of society to one that serves the public good in *collaboration* with an involved community. This change encourages the development of the public good while simultaneously advancing private and public interests within the institution. Creating a new intellectual space to serve the public good requires a change in governance that supports engaged scholarship and the support of a learning community.

As we have read throughout this text, successful governance in higher education relies on well-defined expectations and the allocation and management of resources to respond to those expectations. Asking questions, proposing strategies, and exploring options are inherent tactics to achieve these goals. This perspective "must recognize the potential need for extensive change in the academic structure and function and even in the nature of academic work" (Peterson and Dill, 1997, 3). Jay Dee explored the implications of a loosely coupled relationship in chapter 7 as an alternative framework to define and understand these expectations. He argued that to fulfill the dual demands of public accountability and institutional autonomy, we must rethink the governance relationship between the institution and the state.

In a loosely coupled definition, accountability and autonomy are responsive events, but each retains its individual identity and significance to the organization. An advantage of loose coupling is that it "allows some portions of an organization to persist . . . [and] lowers the probability that the organization will have to—or be able to—respond to each little change in the environment" (Weick, 1976). The structuring of relationships in the governance process is significant, including internal structures between the faculty, administration, and trustees and external relationships between the institution and the state. Craig McInnis provided examples from higher education in Australia in chapter 6 to illustrate that the way in which governance is structured affects how responsive the institution can be to social and political realities. While McInnis specifically focused on how faculty can be more effectively involved in the governance structure, he argued that governance should be an *active* process in terms of stakeholder engagement.

While the authors may disagree on the details of institutional change—Longanecker may find that the tendency for trustees to focus on the broad needs of the public results in mission creep, while Ramaley may suggest that the inherent role of the trustees is to be responsive to the public good—such distinctions matter very little in the context of contemporary social, political, and economic demands on higher education. The demands require a response. William Tierney's discussion of trust in chapter 9 outlined the requirements for a successful response. Even if the relationship between autonomy and accountability is reconceptualized, for example, progressive change between the multiple stakeholders and an effective organizational response is only enabled through a healthy and an engaged organizational culture. Tierney underscored the need for trust in coping with turbulent change and ill-defined expectations: trust within the academy as well as between the academy and its many external constituents. Fostering trust within an academic organization requires outlining a common framework and shared language for the goals of higher education.

Trust has historically existed as an integral factor in the relationship between colleges and universities and the state—the state provided the resources needed for operation, and the faculty, administration, and selected laypersons organized these resources in ways specific to the institution and beneficial to the larger society. Yet this relationship has changed in the new century, and while the means to manage institutions may be unclear, the need for trust to exist between all parties is still essential. Defining expectations is impossible without the trust that all parties will fulfill their obligatory roles. Trust is a prerequisite for risk taking and change.

IMPLICATIONS AND FUTURE GOVERNANCE CHALLENGES

Neil Hamilton has argued, "The university serving its mission of seeking, discovering, and disseminating knowledge is one of humankind's greatest achievements" (1999, 30). He further noted, "This mission can only be achieved through the joint effort of governing boards, administrators, and the academic profession. All three groups are in positions of *public trust* to work cooperatively to achieve this mission" (30). It should be the focus of those engaged in the theory and practice of higher education to facilitate the mutual commitment needed to fulfill the public trust. In the Introduction, William Tierney outlined the challenge presented to the authors: What is the role of the twenty-first-century public university, and how is the changing definition of the public good related to that role? The concept of the public good is not one that those in the university can dismiss or minimize as the situation demands. Instead, the public good is an ideology that underscores the behavior of a public institution and the processes by which the institution operates. Fulfilling the public good requires understanding this ideology and recognizing the shared commitment and dependent relationship between the university and the public.

Organizational change is not a process that occurs by chance. Higher education scholars have considered how organizational change generally occurs, and how it ideally should occur in colleges and universities (see, e.g., Birnbaum, 1988; Clark, 1998, 2004). The preceding chapters have placed the need for organizational change against the pervasive backdrop of the relationship between higher education and the public. The discussion regarding organizational change would only be furthered by an explicit focus on the shared commitment between the two—what does the relationship mean in a time of declining resources and demands for accountability? How might we understand the concept of the public good beyond social resources, which are made available to institutions in terms of fiscal support? How might we reconceptualize public good as not simply financial dependence but as a guiding cultural ideology? Colleges and universities may choose to respond to challenges facing governance and their relationship to the public good in a variety of ways. At a minimum, times of change call for some measured responses. Perhaps, looking back on this era decades from now, we will see these responses and be able to assess the results as well as relate them to the unique history, tradition, and culture of each institution.

The long-term goal of governance for public universities in the interest of furthering the public good is to ensure institutional welfare while also recognizing and advancing social interests. The complexity of demands placed on the university requires an assessment of the processes that may have served the institution quite well in the past. To expect universities to respond to these demands by maintaining the status quo or to overthrow the traditional commitments that public institutions share with the citizenry is unrealistic. The challenge, then, is to maintain public spaces for shared scholarship and the exchange of ideas while transforming governance to enable innovative institutional responses to complex social challenges.

REFERENCES

Birnbaum, R. 1988. *How colleges work*. San Francisco: Jossey Bass.

Burgan, M. 2004. Why governance? Why now? In *Competing conceptions of academic governance: Negotiating the perfect storm*, ed. W. G. Tierney, vii–xiv. Baltimore, MD: Johns Hopkins University Press.

Clark, B. 1998. *Creating entrepreneurial universities: Organizational pathways for transformation.* New York: Pergamon Press.

———. 2004. *Sustaining change in universities: Continuities in case studies and concepts.* Berkshire, UK: Open University Press/McGraw-Hill.

Duderstadt, J. 2000. *A university for the 21st century.* Ann Arbor: University of Michigan Press.

Duderstadt, J., and F. Womack. 2003. *The future of the public university in America: Beyond the crossroads.* Baltimore, MD: Johns Hopkins University Press.

Hamilton, N. 1999. Are we speaking the same language? Comparing the AGB and the AAUP. *Liberal Education* (Fall): 24–31.

MacTaggart, T. J. 2004. The ambiguous future of public higher education systems. In *Competing conceptions of academic governance: Negotiating the perfect storm,* ed. W. G. Tierney, 104–36. Baltimore, MD: Johns Hopkins University Press.

Peterson, M., and D. Dill. 1997. Understanding the competitive environment of the postsecondary knowledge industry. In *Planning and management challenges for a changing environment,* ed. M. Peterson, D. Dill, and L. Mets, 3–29. San Francisco: Jossey-Bass.

Weick, K. 1976. Educational organizations as loosely coupled systems. *Administrative Science Quarterly* 21(1): 1–19.

Contributors

Jay Dee is an assistant professor in the School of Education at the University of Massachusetts, Boston, and is co-director of the New England Center for Inclusive Teaching.

Karri Holley is a clinical professor of higher education at the University of Alabama.

David A. Longanecker is the executive director of the Western Interstate Commission for Higher Education in Boulder, Colorado. He was formerly assistant secretary for postsecondary education at the U.S. Department of Education.

Craig McInnis is a professor of higher education at the University of Melbourne, Australia, where he also serves in the Office of the Deputy Vice Chancellor (Academic).

Kenneth P. Mortimer is a senior associate with the National Center for Higher Education Management Systems. He is a former president of the University of Hawaii and Western Washington University.

Brian Pusser is an assistant professor in the Center for the Study of Higher Education at the Curry School of Education, University of Virginia.

Judith A. Ramaley is the president of Winona State University (MN) and a former visiting senior scientist at the National Academy of Sciences. She also is former president of the University of Vermont and Portland State University.

Colleen O'Brien Sathre is vice president emeritus of Planning and Policy at the University of Hawaii.

William G. Tierney is University Professor, Wilbur-Kieffer Professor of Higher Education and director of the Center for Higher Education Policy Analysis at the Rossier School of Education, University of Southern California.

Jane V. Wellman is senior associate at the Institute for Higher Education Policy and was formerly deputy director of the California Postsecondary Education Commission.

Karen M. Whitney is vice chancellor for Student Life and Diversity at Indiana University-Purdue University Indianapolis. She was formerly associate vice president for Student Life at University of Texas, San Antonio.

Index